Praise for *The Undoing of Death*

"Fleming Rutledge is a powerful and provocative preacher. Proudly evangelical in her proclamation of the gospel, she provides a penetrating analysis of the human condition and a clear affirmation of God's gracious response. Along the way, she invites poets, sages, and rogues to enter the conversation, joining their voices with those of our spiritual ancestors. . . . This collection of sermons, drawn from twenty-five years of preaching, is a valuable resource for all who are concerned about the formation of Christian identity in an increasingly pluralistic and heterodox world."

— MARTHA J. HORNE
dean and president of
Virginia Theological Seminary

"Good Friday and Easter Day attendance has risen to over 3,000 in our parish as Fleming Rutledge has returned over the years to confront our congregation with the news of Christ crucified and raised. The power of God in Fleming Rutledge's words works to raise us from the tomb of our modern anxieties and predispositions to that promised abundant and everlasting life. These sermons are not sentimental escapist fare that ignores or sidesteps the theological reality of our situation. These are, rather, sin-confronting, repentance-inducing, hope-infusing antidotes to our desperate prognosis. This book will restore passion and urgency in the preacher and offer an insightful application of salvation to daily living for all."

— DONALD ARMSTRONG
rector of Grace Episcopal Church,
Colorado Springs

"Fleming Rutledge has an amazing knack for finding your most cherished doubts about the Christian faith. She then lets the gospel encounter these doubts by unveiling your most cherished hopes. By that point in her sermons you realize that you are listening to the risen Lord and not just the preacher."

— M. CRAIG BARNES
senior pastor of National Presbyterian
Church, Washington, D.C.

"Excellent, honest, and compelling sermons are a rare and splendid treasure for the church. Here is a book full of them. Fleming Rutledge's sermons and meditations on Holy Week and Easter go to the very heart of the Christian faith. They portray the drama of the gospel — both the darkness of the cross and the burst of Easter light. They then call believers to a life that takes up that cross and rejoices in that light."

— LEANNE VAN DYK
professor of Reformed theology,
Western Theological Seminary

"These are passionate sermons. They speak arrestingly and thoughtfully of the passion of Jesus and of the passionate love of God. They tell us how and why the power of that crucified love intervenes in contemporary lives and how, in Fleming Rutledge's phrasing, 'the cross is backlit by the dawn of God's new day.'"

— FREDERICK H. BORSCH
Bishop of the Episcopal Diocese
of Los Angeles

"Fleming Rutledge's sermons are thoughtful, compelling, biblical, and personal — a welcome combination for the church today. The power of the Word preached with intelligent warmth is all too rare in the pulpit, but it is so very evident in *The Undoing of Death*."

— CAROL ANDERSON
rector of All Saints' Episcopal Parish,
Beverly Hills

The Undoing of Death

SERMONS FOR HOLY WEEK AND EASTER

Fleming Rutledge

WILLIAM B. EERDMANS PUBLISHING COMPANY
GRAND RAPIDS, MICHIGAN / CAMBRIDGE, U.K.

© 2002 Wm. B. Eerdmans Publishing Co.

All rights reserved

Wm. B. Eerdmans Publishing Co.
255 Jefferson Ave. S.E., Grand Rapids, Michigan 49503 /
P.O. Box 163, Cambridge CB3 9PU U.K.

Printed in the United States of America

06 05 04 03 02   5 4 3 2 1

ISBN 0-8028-3969-x

www.eerdmans.com

To my beloved daughters

Heyward Rutledge Donigan
and
Elizabeth Heath Rutledge

with thanksgiving for all that they mean to us
and commending them always
to the eternal care of the crucified and risen Christ

Contents

Contents

❦

Contents

Contents

Contents

Illustrations

———∞∞∞———

Illustrations

Author's Foreword

———— ⸎ ————

Holy Week and Easter preaching is by any standard the most challenging of the Christian year. The intensity of the season, the uniqueness of the content, and the high expectations of congregations place special demands on those who deliver the messages. It has been my privilege and solemn responsibility to preach on Good Friday — in various congregations across the United States — for twenty-six consecutive years (1976-2001). This volume is culled from those experiences and from the accompanying Holy Week and Easter sermons that were delivered, in many cases, in those same congregations.

The meaning of the Crucifixion demands careful and thorough exposition of a sort that is not possible in a Sunday sermon. That is why the traditional three-hour Good Friday service, where it is offered, remains an invaluable opportunity. Good Friday preaching, however, seems to be going out of fashion. Three-hour preaching services have become harder to find. Liturgies for the day have become more elaborate and, in many cases, have replaced sermons altogether. The books of Kenneth Leech have been of exceptional value to me since I discovered them about five years ago, and I urgently recommend *We Preach Christ Crucified* in particular, but I cannot agree with his opinion that there need not be any preaching on Good Friday because the liturgy is enough.[1] The reason that the liturgy is not sufficient by itself is that the Cross is not self-interpreting. As St. Paul clearly expected his congregations to understand, God has given us the apostolic gift and task of proclaiming "the word of the Cross."

A great deal of controversy, polemic, and even hostility surrounds the preaching of the Cross in the mainline churches today. There is a certain amount of "political correctness" associated with Holy Week preaching; various litmus tests are applied. I beg the reader who is predisposed to one or another view of the Cross and Resurrection to withhold judgment until he or she has read more than one of these collected sermons. Those who are looking for the "substitutionary atonement" will indeed find it here, but not in the strict scholastic form which has come to be called "penal substitution." The prominent Christus Victor theme plays a large role in these sermons, especially the Easter ones. The exemplary or "subjective" motif will be found also, though to a lesser degree. It is my intention and my hope to provide a rich variety of interpretations, because that is what the New Testament and the tradition offer us. The emphasis is on metaphors and images, rather than rationalistic "theories." Atonement for sin, Christ's sacrificial self-offering, and the price God paid for our redemption are stressed, but so are the motifs of deliverance from oppression, victory over death, triumph over evil, and Jesus' solidarity with the outcast and wretched of the earth. Anyone who reads this collection as though it were a narrow brief for one interpretation over against another will be misunderstanding my intention.

Many of these sermons are brand new; others — especially the Good Friday ones — have been rethought and reworked over a period of many years. None have ever been published before. Of necessity, there is a small and — I think — inconsequential amount of repetition in these sermons because the themes and texts remain the same over the years. "Christ died *for our sins,*" for instance, is a recurring motif, as is the unique significance of the Crucifixion and the Resurrection as a *real event,* not a religious idea. No two passages, however, are exactly the same and, if the sermons are read in small doses as most readers will prefer, it will be seen that repetition is deliberate, for the sake of emphasis.

Some will, perhaps, be disappointed to find that I have not followed the hallowed tradition of preaching on the Seven Last Words. I can only explain this by saying that when I first began preaching on Good Friday in the mid-1970s the custom seemed to me to be overworked and a bit tired. I thought that a different approach might be refreshing. At this point it may be that a return to the formula might be a good thing, and that remains a possibility for future Good Fridays. In any case, there is great emphasis here on two of the Words: the Cry of Dereliction ("My God, my God, why hast thou forsaken me?") and "It is finished." Other Words are addressed briefly in "The Hour of Glory" and "Lead Us to Calvary."

Alert readers will note that Kenneth Woodward, religion editor of *Newsweek,* is quoted more frequently in these sermons than any other writer. This may seem odd, but there is a reason for it. Every year at Eastertime for a number of years, Mr. Woodward has done a cover story about Jesus or God or religion in general, and he can be counted upon, not only to contribute something timely, but also to say something genuinely theological. His articles are therefore a particularly valuable resource for the Holy Week preacher.

Suggestions for Reading the Sermons

The arrangement of the sermons in groups according to the holy days presents some advantages and some disadvantages. Different readers will approach the contents in different ways. For example: preachers reading for sermon ideas, as I might do myself, will perhaps go straight to a specific section — Maundy Thursday, for instance — and read more than one sermon at a sitting. This method is not recommended for most other readers, however. I suggest the reading of one sermon at a time from each section, perhaps in sequence according to that of Holy Week itself.

With an eye to encouraging the freedom of the reader to choose from the various sections, I offer this story:

Back in the 1980s when the AIDS epidemic was at its height in America and nothing had yet been developed to combat it, I visited a man who was in the hospital with no prospect of leaving it in this life. He was a devout Christian and he knew he was dying. We had a long visit and talked about the Bible, the Lord, and the faith. I ventured a few thoughts about the solidarity of Christ in his Passion with those who are suffering. After a while my parishioner said, to my surprise, "I don't really want to think about the crucified Christ. It upsets me."

I was surprised, but not without resources for responding. How grateful I was to be able to say without a moment's hesitation, "That's all right; let's think about the Resurrection!" The next day I sent him a copy of Matthias Grünewald's resplendent painting of Christ exploding from the tomb. This is by way of saying that if the reader begins to feel herself getting bogged down in the Holy Week sections, she is by all means encouraged to skip to the Easter ones. The light of Easter Day now shines in perpetuity on the week of the Passion and gives us hope even in the midst of the darkest night. For those who believe in Jesus, the Cross is backlit by the dawn of God's new Day.

It may be helpful for the reader to note that these sermons were preached in several different types of settings. The Sunday sermons, which are marked as such, were written with the Sunday congregation in mind. The weekday sermons for both Holy Week and Easter Week are more demanding in certain respects, because those who come for the preaching of the Word on weekdays tend to be more experienced in hearing and more intentional in their commitment. The Good Friday meditations are somewhat shorter, more reflective, and more open-ended, with each one leading up to the next. It is recommended that each of the sets of Good Friday meditations be read all at once in sequence, but *only one set at a time*, because reading two or three sets at a sitting would be too heavy a dose.

Dates are given for a few of the sermons. That is because they are very much the product of their specific time — with illustrations from that moment. Most are not dated because they can be read independently of any particular year.

About translations: The shape and rhythm of sentences, I believe, is more important for effective communication than an overly scrupulous effort to meet our present culture's demands for ideological correctness. There was a great outcry from lovers of literature when the Revised Standard Version first appeared (how long ago it seems!), but today there is general recognition that it retains much of the cadence of the King James Version, without the numerous errors. I therefore use the RSV most of the time, but occasionally I shift into the KJV for its greater rhetorical power. Other translations have been used a few times and have been identified accordingly.

About capitalization: I sometimes capitalize words to emphasize certain points (a dimension available in print though not, obviously, in delivery). In particular, I have frequently (not always) capitalized Sin and Death to underscore their independent status as Powers, separate from the human being and not susceptible to human choice — a theme of Paul's letters, especially in Romans 7 and elsewhere in that letter. Death is clearly depicted as a Power in John's Gospel, and some of the sermons draw on that theme — especially the title sermon, "The Undoing of Death."

About endnotes: I have used endnotes instead of footnotes in order to present a cleaner page for the general reader. There is much material in them, however, for the use of those who are interested in further study of particular issues and themes.

About the epigraphs: All but one of the quotations on the chapter-head pages are taken from John Donne's sermon, "Death's Duel," preached in the presence of Charles I in St. Paul's Cathedral, London, on the 25th of February 1631. There has perhaps never been any other preacher to rival Donne in English; this is my way of paying homage to him. The other epigraph, from Gerard Manley Hopkins, is identified on the Easter Day page. It is encouraging to note that in these postmodern times this poet continues high in critical esteem.

Conclusion

One crucial point remains to be made. In a projected future book about the Crucifixion, the final, climactic series of chapters will be devoted to cruciform, or Cross-shaped, ethics. If the Cross is not acted out in life with special regard for those with whom Christ identified himself in the manner of his death — the "low and despised" among us (1 Corinthians 1:28) — it becomes blasphemous, like the crosses burned by the KKK, or those erected by the Serbian Orthodox over the ruins of Muslim homes. In my opinion, however, the working out of Christian ethics is best done in the Sunday teaching and the day-in, day-out life of the congregation. The preaching of Holy Week has its own special character. It is like that of St. Paul to the Galatians where he "publicly portrayed Jesus Christ before your eyes as crucified" (Galatians 3:1). Therefore the central aim of the Holy Week and Easter Day sermons is to concentrate on the good news (the *kerygma* or *evangel*) itself, that root from which all else grows. This is not to say that there is no specific reference to ethical problems in the Holy Week sermons collected here, but they do not take center stage. The alert reader will notice that there is an increasing amount of ethical content in the Eastertide sermons. The relationship of the *kerygma* — the gospel — to ethics is beautifully proclaimed in Colossians 1:3-6, 9-10:

> We always thank God, the Father of our Lord Jesus Christ, when we pray for you, because we have heard of your faith in Christ Jesus and of the love which you have for all the saints, because of the hope laid up for you in heaven. Of this you have heard before in the word of the truth, the gospel (*evangel*) which has come to you, as indeed in the whole world it is bearing fruit and growing — so among yourselves, from the day you heard and understood the grace of God in truth. . . . And so, . . . we [apostles] have not ceased to pray for you, asking that you may be filled with the knowledge of his will in all spiritual wisdom and understanding, *to lead a life worthy of the Lord, fully pleasing to him, bearing fruit in every good work and increasing in the knowledge of God.*

[xx]

In order to lead "a life worthy of the Lord," we need to "increase in the knowledge of God" and especially the nature of his sacrifice. In order to enter into his life of self-giving love, we need to know more about the meaning of his death for us and the power of his Resurrection for new life. May God be pleased to increase our knowledge of what he has done for us through Christ, that we may love him more dearly and, living out of his love, may bear fruit for his glory.

Acknowledgments

Over the past twenty-six years I have had the priceless gift of invitations to preach during Holy Week in parishes all over the United States. It has been an extraordinary privilege. To each of these parishes I owe a debt of thanksgiving. Many of them are listed on the last page of the Good Friday section.

A very special mention must go to our daughter Elizabeth Heath Rutledge, who painstakingly read much of the manuscript, caught typos, made suggestions for clarification, and reminded me time and again that there simply is no answer to the problem of suffering and that we must always live in the midst of painful ambiguity. Her devotion to this project has meant more to me than I can possibly say. I am also deeply grateful to Pennie Curry, Dorothy and Louis Martyn, George and Deborah Hunsinger, Francine and Doug Holmes, Ellen and Dana Charry, Jim Kay, Laura Saunders, Ellen Davis, Wallace Alston, David Tracy, Aldo Tos, Susan Grove Eastman, Susan Crampton, Richard Hays, and my dear sister Betsy McColl, among many others who have believed in my vocation and sustained me through many times of drought. Hugh Nissenson, though he describes himself as a Jewish unbeliever, has encouraged me tremendously with his unflagging enthusiasm for the sermon as an important form of American literature. The faith placed in me by three departed mentors, Paul Lehmann, Joseph Mitchell, and Peter Forbath, has played a larger role than they could have imagined. These comrades and many others are part of the cloud of witnesses that God has graciously given to surround this undertaking.

It has been a great pleasure to work with Eerdmans for the third time. I especially appreciate the style, grace, and brio that Sam Eerdmans brings to the care and feeding of Eerdmans authors (learned, surely, from William B. Eerdmans himself). Andrew Hoogheem performed heroic feats at the last minute tracking down the illustrations; I am very grateful to him for his knowledge, his discernment, and his caring about the images almost as much as I did. Many thanks as well to Bruce Robinson, Kathryn Vander Molen, Charles Van Hof, Allen Myers, Todd Tremlin, Amy Kent, and Jennifer Hoffman, whose professionalism and commitment to the best in Christian publishing continues to amaze.

Many authors end their acknowledgments with heartfelt thanks to their spouses for their endless patience and support. I never fully understood the depth of these tributes until now. It is very difficult to live with a writer. Add to that the peculiarity of living with a preacher, and you have some sense of what is required for a marriage to survive the production of a book like this. My husband Dick has championed my work as though it were one of the most important missions of his life. I am truly thankful for him.

PART ONE

The First Day of Holy Week: The Sunday of the Passion, Commonly Called Palm Sunday

———— ✾ ————

All his life was a continual passion.

JOHN DONNE

A note about the Palm Sunday sermons in this book

———∞∞∞———

In the Episcopal church, as well as other liturgically-oriented traditions, a procession with palms is staged with great festivity at the
beginning of the service; the central feature of the day, however, is
the solemn, dramatic reading of the Passion narrative shortly afterward. The Biblical text is from one of the Synoptic Gospels (Matthew, Mark, Luke), alternating in a three-year cycle (John's version
is read on Good Friday). The narrative is divided into parts with a
narrator and various actors taking the roles of Jesus, Pilate, Peter,
and so forth. The congregation takes the part of the crowd, which
means that they are called upon to shout "Crucify him!" at the appointed moment.

The Tears of Palm Sunday

———❦———

And when he drew near and saw the city he wept over it, saying, "Would that even today you knew the things that make for peace! But now they are hid from your eyes. For the days shall come upon you, when your enemies will . . . hem you in on every side, and dash you to the ground, you and your children within you, and they will not leave one stone upon another in you; because you did not know the time of your visitation."

(LUKE 19:41-44)

P alm Sunday is a very strange day. Its proper name is the Sunday of the Passion, because the story of Jesus' suffering and death is always read. I remember a teenaged boy, an acolyte in my former church, standing with the cross at the head of the palm procession. He turned to me and said, "I don't understand what I'm supposed to be feeling." He well captured the ambivalence of the day. Crowds are attracted by the festivity and then get hit over the head with the story of the Crucifixion. Today we learn in a visceral, uncompromising way that the crowd who hailed Jesus as Messiah and King on Sunday shouted "Crucify him!" on Friday. It is not a day for the faint of heart.

Let us take our cue from St. Luke and the other evangelists, since the center of every Palm Sunday service is the reading of the

[3]

Rembrandt: The Raising of the Cross

This painting could be entitled "I crucified thee." Rembrandt has put himself into the picture as one who participates in the deed. His expression tells us that he is assuming full responsibility for what he is doing. This corresponds to the action of worshippers on Palm Sunday who cry out the words "Crucify him!"

In the nineteenth century, American Christians revered Rembrandt with a good deal of pious sentimentality, and a hagiography grew up about him. As a reaction and a corrective, later twentieth-century art historians debunked this, showing that Rembrandt was just as much influenced by power and patronage as any other artist and was perhaps not a sincere Christian at all. On balance, however, it seems improbable that the profound spiritual insight demonstrated in this painting could have come from a source other than personal commitment.

Passion narrative from the Gospels of Matthew, Mark, or Luke. This week more than any other, we come to the center of what they want to communicate to us. We have just heard Luke's version of the Passion. All four of the Gospels move toward this climax. All four of them give much more attention to the suffering and crucifixion of Jesus than they do to any other part of his life. This is not an accident. From the earliest days of the church, it was understood that Jesus' life gained its significance from his death. The apostles and evangelists wanted their readers to understand the meaning of this death more than they wanted anything else in the world.[1]

Each day this week, those of you who can make the commitment will move deeper into the heart of these events. We can promise that if you do, you will find yourself blessed in a deep way, but not everyone is willing. The "word of the Cross," as St. Paul called it, has always been an offense. It has never been a palatable message. My husband called me on the phone Thursday from home; he said he had a sermon illustration for me. He had been to a local shopping center, and in the window of a gift and card shop he saw this sign: "We make Easter easy!" I guess that meant they were offering one-stop shopping for all the eggs, flowers, cards, and bunnies you might need, but it struck my husband and me both as an absolutely classic example of the human tendency to flee as far away from the Cross as we possibly can. The churches are no exception. In at least one sense it's true that Easter is easy. Everybody loves Easter. Only the elite corps shows up for Maundy Thursday and Good Friday.

You could say that Palm Sunday is the Trojan horse of the Christian year. We get lured in by the festivity, but before we know it we are being assaulted by the long dramatic reading of the Passion. Palm Sunday is not a day unto itself. Palm Sunday is the introduction to Holy Week. A lot of people have not had the opportunity to understand this; perhaps some of you are in that category today. I've always been curious about the reaction of unsuspecting churchgoers to the Palm Sunday liturgy. Last year on Palm Sunday, I was at the church door at the end of the service, shaking people's hands, when a woman leaned forward and said to me in a confidential tone of voice, "I never say, 'Crucify him!' I just can't do it." She obviously expected me to congratulate her. Unfortunately, she had missed the whole point. She saw herself as one of the virtuous, above the common herd. She meant well, but she did not understand Jesus' saying, "I did not come to call the righteous, but sinners."

When Jesus came into Jerusalem riding on that donkey, he was received with something like the sort of acclaim that celebrities receive today. Jesus was mobbed, so to speak. His head, however, was not turned. He seems to have known exactly what was happening to him. In St. Luke's version of the Palm Sunday story, he tells us that "when he drew near and saw the city he wept over it, saying, 'Would that even today you knew the things that make for your peace! But now they are hid from your eyes. For the days shall come upon you, when your enemies will . . . hem you in on every side, and dash you to the ground, you and your children within you, and they will not leave one stone upon another in you, because you did not know the time of your visitation'" (Luke 19:41-44). Here is the purpose of the Palm Sunday liturgy: for the church to know the things that make for [her] peace, to know the time of [her] visitation. And strangely enough, it is in precisely the agony of the Cross that the church finds her peace.

This is one of only two times in the four Gospels that we are told Jesus wept.[2] Surely this is extraordinary. The Gospel of Luke says he is weeping for the city. What is the city? It is God's holy city, or was supposed to be; but what a long, long history of disobedience and disappointment! How Jerusalem had abandoned her holy calling! For a thousand years God had been preparing her through the prophets to meet her Messiah, her Savior, her Redeemer; now, as the Messiah at last appears, she is going to arrest him on a trumped-up charge, try him in the middle of the night, flog him nearly to death, and execute him the way we execute serial killers and terrorist bombers, though in an infinitely worse manner. Yet Jesus does not weep for himself. He weeps for the city. He weeps for those who will soon shout "Crucify him!" In other words, he weeps for us.

Did anyone ever weep for you? Did your mother shed tears because you did something that disappointed her? Did your father

Dürer: Christ's Entry into Jerusalem

This woodcut from Dürer's *Small Woodcut Passion* is typical of most representations of the Triumphal Entry in highlighting the contrast between the imperial figure of Christ and the absurdity of the little beast he rides upon, with his feet almost touching the ground.

weep for you because you got into trouble? Or did a daughter weep because her father abused her? Did a son weep because his father blamed him for something he never did? Did you weep for a friend lost on the battlefield or in an air crash? Did you weep for a child lost in the drug culture or for a grandchild kicked out of school? Did you weep for someone committing a hideous injustice? Everyone has grieved for the young victims in Jonesboro, but what about the two boys in jail? Do we weep for them too?[3] All these tears and every tear that has ever been shed by anyone anywhere are rolled up into the tears of Jesus. Jesus weeps for us. The Son of God weeps for you.

Recently I saw a 60 *Minutes* program about the unspeakable massacres that have been going on in Algeria. Christiane Amanpour interviewed a man who had watched the military come in and murder his whole family, his wife and children. He showed Ms. Amanpour the locations, the bloodstains, the place where he hid and watched, unable to do anything to save them. He described all this in a dispassionate tone, as though he were a journalist or tour guide, so that we, the television audience, wondered why he did not seem to be feeling anything. After he finished his description, the camera left him and went on to show other things. A few minutes later, however, it returned to reveal him sitting at a little table with his head bowed. Moving in, the camera revealed him to be silently weeping. The tears fell down his face and dropped on the table. No words were necessary. In those silent tears there was a whole world of inconsolable sorrow. Tears are eloquent. Tears speak. Judges look for tears when they are looking for a reason to give a lighter sentence. Jesus' tears encompass the entire human tragedy; he weeps for the Algerian man and his family, *and also* for the killers of this man's family. In the tears of the one man Jesus, God's complete solidarity with human pain, yes, *but also with human sin* is shown. And yet we do not know the time of our visitation. We don't want a crucified Messiah. In one way or another, we want to make Easter easy.

Why is it that we don't like the Cross? Why would we just as soon skip Good Friday and come back to church on Easter Day when everything will be beautiful? Well, there are a lot of reasons, but the one that becomes clear on Palm Sunday is that really coming to terms with the Cross means understanding that the good religious people, you and I, are responsible for our Lord being there. That's why we play the part of the crowd in the Passion narrative. "Crucify him!" I truly feel sorry for the woman who could not bring herself to say it. She does not understand that the Cross is what makes for the church's peace. She does not want to understand that Jesus weeps for her. But that is to miss the whole point, and missing the point is to miss the opportunity to be remade from the inside out.

Easter was not "made easy" for Jesus. "Behold, and see if there be any sorrow like unto his sorrow," says the book of Lamentations (1:12 KJV).[4] Easter cost the greatest price that has ever been paid in the history of the universe. And yet — miracle of miracles — for us, Easter is *free*. It cost us nothing; it cost God everything. We did not deserve God's ultimate sacrifice, but God paid it out of his vast storehouse of unconditional love. Your tears and mine are merely sentimental most of the time, but the tears of Jesus are wrung out of God's inmost heart of yearning compassion. The Messiah weeps for the sin that brings him to Jerusalem to die for her redemption. It is our complicity in sin that brings him there; it is our sin that he bears away from us like the scapegoat going into the wilderness. He weeps for you and for me. *The Lord has laid on him the iniquity of us all* (Isaiah 53).

Dear people of God, I have seen your work of faith and labor and love for one another. It is because "I know your works"[5] that I have faith in you this morning, that you will not want to miss the time of your visitation this week. These are "the things that make for your peace." Peace is found, not in escape, not in denial, not in false hope, but only in the Cross. What load are you carrying? Bring it to him. He has borne it already. What secret tears are you bottling up? He knows. He understands. He is taking it with him as he begins his journey to Calvary. "Shun not suffering, shame, or loss; learn of him to bear the cross."[6]

AMEN.

Postscript: In April 2001, *The Atlantic Monthly* featured a cover story by David Brooks, author of *Bobos in Paradise,* a well-received study of "bourgeois bohemian" baby boomers. In the *Atlantic* article, entitled "The Next Ruling Class: Meet the Organization Kid," Brooks described America's young elite and their attitude toward religion (specifically, Christianity). Robert Wuthnow of the Princeton faculty notes that they are much more interested in "spirituality, as they call it" than students a generation ago, but (the reporter continues) "the character of their faith tends to be unrelievedly upbeat." Again Wuthnow: "You never hear about sin and evil and judgment. It's about love and success and being happy." This is disturbing on a number of counts. For one thing, it means that they don't know very much about love, because real love *(agape)* inevitably brings suffering. For another, it means that although they may be busily (and admirably) serving at soup kitchens and building houses for Habitat for Humanity, they have little sense of the structures of sin and evil that pervade human society everywhere and cause so many to remain impoverished and downtrodden. In particular, Wuthnow's analysis means that their "spirituality" has no Cross at its center. The author, David Brooks, concludes: "These are some of the best and brightest our high schools have to offer . . . but they live in a country that has lost, in its frenetic seeking after happiness and success, the language of sin and character-building through combat with sin."[7] Notably, in a CNN interview on October 30, 2001, David Brooks stated that this generation of young elites had perhaps been dramatically altered by the aftermath of September 11. Surely there is an opportunity for the churches here.

The New World Order

———⚬≈⚬———

Text: The Passion According to St. Mark

Of all the days in the Christian year, this is certainly the most disconcerting. Even the most seasoned churchgoers tend to forget, each year, exactly what we are in for when we come to church for this occasion. We start out in a gala mood; Palm Sunday has always been a crowd-pleaser. The festivity of the triumphal procession, the stirring music, the palm branches, the repeated hosannas all suggest a general air of celebration. It comes as a shock to us, year after year, to find ourselves abruptly plunged into the solemn, overwhelmingly long dramatic reading of the Passion narrative. It's a tough Sunday. It begins in triumph and ends in catastrophe. We come in prepared for a party, and we leave as if we were going to a funeral. We come in joyful and we go out stricken. All in all, it is a most perplexing day — and for those who are unprepared, it can be downright threatening.

It would be tempting, on this day, to follow good American practice and tone down the depressing parts — "accentuate the positive, eliminate the negative." Many American congregations have attempted this. Were it not for the ancient liturgical wisdom given to the church, it would be perfectly possible to go to Sunday services two weekends in a row — Palm Sunday and Easter Day — without ever having to face the fact that Jesus of Nazareth was abandoned, condemned, and put to death as a common criminal on the Friday between. Our historic liturgy, however, guards against this fatal misunderstanding. From early times the Christian church has placed the Passion narrative squarely in the center of all that we do on this deceptively festal day. The proper liturgical name for this day is not really "Palm Sunday"; it is "the Sunday of the Passion." In this way, the church announces for all to hear that the Crucifixion of Jesus is the main event. There is no passage from Palm Sunday to Easter without Good Friday.

The proclamation of the Christian church about the significance of Jesus' death is so staggering that one sometimes wonders how it has all become so commonplace. Christians have put forth this message for two thousand years with sufficient urgency to compel the faith of millions, yet even regular churchgoers tend to forget how colossal the claim of the Cross really is. According to the New Testament, the Crucifixion of Jesus is the turning point of universal history.[8]

There has been a certain amount of cynical commentary in the media this month about President Bush's phrase, "new world order." I saw a trenchant political cartoon on the subject last week. The scene depicted is a restaurant. Seated at the table are two men, one a Palestinian, the other an Israeli. George H. W. Bush is the waiter, holding his little pad and pencil. He says to them, "May I take your New World Order?" The Israeli and the Palestinian, glowering at each other with ferocious expressions, say, "The same."

The claim of the Christian gospel is that the Crucifixion of Jesus was the inauguration of the New World Order (not "a" but "the"). Yet everything seems to be exactly the same. The headlines in the newspapers are as depressing as ever:

Woman and Daughter Kill Mother, Kidnap Baby

Soldier Who Served in Gulf War
Shot Dead on Detroit Street

Economic Boom in Milwaukee Leaves
Low-Income Groups Behind

Programs for Handicapped Children Facing Deep Cuts

United Nations Report Describes
Near-Apocalyptic Devastation in Iraq

Monrovia, Liberia — The "City of Dreadful Sights"

New World Order? On the contrary, it seems that the more things change, the more they remain the same.[9] The contradictions of Palm Sunday are mirrored in the news. Mixed in with the stories about crime, violence, poverty, war, and death we will find another type of headline:

Local Churches Prepare to Observe Holy Week

Music of the Season Keeps Organists and Choirs Busy

Pope John Paul II Washes Feet in Solemn Ceremony

Jerusalem Prepares for Influx of Holy Week Pilgrims

What do these two groups of headlines have to do with one another? Does the Christian church just continue to go its irrelevant and outmoded way, quaintly pursuing its picturesque customs while the real world goes about its real business? Or could it be that the haunting contradictions of Palm Sunday are somehow reflected in the evil and suffering of the world, strangely related in precisely the same way that the ugliness of the crowds on Friday is related to their hosannas on Palm Sunday?

A revealing event, in recent years, was the discovery of the torture chambers of President Touré of Guinea. He had fooled almost everyone with his cultivated, elegant ways — very few knew, until the discoveries after his death, that hundreds, perhaps thousands, had died in his prison of horror. The details were revolting in the extreme. In one tiny, windowless cell, a prisoner had written *in his own blood* these words: "God save me."

This week, the church of Jesus Christ gathers around the heart, the center, the guts of its claim to know the truth. Today, we bear this testimony in the full gaze of public, secular, worldly opinion — the Son of God is going to die a godforsaken death and, in this death, the truth about God and man and human destiny is fully revealed. We dare not say this, we must not say this, we can not say this, unless the death of Jesus Christ is somehow connected with the terrible, bloody cry of that nameless victim: "God save me." If the truth about Jesus Christ cannot be uttered in the face of such unspeakable and hopeless suffering, then it should not be uttered at all.

I had a dear friend, whom I will call Sarah. When she was in her thirties she developed rheumatoid arthritis and aplastic anemia and a host of other ills. For thirty years she suffered more physical pain and more crippling disabilities than almost anyone else I have ever known. We prayed for her constantly, to no apparent avail. Her husband said, "Every time we pray, she gets worse." I have never ceased to think about this friend, Sarah, whom I loved. If the Christian faith has nothing to say to her, it has nothing to say to anyone. What hope is there, ultimately, for humanity? What word of comfort is there for those who can only get worse? What can be said in the face of an inscription written in blood — "God save me" — in view of the fact that the prisoner clearly was *not* saved in this world? If we Christians cannot respond in word and deed to questions such as these, if our faith in Jesus Christ falls apart under such challenges, then it is not a faith worth having.

You have just participated in the reading of the Passion narrative from Mark. Listen again to this portion:

> They that passed by railed on him, wagging their heads, and saying, Ah, thou that destroyest the temple, and buildest it in three days, save thyself, and come down from the cross. Likewise also the chief priests mocking said among themselves with the scribes, He saved others; himself he cannot save. Let Christ the King of Israel descend now from the cross, that we may see and believe. And they that were crucified with him reviled him.

And when the sixth hour was come, there was darkness over the whole land until the ninth hour. And at the ninth hour Jesus cried with a loud voice, saying, *Eloi, Eloi, lama sabachthani?* which is, being interpreted, "My God, my God, why hast thou forsaken me?" (Mark 15:29-34 KJV)

Here, in Jesus' Cry of Dereliction, which has never been fully plumbed, is the proving ground of our faith. The Son of God, in the Garden of Gethsemane, cried to the Father "God save me!" and the answer came that there was to be no escape. If there is one thing certain today, it is this: we do not proclaim a God who has remained remote from the agony of his creatures. "My God, my God, why hast thou forsaken me?" In those words from the Cross we see the deepest identification of Jesus the Messiah with the outermost limit of human suffering. He truly wrote the words "God save me" *with his own blood.* St. Mark wants us to see that it is precisely in this extremity that Jesus is Lord. Mark's whole Gospel is constructed so as to come to its climax with Jesus' dereliction and shameful death. It is in this condition of utter abandonment that Jesus is seen most fully and most truly to be Son of God.[10]

Jesus' Cry of Dereliction on the Cross is not just the heartbreaking lament of an abandoned man. It is that, but it is not only that. What we see and hear in Jesus' death is not just his identification with the wretched of the earth. It is that, but it is not only that. What we see and hear in Jesus' death is the decisive intervention of God to deliver his children from the unspeakable fate of ultimate abandonment. It is the strangest imaginable teaching on this most strange of all days. The testimony of the four evangelists, the testimony of the Christian church, is that in this event, in this godforsaken death, the cosmic scale has been conclusively tipped in the opposite direction, so that sin and evil and death are not the last word and never will be again.

Can we expect people to believe this today? Where is the evidence? The Christian message proclaims a New World Order; the data suggest that nothing is changed — the customers are still ordering up the same old violence, brutality, vengeance, and death. As long as there are people writing "God save me" in their own blood, how can we speak of deliverance in Jesus Christ? Do we just have to fall back on blind faith? Do we just say that God will make everything right some day?

I am convinced that we can say more than that. Even as I am confronted with the intolerable fact of these words in blood, I am reminded also of the reasons that I believe in the reality and the power of Jesus Christ even now in this "present evil age" (Galatians 1:4), even while it is still hidden in the weakness of the servants of God.

I believe that the Cross of Christ inaugurated the New World Order of God. It brought something into the world that was not there before. I believe in it because of those who follow that Way. I think for instance of Susan Leckrone, a member of our New York City congregation, who at this moment is in Monrovia, Liberia ("the city of dreadful sights"), bathing out of a bucket because there is no running water, using her skills as a nurse to bring the love of Jesus to the victims of an atrocious civil war. She writes back and tells us that the Christians there are still praising the Lord.[11]

And I believe because of a story I read about the Civil Rights movement. The freedom fighters discovered somewhere along the way that one of the greatest weapons against evil is subversive humor. Bayard Rustin tells it:

> When the Ku Klux Klan marched into Montgomery and we knew they were coming, Dr. [Martin Luther] King and I sat down and thought it over. And we said, 'Ah! Tell everybody to put on their Sunday clothes, stand on the steps [of the church], and when the Ku Kluxers come, applaud 'em.' Well, they came, marched three blocks, and unharassed, they left. They could not comprehend the new thing. They were no longer able to engender fear.[12]

That is the new thing. That is the New World Order. There are witnesses all over the world whose lives are a testimony to its reality and power. I think of John Perkins, of Mendenhall, Mississippi, who wrote that "the night some police officers beat me almost to death was the night God gave me compassion for whites." I think of Dietrich Bonhoeffer, whose fervent prayers in the Nazi prison moved observers so deeply in the hour before he was hanged. I think especially of Bishop Tutu, small of stature and black of skin, who loves his enemies and blesses those who curse him because his steady vision of the heavenly city, the true New World Order, gives him strength to do battle with apartheid day in and day out.[13] And finally I think of my dear friend Sarah and her husband Sam.[14] I was with her just before she died. I believe that in many ways she thought God had abandoned her. But she never, never for one minute let go of the church, the prayers and the faith of those who loved her, above all that of her husband, who had enough faith for a hundred. She died on Easter Day, 1986. On her tombstone, Sam had these words engraved: "Welcome, happy morning."

My dear brothers and sisters in Christ:

With all my heart, with all my mind, with all my strength I desire to convey to you that this week, while the world goes about its business, the meaning of existence is revealed to those who have eyes to see. The true significance of the headlines comes to light as Jesus of Nazareth goes his solitary way. Today in the reading of the Passion, Thursday night as Jesus eats his Last Supper and goes forth to be betrayed, Friday noon as he hangs exposed and naked on the Cross and pours out his life, *God is acting.* In the events of this week, the cries of those who suffer have been heard by the only One who could, the only One who can, the only One who will deliver on his promise that there will be a happy morning. But it only comes — it *only* comes — by means of his death. Let us follow him then, this week, to the foot of his Cross. Let us come together in mind and heart to behold our Lord as he gives himself up for the sake of the whole world. Let us come in heart and soul and mind, in faith and in trust, to confess that "truly this man is the Son of God."

AMEN.

Lead Us to Calvary

———❦———

This is your hour, and the power of darkness.

(LUKE 22:53)

To-day shalt thou be with me in paradise.

(LUKE 23:43)

We have all been following the news about the troubles in the Holy Land. I wonder if you have noticed that the news articles have seemed more and more to have less and less to do with Christianity. I read an article last week, quite a good one, in which the author (a Jew) seriously proposed that the city of Jerusalem be divided, West and East, between Jews and Palestinians. From a realistic political standpoint, his discussion made a lot of sense, but what struck me most was that in the entire eight-page article there was no mention, not even a hint, that Jerusalem had any importance for Christians.[15] It was as though Christianity did not even exist in the city of its birth.

A related thought occurred to me as I picked up my clothes at my favorite Chinese laundry a few days before Ash Wednesday, that is, before Lent had even begun. The place was bedecked from stem to stern with bunnies, eggs, and best wishes for a happy Easter. The

[18]

friendly Chinese owners were obviously not aware of any liturgical violations; they assume that this is what Americans expect. My sense of something askew was compounded when I spent some time in various locations going from store to store looking for Easter cards. The proportion of cards having to do with the Resurrection of Christ was minuscule or nonexistent compared to the racks and racks of secular cards. Even some of the *church* bookstores had far more cards with generic messages about springtime and the renewal of nature than they did real Easter cards. Again, it seemed as though real Christianity did not exist.

In recent months I have read several articles about how the most compelling stories being told in our culture today are the stories told by advertisers. All of us, without necessarily knowing it, have allowed these stories to tell us who we are, what we want, what our goals of life should be. Wearing Polo clothes offers the hope of entering Ralph Lauren's world of moneyed ease. Buying a Range Rover means the possibility of a limitless horizon. Cosmetic surgery, in particular, has created within the last ten years a burgeoning advertising category all by itself; youth and good looks are forever within the reach of your surgeon's knife — for a price, of course. No one in America is untouched by these false narratives. Even if one is theoretically a believing Christian, the messages from the mass media are capable of overwhelming the messages from Holy Scripture and the sacraments of the church. It's almost as though Christianity didn't exist.

The point of all this is that you, the people of this congregation, have made a very important choice today. You have come together this morning as a community of those who are being shaped by *this other story,* the story of some strange events that happened in the city of Jerusalem 2000 years ago. We are here to learn once again that, no matter what the secular culture may tell you, the story of Jesus is still the greatest story ever told and always will be. If you believe this, or if you think you *might* believe it, or if you are in any way drawn even to the *possibility* of believing it, then you will want to be here for all of the Holy Week events — Thursday and Friday in particular — in order to be grasped by what Easter really means. (And by the way, the Maundy Thursday service is family night. With its incomparable drama and intimate scale, it is especially suited for older children.) Christians today are surrounded on all sides by alternative stories, many of them very seductive and powerful. All the more reason for immersing ourselves in *this* story, *this particular narrative* of Jesus and his execution in Jerusalem, for without it, there is no Christian church, no Christian faith, and certainly no Easter.

The gospel that we proclaim tells us that all those years ago, in that specific Roman province called Judea, certain events occurred that have universal meaning. Our relationship to that particular locale is paradoxical; it *is* and *is not* central to our saving story.[16] No matter what vicissitudes may trouble the actual geo-political city of Jerusalem, the meaning of the story of Jesus remains intact. I don't mean to disparage the importance of finding a solution to the problems of modern Israel. It is all very troubling to anyone who loves the land of the Bible. As the Psalms teach us, we Christians should pray earnestly for the peace of Jerusalem (Psalm 122:6), and work for it and give for it, as we always do on Good Friday. But there are two Jerusalems — the earthly one and the transcendent, perfected Jerusalem that belongs to the future triumph of God.[17] On Palm Sunday two thousand years ago, the earthly Jerusalem was bisected by the heavenly one, with eternal consequence for the whole world.

You know the story, how Jesus of Nazareth, a poor itinerant preacher from the unpromising region of Galilee, came into the city at the head of a rather ridiculous procession. With seeming foreknowledge, the Master commanded his disciples to borrow a donkey (they were too poor to own one), which he mounted and rode into the city as the disciples, joined by the rabble of the city, greeted him as Messiah: "All glory, laud and honor, to thee, Redeemer, King!" How much thought did most of us give to those words as we sang them a few moments ago? How much thought did the crowd in Jerusalem that day give to them? Those who shouted "Hosanna!" on that first Palm Sunday were essentially the same as those who yelled for his death on Good Friday. The liturgy of Palm Sunday is set up to show you how you can say one thing one minute and its opposite the next. This is the nature of the sinful human being.

Palm Sunday is the first scene in the final drama of the salvation of the world. The story of Holy Week begins here. Jesus knowingly stages his own entrance into the city where he will meet his destiny, deliberately arranging to ride, not on the war horse that a military conqueror would use, but on the lowly beast of burden that was prophesied by Zechariah: "Behold, your king is coming to you, humble, and mounted on a donkey" (Zechariah 9:9). Jesus is dramatizing two things: he is indeed the Messiah that the prophets foretold, but at the same time he is not at all the sort of Messiah that people were hoping for. The second lesson from Philippians is perfectly chosen for today; listen again to the way that St. Paul tells the whole story in two sentences: "Christ Jesus . . . though he was in the form of God, did not count equality with God a thing to be grasped, but emptied himself, taking the form of a servant, being born in the likeness of men. And being found in human form he humbled himself and became obedient unto death, even death on a cross" (Philippians 2:5-8).

The Palm Sunday liturgy has a sort of genius about it. It combines the festivity of the palm procession with the dreadful story of the Crucifixion. I would imagine that anyone coming to the Palm Sunday service unprepared would be in quite a state of shock. No one is off the hook today. All of us who sang "Thou art the King of Israel, thou David's royal Son" shouted shortly thereafter, "Crucify him!" Indeed, the evangelist Luke sharpens the point by adding, "They [the people] were urgent, demanding with loud cries that he should be crucified" (Luke 23:23). It can't be said too often; those who clamored for Jesus' death were not "the Jews." They were us. There is a sense in which the most important Sunday to be in church is Palm Sunday, because no other Sunday places *us* so squarely in the middle of the action. You know that "Palm Sunday" is really a nickname. The real name of this day is the Sunday of the Passion. That is why we sang just now, "Lest I forget, lead me to Calvary."[18]

Lead us to Calvary.[19] There are two ways to go there. One way is to go as spectators, there for the show, not acknowledging our complicity in any way. The other way is to go as penitent sinners knowing our need for Christ even as we acknowledge our acquiescence in his death. The surest way of doing this is to understand our place in the story. I call your attention to one verse in the Passion story according to St. Luke:

> Jesus said to the chief priests and captains of the temple and elders, who had come out against him, "Have you come out as against a robber, with swords and clubs? When I was with you day after day in the temple, you did not lay hands on me. But this is your hour, and the power of darkness." (Luke 22:52-53)

This is your hour, and the power of darkness. Let us focus on this verse for a moment. All four evangelists picture Jesus squarely in the center of the struggle between two cosmic powers. The forces of evil are going to be unleashed against him in full strength. C. S. Lewis once wrote that "the mere sight of the devils was one of the greatest among the torments of Hell . . . at the bottom of all worlds that face is waiting whose sight alone is the misery from which none who beholds it can recover."[20] Jesus has been banishing demons, demonstrating his power over them, all during his ministry; now he is about to give himself over to them. No wonder he prayed on Thursday night, "Let this cup pass from me."

In a bookstore a few months ago I found a book of paintings of the Crucifixion. I bought it and brought it home and began looking through it. The pictures were arranged in chronological order with the early ones first. I had seen most of the images in the first half of the book before; they had nothing particularly new to say to me. They all looked more or less the same. As I turned the pages toward the end, however, the more modern versions began to engage my attention. One in particular I will never forget. Even if we had an overhead projector we would not show it in church; it is too horrible. It looks somewhat as the Crucifixion must have really looked. For one thing, the Lord has no loincloth, as he certainly would not have had in real life. For another, the viciousness and cruelty of cru-

[22]

Lovis Corinth: Large Martyrdom

This picture, almost too dreadful to look at, is valuable for its unsparing depiction of the surpassing brutality of the method. This is what crucifixion was really like, and this was the depth of depravity and inhumanity required to carry it out.

cifying a human being is made plain in a way that I had not seen before. We see the Roman soldiers going about their work in the most unsparing way. It is an illustration of the saying, "This is your hour, and the power of darkness."

Most of us have never seen anyone tortured to death and, God willing, we will never have to. But we are implicated in the powers of darkness just the same. Yesterday there was an article in *The New York Times* about the movement to save the nuclear sites where the bombs were developed as tourist attractions. One U.S. Senator said of the B Reactor, where plutonium was made for the Nagasaki bomb, "It would not be a place to spend a fun day; it would be sort of like the Holocaust Museum." But the president of the B Reactor Museum Association spoke with pride of the technological achievement. "When you stand in front of the reactor, you realize this is what humans can do. . . ."21 Yes. When you look at a picture of the Crucifixion, you realize this is what humans can do. Without doubt, the Romans were proud of their ability to keep order in the Empire with the gruesome method of death they had devised, and they went about it in the same efficient way. It was distasteful, certainly, but these undesirable people had to be disposed of, as a deterrent. That is the way the human species thinks. As many theologians and virtually all great literary artists have seen, we human beings live according to the whims of the Power of Death. *This is your hour, and the power of darkness.* Jesus gave himself up, body and soul, to these Powers of darkness. He prepared himself to look into the face of the Devil. This is the way that God chose to save us from that power that held us in bondage, by submitting to it himself. *This is your hour, and the power of darkness.*

During this coming week, the church commemorates and dramatizes the victory of the Son of God over the dark Powers. I beg you, do not let any secular story or alternative story take priority over this one in your hearts and minds. "Lest we forget, lead us to Calvary." The church does not try to deceive you. We are summoned to stare evil in the face. We are summoned to watch at our Lord's side. We are invited to see what human beings can do. We will see ourselves as Judas, who betrayed the Lord; as the religious leaders who condemned him; as Peter, who denied him; as the crowd who shouted "Crucify him!" and as the thief who mocked him. But St. Luke, in his Passion narrative, invites us to see ourselves also as the other thief, the one who made no excuses, but threw himself on the mercy of the Son of God. When the repentant thief heard the other one cursing Jesus, Luke tells us, he "rebuked him, saying, 'Do you not fear God, since you are under the same sentence of condemnation? And we indeed justly; for we are receiving the due reward of our deeds; but this man has done nothing wrong.' And he said, 'Jesus, remember me when you come into your kingdom.' And Jesus said to him, 'Verily I say unto thee, today shalt thou be with me in paradise'" (Luke 23:40-43).

Let us be that thief today. Come to the banquet table of this King who loves us and gives himself for us so that the hour of darkness, having exhausted itself upon him, will have no power to claim those whom he calls to his everlasting Jerusalem, now and forever.

AMEN.

A Procession of Fools

———◦⊷∞⊶◦———

Text: The Passion According to St. Matthew

What do you think people thought we were doing just now? There was a time when whole towns in Europe would turn out for Palm Sunday processions and everybody knew what it was all about.[22] Nowadays, the Palm Sunday congregations are a small minority of the total population. Most people who happened to be driving by while we were attempting to sing "All Glory, Laud and Honor" without accompaniment, in various keys and at various tempos, either did not know what we were doing or did not especially care. I imagine a conversation in a passing car:

> Kids: "Dad, what are those people doing?"
> Dad (a lapsed Episcopalian): "It's Palm Sunday. They're pretending to wave tree branches or palm trees or something."
> Kids: "Why?"
> Dad: "Because Jesus was in some kind of a parade."
> Kids: "What for?"
> Dad: "I forget. Ask your mother."
> Kids: "Can we go to McDonald's?"

Note to the reader: This sermon has been lengthened somewhat for the present volume, in order to include more about Desmond Tutu and the Truth and Reconciliation Commission in South Africa.

Maybe I am not giving you enough credit, but didn't some of you feel just a teensy bit foolish just now? If you had children with you, that made it OK — you knew it was good for the children — but if you didn't, you might have wondered, "Do I really want to be doing this?" Maybe that's why some of you slipped into the church just a tad late.

The first Palm Sunday apparently involved a reasonably large, enthusiastic crowd of hosanna-shouters.[23] St. Matthew tells us that "the whole city was shaken" (21:10).[24] This evangelist wants us to know that the Messiah of Israel is entering his capital city. Try as we may, we cannot reproduce that degree of high drama in our liturgical processions. I don't mean that we shouldn't have them; I'm just suggesting that we have to make an extra effort to understand that what happened to Jesus on the first day of his final week on earth was replete with meaning on a number of levels not readily apparent in our little re-enactment. You have already sensed those layers of meaning, I feel sure, because you have participated not only in the palm procession but also, just now, in the solemn reading of the St. Matthew Passion.

"When Jesus had finished all his teaching," Matthew tells us, "he said to his disciples, 'You know that the Passover is coming, and the Son of Man will be delivered up to be crucified'" (26:1-2). This is the predominant note of the day. Even in the midst of the palm procession, there is a note of foreboding; the beautiful hymn that we will sing in a few minutes evokes it:

Ride on! ride on in majesty!
In lowly pomp ride on to die! . . .
The angel armies of the skies
Look down with sad and wondering eyes
To see the approaching sacrifice.[25]

Wrenching paradox! The King of glory is "betrayed into the hands of sinners" (Matthew 26:45). No one knows it better than Jesus himself. He chooses it. As he himself says to Peter in the garden at the time of his arrest, "Do you not know that I could appeal to

my Father, and he would at once send me more than twelve legions of angels? But then how would the Scriptures be fulfilled, which say that all this must take place?" (Matthew 26:53-54). There will not be any angelic interventions. The angel armies will look on "with sad and wondering eyes" but they are forbidden to come to rescue him. The great Giotto, in his frescoes of the life of Christ in the Scrovegni (Arena) Chapel in Padua, shows angels protecting Jesus in the early episodes and then, in the fresco depicting the dead Christ, shows the angels in wrenching attitudes of extreme grief. If it is possible to identify with angels, this is the occasion to do it; we sense their agonized impotence as they are forced to hover nearby without taking any action. More than any rendering that I know, this painting conveys the sense of the divine hand withheld, by the choice of the Son himself. God has chosen a way that is precisely antithetical to the way that we would have done it. As Jesus stands before Pontius Pilate with his hands tied behind his back, the kingdom of this world is confronted face to face with the shocking

Ephitaphios of Thessaloniki *(left)*
Giotto: Detail from Pieta (Lamentation) *(above)*

Both of these images convey a powerful sense of the unthinkable horror of the Crucifixion of the Son of God. They differ, however, in their effect; the icon is typically hieratic and stylized, whereas Giotto's angels are humanized and work more immediately on our emotions. This stylistic innovation of the Italian Renaissance, begun by Cimabue and brought to maturity by the genius of Giotto, is one of the most important developments in art history. Icons in the Byzantine style have for some time been increasingly admired on their own terms, however.

image of the kingdom of God bound and defenseless. The power that manifests itself in strength is confronted by the power that manifests itself in weakness.

The evangelist Matthew is known for his emphasis on Jesus' identity as the royal Son of God, the scion of David, the kingly Messiah. It is especially clear in Matthew's version that Jesus is in imperial control of every detail of his entry into Jerusalem on the back of the donkey. It is a most curious sight, this procession. Not only does the "king" ride on an absurd animal, but his close followers make a distinctly downscale impression — they are a retinue of fishermen, tax-collectors, dubious women, street people, mental cases, and riffraff of various sorts. It has a truly ridiculous aspect; we need to remember that and not try to glamorize it. Jesus, however, has planned the whole thing. This is his way of demonstrating just what kind of king he is. He has arranged this peculiar parade in order to teach that his kingdom is utterly different from earthly empires and has nothing in common with worldly pomp; indeed, he enters the city in terrible and shameful poverty.[26] And so, a king; but one who forces us to ask, *what kind of king?*

Matthew continues, "Jesus stood before the governor; and the governor asked him, 'Are you the King of the Jews?' . . . but [Jesus] gave him no answer, not even to a single charge, so that the governor wondered greatly" (27:11-14). This unnerving silence of Jesus at his trial is recorded by all four evangelists. He will not respond to the way the questions are framed. He will not allow himself to be defined by human preconceptions of his kingship. The meaning of his kingly rule will be revealed only by his suffering as he gives himself up to the tender mercies of the powers of this world. It is his free and sovereign choice to relinquish all his divine prerogatives and submit to the treatment described to us by the evangelist:

> Then the soldiers of the governor took Jesus into the praetorium, and they gathered the whole battalion before him. And they stripped him and put a scarlet robe upon him, and plaiting a crown of thorns they put it on his head, and put a reed in his right hand. And kneeling before him they mocked him, saying,

"Hail, King of the Jews!" And they spat upon him, and took the reed and struck him on the head. (Matthew 27:27-30)

Can we get our minds around this? The heavenly Son of the almighty Creator has given himself up to being spat upon by wretched human creatures, creatures who in fact are by their actions forfeiting the designation of human being; creatures caught up in a heedless, untrammeled display of barbarism; creatures whom he nevertheless loves and for whom he is prepared to suffer this vile humiliation, this public rejection, this hideous death.

The people who shouted "Hosanna to the Son of David!" were apparently able to imagine this unlikely Messiah on Palm Sunday — but not on Friday. The lesson of the donkey had not stayed with them very long, if indeed it registered at all. If Jesus was not to be the kind of swashbuckling leader they wanted, then "let him be crucified" (27:22-23). You and I would have done the same; that is why we have played both parts today. We are no different from the crowds in Jerusalem; we want to see believable demonstrations of divine power and kingly authority. "King of Israel, indeed!" (27:42 NEB) we shouted; "Let him come down from the cross" — let him show off his power, let him strike down his enemies — "and then we will believe in him. Come down from the cross and save yourself, if you really are the Son of God" (Matthew 27:42).

But he did not come down. And so now, as the discrepancy between kingship as we understand it in this world and the situation of the man on the Cross could not be more stark, we come to the deepest place in the Passion narrative.

From midday a darkness fell over the whole land, which lasted until three in the afternoon, and about three Jesus cried aloud, "Eli, eli, lama sabachthani?" which means, "My God, my God, why hast thou forsaken me?"

Did you fully take this in when we read it? There is no other "word from the Cross" in Matthew's Gospel, nor in Mark's either. Wouldn't you have thought that these two evangelists would have softened it up a bit? Apparently Luke thought it was too much, because he omitted it altogether.[27] Matthew and Mark, however, preserved it alone among the Seven Words. For these two evangelists, the Cry of Dereliction seems to hold the key. Here we find the contradiction which opens up for us the most profoundly anti-religious aspect of our faith. We should realize that there is no sense in it. Many have tried to give it sense, but with little success.[28] You can study the history of religion until you are exhausted and you will never find anything like this. God against God? God forsaken by God? A crucified God? We have not pondered the Cross of Christ closely enough if we have not been repelled at least to some degree by this scandal.[29] That is what St. Paul called it: a scandal (*skandalon* in Greek). He also called it foolishness: "The word of the cross is foolishness to those who are perishing. . . ." But, he continues, "it is written, 'I will destroy the wisdom of the wise, and the cleverness of the clever I will thwart.'. . . Has not God made foolish the wisdom of the world? . . . for it pleased God through the foolishness of what we preach to save those who believe" (1 Corinthians 1:18-21).

So perhaps we are right to have felt a little foolish a while ago. Paul continues: "Where is the wise man? Where is the scribe? Where is the debater of this age? . . . For Jews demand signs and Greeks seek wisdom, but we preach Christ crucified, a stumbling block (*skandalon*) to Jews and foolishness to Gentiles, but to those who are called, both Jews and Greeks, Christ the power of God and the wisdom of God. For the foolishness of God is wiser than human wisdom, and the weakness of God is stronger than human strength" (1 Corinthians 1:20-25).

There is a dimension here that is almost beyond words, and yet we must try to put it into words. Many people are just not willing to look at this dimension; if we were willing, we would not give our support so readily to the death penalty in this country. What we see and hear in Jesus' death is not just his solidarity with the victims of this world. It is that, but it is not only that. What we see and hear in the Cry of Dereliction is Jesus' identification in his Cross *not only* with the innocent victims of this world *but also* with their torturers.

That scandalous insight is especially important to St. Paul, who knew it to be the reason that the Cross is so radical. What Jesus assumes on the Cross is *not only* the suffering of innocents *but also* the wickedness of those who inflict suffering, and here Luke is important because he incorporates the idea into a Word from the Cross: "Father, forgive them; for they know not what they do" (Luke 23:34). This means that Jesus, in his death, makes himself one, not only with my *pain*, but also with my *sin* — because I myself, and you yourselves, and all of us ourselves, are *sometimes victims* of others and *sometimes torturers* of others and *sometimes both*, and when we recognize this we are, as Jesus said to the scribe, "not far from the kingdom of God" (Mark 12:34).

The most striking form of Christian witness in the world — the one thing that the world even at its worst will occasionally recognize — is the forgiveness of a perpetrator by a victim. That was the power of the American Civil Rights movement. The leaders, who were mostly Christians, would not allow the marchers and demonstrators to act out of hatred toward white people. One of those leaders was Mrs. Fannie Lou Hamer.[30] Beaten almost to a pulp in a Mississippi jail, ridiculed by upper-class blacks because she was an illiterate sharecropper, risking her life daily to train volunteers in the voter registration movement, yet living out of "a deep river of faith," she said, "It wouldn't solve any problem for me to hate whites just because they hate me. Oh, there's so much hate, only God has kept the Negro sane. . . . You have to love them [whites] for they know not what they do."[31]

Even the world at its worst recognizes the moral force in this. That is why Nelson Mandela will forever be accounted one of the most remarkable leaders in history. Think of it: a man imprisoned for no crime but only for his convictions, emerging after twenty-seven years of incarceration without a single trace of bitterness or vengefulness, whose first public gesture was to invite his white jailer to his inauguration as his honored guest. That is why the whole world defers to him; it has been said that more heads of state want to be photographed with Mandela than anyone else on earth. But Archbishop Desmond Tutu of South Africa is equally remarkable, in some ways even more so because he was on the front lines of the struggle for so long and for decades had to endure being misunderstood and vilified by people on both sides of the conflict. Not for one minute during all that time has he ceased to be the theological spokesman for nonviolence and reconciliation. In his book *No Future Without Forgiveness,* he tells the story of his chairmanship of the Truth and Reconciliation Commission, charged with uncovering the atrocities that occurred under the apartheid system.[32] There were two types of testimony before the commission: the wrenching personal stories of the victims and their families, and the depositions of the perpetrators who sought amnesty by confessing their crimes. The commission focused especially on enabling the wrongdoers to repent and publicly ask forgiveness. Bishop Tutu writes:

> We were constantly amazed in the commission at the extraordinary magnanimity that so many of the victims exhibited. Of course there were those who said they would not forgive. That demonstrated for me the important point that forgiveness . . . was neither cheap nor easy. . . . True reconciliation is not cheap. It cost God the death of His only begotten Son. . . .
>
> In forgiving, people are not asked to forget. . . . Forgiveness does not mean condoning what has been done. . . . It involves trying to understand the perpetrators and so have empathy, to try to stand in their shoes and appreciate the sorts of pressures and influences that might have conditioned them.
>
> Forgiveness is not sentimental. . . . Forgiveness means abandoning your right to pay back the perpetrator in his own coin, but it is a loss that liberates the victim. . . .

And then Tutu continues,

> Does the victim depend on the culprit's contrition and confession as the precondition for being able to forgive? . . . Jesus did not wait until those who were nailing him to the Cross had asked for forgiveness. He was ready, as they drove in the nails, to pray to his Father to forgive them and he even provided an excuse ["they

do not know what they are doing"}. If the victim could forgive only when the culprit confessed, then the victim would be locked into the culprit's whim, locked into victimhood. . . .[33]

Here in our own day is a dazzling example of the foolishness of God. Bishop Tutu's account of the TRC is full of references to the criticism and scorn that its members endured, but his book will stand forever as a companion for those who seek to follow the Messiah on the donkey. Here is the radical core of Holy Week: on the Cross, our Lord takes the part of those who are condemned and god-forsaken, those who are on Death Row, those who have been abandoned even by their families, those who are cast out of society and have no one to take their part. The Cry of Dereliction, combined with Jesus' prayer for the forgiveness of the perpetrators, brings us into the very heart of the God who has extended his love into the darkest places of the human soul, even into Hell itself.

Did you feel foolish, earlier? That is your clue:

We preach Christ crucified, a stumbling block *(skandalon)* to Jews and foolishness to Gentiles, but to those who are called, both Jews and Greeks, Christ the power of God and the wisdom of God. For the foolishness of God is wiser than human wisdom, and the weakness of God is stronger than human strength. (1 Corinthians 1:23-24)

So yes, we are a procession of fools today. *Hosanna to the Son of David! Blessed is he who comes in the name of the Lord! Hosanna in the highest!*

AMEN.

PART TWO

Monday, Tuesday, and Wednesday of Holy Week

⤜∞∞⤛

That God, this Lord, the Lord of life, could die, is a strange contemplation; that the Red Sea could be dry {Exodus 14:21}, that the sun could stand still {Joshua 10:12}, that an oven could be seven times heat and not burn {Daniel 3:19}, that lions could be hungry and not bite {Daniel 6:22}, is strange, miraculously strange, but super-miraculous that God could die; but that God would die is an exaltation of that.

JOHN DONNE

Note to the reader

—⊗⊗⊗—

These sermons were delivered to weeknight congregations, for the most part made up of people whose presence on a weeknight was indicative of a high degree of commitment and a willingness to work harder at listening. Moreover, the services were preaching services with one or two hymns and a few prayers, not the longer Eucharistic service. The sermons in this section are therefore longer and more dense than the Sunday sermons in this collection.

Monday in Holy Week 1989

The King's Ransom

———— ∞∞∞ ————

The Son of Man came not to be served but to serve, and to give his life as a ransom for many.

(MARK 10:45)

You know that you were ransomed from the futile ways inherited from your fathers, not with perishable things such as silver or gold, but with the precious blood of Christ, like that of a lamb without blemish or spot.

(1 PETER 1:18-19)

You were bought with a price.

(1 CORINTHIANS 6:20; 7:23)

For many people who have been fascinated by the Shroud of Turin, it has come as a disappointment to learn that it is only eight hundred years old. Others, however, are relieved. In view of the fact that some Roman Catholic leaders are saying the shroud is still worthy of veneration and capable of producing miracles, it seems that there is still a lot to be said for the Reformation. For example, one statement from the Protestant wing of the church reminded us that even if the carbon tests had shown that the linen dated from the first century, there still would be no proof that it ever covered the body of Jesus.[1] Belief in Jesus does not come from venerating relics, which can be invested with whatever the believer wants to believe; it must be rooted and grounded in Scripture, tested and retested by Scripture, thought and rethought in every generation, but always with the "living and active" Word of God as our guide (Hebrews 4:12).[2]

Speaking of relics and the Middle Ages, however, I happen to be a big Joan of Arc fan. Over the years I have read a good deal about her, including especially the transcripts of her responses at her trial which bring her closer to us than most historical figures can ever be. In reading about her life, though, I found myself thinking more than once, "Thank God for the Reformation!" Remarkable and devout as she was, she could not read a word; the Bible was a closed book to her. She knew almost no theology, and all the stained glass and relics in the cathedral of Rheims could not teach it to her.[3] Similarly, there are no paintings or sculptures of the crucified Jesus that can teach us its inner meaning. If one has the meaning in mind, the images take on great depth and resonance; if not, however, they remain two-dimensional.

Many letters are being written to various magazines about the controversial Nikos Kazantzakis movie, *The Last Temptation of Christ.*[4] Almost all the letters that I have read praised the film. The writers found it "extraordinary," "profound," "deeply moving," and so on. More than one spoke of it as a "spiritual experience."

But what is the *content* of those spiritual experiences? What do they move us to think and feel? What do they propel us to do? One woman wrote that the movie caused her to "feel great compassion for Jesus Christ." That is a beginning, I suppose, but let's contrast it with the Palm Sunday experience. On Palm Sunday, the focus is not on our compassion for Jesus. The liturgy of Palm Sunday is designed to deny us the luxury of looking on as a spectator, compassionate or otherwise. Rather, it draws us right into the story and makes us participants. Furthermore, it forces us to see that our participation was not benign. We shouted "Crucify him!" on Palm Sunday, and we sang a hymn that included the words, "I crucified thee."

Since Joan of Arc's martyr's death, she has been revered in France. Alexandre Dumas *(père)* wrote, "Joan of Arc is the Christ of France; she has redeemed the crimes of the monarchy, as Jesus redeemed the sins of the world."[5] Is that a legitimate statement? If not, why not? Where do we go for guidance in this matter? How are we to evaluate this sort of claim? Do we look at paintings? Do we go to the movies? Do we read history? Where do we go for information?

Did you know that there is no information about the human Jesus whatsoever except in the New Testament?[6] We do have some tiny scraps of data about John the Baptist from early sources, but nothing about Jesus from any contemporary extrabiblical piece of writing.[7] It has been shown over and over that we have no access to Jesus outside the scriptural witness, yet people persist in constructing a Jesus to suit themselves. Just last week I was buttonholed in a restaurant by a woman who dropped out of one of our Bible classes a long time ago. She couldn't say enough about how wonderful *The Last Temptation of Christ* was and how important it was for me to see it. I wish I had had the presence of mind to tell her that I would go to the movie if she would come back to the Bible study group. The trouble with that is, of course, it isn't really an equal exchange; the movie offers a mere two hours of more or less thought-provoking entertainment, whereas the Bible summons us to a whole lifetime of study and transformation.

This Monday of Holy Week, let us continue what we began yesterday, on Palm Sunday. Let us probe more deeply into the story of Christ's Cross and what it means for us. Today's Biblical text is a most remarkable one. The speaker is Jesus himself, interpreting his own death:

> The Son of Man came not to be served, but to serve, and to give his life as a ransom for many. (Mark 10:45)

Let's try a little exercise. Substitute the words "Joan of Arc" for the words "the Son of Man." "Joan of Arc came to give her life as a ransom for France." It sounds strange, to me at least. Came from where? Came to where? Came from the French countryside? Came to Chinon? Orleans? Rheims? Who was holding France hostage? Was Joan's death a ransom paid to the English? How could that effect the "salvation" of France? Was France indeed "saved" by her death? Perhaps these kinds of questions will help us see that Jesus' simple-sounding statement is not so easy to interpret.

"The Son of Man came to give his life as a ransom for many." To begin with, who is the Son of Man?[8] In Jesus' time, "Son of Man" was a numinous title referring to a hoped-for heavenly figure, a messianic personage yet to come, invested with divine power and privilege. When Jesus says "the Son of Man came," it's equivalent to saying "the Messiah has come down from heaven." In other words he came, not from Bethlehem or Nazareth or rural France, but *from God.* The use of the term "Son of Man" would have reminded the disciples of the seventh chapter of the book of Daniel, with its thrilling description of the majestic figure of the Son of Man "coming with the clouds of heaven" and having all power and dominion given to him. From there one readily goes on to imagine this divine figure riding out gloriously in front of a victorious cohort of angels and archangels. But that is not what Jesus says. He says the opposite: "The Son of Man did not come to be served, but to serve, and to give his life as a ransom for many."

This word "ransom," now. Think about it for a moment. What is the purpose of a ransom? Clearly it is for deliverance. The basic idea is this:

1. A person or group has come under the control of another power.
2. The person or group has lost its freedom to act.
3. The person or group finds its own strength completely inadequate.
4. *Therefore:* Freedom can be gained only through the intervention of an outside power.

The most obvious modern analogy is that of hostages locked in a building. They can't free themselves. An anti-terrorist squad has to come in from outside. By analogy, when Jesus says he has come, he doesn't mean he has come from another geographical place, but from *another sphere of power.* Think of occupied Europe held hostage under the Nazis. There were valiant resistance movements here and there, but as long as they operated from within the Nazi realm, there was no real hope. There had to be an *invasion,* a landing which would liberate them from the occupying forces. C. S. Lewis's Narnia stories are based on the same premise. The inhabitants of Narnia are in thrall to the wicked queen of Narnia and cannot escape her power; they must wait for the mighty lion, Aslan, to land. Once the invasion has begun, they know they will be freed. The New Testament sees the situation very much in these terms. The creation is not free; nature and human beings alike are not free; we are all under the sway of occupying Powers: Sin, Evil, Death. Only an invasion by the Creator himself can save it. This is the meaning of St Paul's saying, "The creation itself will be set free from its bondage to decay and obtain the glorious liberty of the children of God" (Romans 8:21). He depicts the whole creation "groaning in travail" as it waits. In the Incarnation of the Son of God, the invasion has begun; in the Crucifixion the beachheads are secured; in the Resurrection we see the firstfruits of the final liberation.[9]

None of this can be learned from movies, or the veneration of relics, or television documentaries about the latest scholarly theories concerning Jesus. Only from Scripture heard in the context of the worshipping community do we learn these things about our bondage and our deliverance. Only in Scripture does the meaning of Christ's sacrifice come clear. In him, a Power strong enough to conquer Sin and Death has appeared — definitively, conclusively, finally.

Wait a minute, though; haven't we wandered off the subject? First we were talking about a ransom, now we're talking about an invasion. Aren't we mixing metaphors? Well, yes, we are; but that's because the Bible does it all the time. For instance, Jesus himself, in his Good Shepherd discourse (John 10) first says he is the door of the sheep, and then just a couple of verses later he says he is the shepherd. The Epistle to the Hebrews has the scapegoat in Leviticus mixed up with the sacrificial lamb. It's fluid; the interwoven images make it possible for us to evoke several things at once, for which the preacher is very thankful.

Certain literal-minded people have made it difficult for us over the years, however. There were important early theologians who thought Jesus' death was a ransom paid to the devil.[10] Most ordinary Christians to this day, however, have probably understood the "ransom saying" for what it is: a figure of speech. Vincent Taylor called it a "luminous hint."[11] This evening we are here to go beneath the surface of the saying and look at the deep underlying meaning. The emphasis in the idea of a ransom is *deliverance by purchase*.[12] The First Epistle of Peter clarifies it: "You know that you were ransomed from the futile ways inherited from your fathers, not with perishable things such as silver or gold, but with the precious blood of Christ, like that of a lamb without blemish or spot" (1 Peter 1:18-19). Here too we find a blend of images — the ransom with the sacrificial lamb. This verse contains the idea of original sin ("futile ways"), holding us in bondage as it did our parents and grandparents and so on back as far as we can trace the human species. St. Paul, especially, sees humanity in bondage to hostile Powers and depicts the Cross as the moment of deliverance. Twice in close succession, as though to emphasize it, he writes to the Corinthians: "You were bought with a price" (1 Corinthians 6:20; 7:23). Again, the idea of a ransom or price is a metaphor, conveying the idea that the price to be paid is of equivalent value to that which is redeemed.[13] Here is the key to our participation in the story. We were held hostage to Sin and Death. These two Powers rose up with all their might, wielding their weapons so effectively that all the best people fell in line to acquiesce in the execution of the Son of God. On Good Friday — and here we are going to mix the images to the nth degree — he became two things at once: he is the one-man anti-terrorist team, and he is the hostage who steps forward and volunteers to be killed. He is both at the same time.[14]

If you say this doesn't make any earthly sense, you are right. We are stretching for words here. The mysterious ransom saying of Jesus cannot be forced into rational categories. What it tells us is this: God is *personally involving himself* in the rescue of his enslaved children, at the highest level of sacrifice the world has ever seen. It is not just that he has come to set us free. It is more than that. He has in some hitherto unimaginable way actually substituted himself for us, as though our blighted little lives were actually worth this gift of infinite value, this outpouring of the divine life of God, this undergoing of ultimate humiliation, this entrance into Hell — for us. Only by looking at the Cross of Christ do we learn the magnitude of the forces that held us in bondage. We escaped; he was immolated. The size of the "ransom" is equivalent to the size of our enslavement. That is the payment of equivalent value. That is what we are worth to him.

And so, you see, the price for our complicity in his Crucifixion has already been paid. The universal human condition is one of bondage under the reign of Death; but in his own death and Resurrection the Lord has overturned that reign. He has established himself for ever over the dark Powers. He can never be overthrown. "He reflects the glory of God and bears the very stamp of his nature, upholding the universe by his word of power. When he had made purification for sins, he sat down at the right hand of the Majesty on high" (Hebrews 1:3).

"Aslan has landed."[15] Everything is different now. Our struggle continues, but as the English say, we are "in very good heart." D-Day is not the end; in World War II the desperate Battle of the Bulge still remained to be fought, but when you know the enemy is on the run, you fight with a defiant confidence. Winston Churchill said to the British people in 1942, "This is not the end. It is not even the beginning of the end. But it is, perhaps, the end of the beginning." Expanding his words, we may rightly say that the Crucifixion and Resurrection of Jesus Christ is truly the beginning of the End, when the kingdom of God will be all in all.

Flannery O'Connor wrote, "My subject in fiction is the action of grace in territory held largely by the Devil."[16] Almost all of her stories illustrate the subversive nature of God's work, moving in on us when we least expect it.[17] This invasion of grace is exactly what St. Paul is writing about. What he says to the Christians in Rome is a living Word for us in our struggles two thousand years later:

If God is for us, who is against us? He who did not spare his own Son but gave him up for us all, will he not also give us all things with him? . . . Who shall separate us from the love of Christ? Shall tribulation, or distress, or persecution, or famine, or nakedness, or peril, or sword? (Romans 8:31-35)

See how Paul envisions the Christian life as a battle? Feeling compassion for Jesus is all right as far as it goes, I suppose, but it is misdirected. It would be nearer the mark to stress Jesus' compassion for *us,* but that, too, is insufficient. On the Cross, Jesus is not just *showing compassion;* by paying the ransom of his own life and descending into Hell for us he is *effectively delivering us* from the malevolent Powers that would destroy humanity. Nothing like that has ever happened in any other death.

Perhaps this message is not for you on this particular night. If you are in search of a spiritual experience, this may not be it. If you are interested in a more generic religious message, it may be that this news of Jesus' agonizing death on the Cross as the means of deliverance from the Powers of Sin and Death will pass you by tonight. But if you have any sense of your own vulnerability at the hands of those occupying Powers, if you know what it means to live on the fragile border where health and well-being are under threat from weakness and decay, if you sometimes feel that you are in a prison beyond your power to escape, then this coming of the Son of Man is for you.

We can say still more. Great figures like Joan of Arc have left places of safety and familiarity and ventured out to fight against wickedness and corruption. Throughout the ages, Christian people whose names are not recorded but who care deeply about liberty and human flourishing have joined God's Allies in the struggle against the enemies of his people. If you are reasonably happy in your own existence but bear a burden in your heart because of what is happening to others, then you too are being called into Christ's army of resistance. If you "hunger and thirst after righteousness" (Matthew 5:6), *not only* for America and England and France and people who are essentially like yourself *but also* for the two-thirds world of suffering black and brown people who live and die on the margins, then you are ready to enlist in the Lord's underground. It may sound too grand and large for you; you may think someone else can do it better than you; it may be that you think there is no role for the small deed, the little contribution, the quiet gesture. Never, never think that. The big stuff has already been done by the Lord of heaven and earth. He has already come with the heavy artillery. Our part is mostly to be foot soldiers. Just remember: the heavy artillery is not the weapons systems of the world. The weapons of Christ are those of suffering love.

It may appear that small deeds done by ordinary people are of no use. It may appear that we are struggling for nothing in the face of an indifferent or hostile world racing past us and over us on its way to greater conquests. Paul writes, "As it is written, 'For thy sake we are being killed all the day long; we are regarded as sheep to be slaughtered'" (Romans 8:36). Is that the way it is?

No! says Paul. Never, never think that. The Lamb of God has been slaughtered for us already; that is why

> . . . in all these things we are more than conquerors through him who loved us. For I am sure that neither death, nor life, nor angels, nor principalities, nor things present, nor things to come, nor powers, nor height, nor depth, nor anything else in all creation, will be able to separate us from the love of God in Christ Jesus our Lord. (Romans 8:37-39)

The Messiah Comes to His Temple

———— ✦ ————

*The Lord whom you seek shall suddenly come to his temple . . .
but who shall stand when he appears? For he is like a refiner's
fire. . . .*

(MALACHI 3:1-2)

*Take these things away; you shall not make my Father's house a
house of trade.*

(JOHN 2:16)

When Jesus came among us in the first century A.D., he
came in a specific historical context. We need to remember that, for it is one of the basic facts of our faith. The various
searches for the "historical Jesus" over the past century or two
have led us down some blind alleys, but we may be thankful for
the reminder that Jesus was not just a generic religious figure but
a very specific Jew in the occupied territory of Palestine under a
readily identifiable Roman government. This is very important
for us to recognize, especially the Jewish part. Holy Week was for
hundreds of years an occasion for outbursts against the Jews, a
shameful legacy that we must continually hold in our minds so as
never to repeat it.

The Hebrew Scriptures were the only Bible that Jesus and his disciples knew, the Bible that all Jews knew by heart and lived from every day of the year. Some parts of the Scripture, however, were more palatable than other parts, just as they are today. This evening we are going to look at a powerful but unsettling tradition ranging throughout all the Hebrew prophetic literature that everybody knew but few wanted to think about. As we proceed, you will notice that this tradition is just as applicable to us today as it was to the religious people of Jesus' time.

This prophetic tradition had two features. The first was that God was rightfully angry with his chosen people because, in spite of all his patience and loving-kindness, they were more attentive to their forms of worship than they were to the righteousness of God. In Isaiah we find these words:

> What to me is the multitude of your sacrifices? says the LORD; I have had enough of burnt offerings. . . . Your appointed feasts my soul hates; they have become a burden to me, I am weary of bearing them. . . . Even though you make many prayers, I will not listen. (Isaiah 1:11-15)

Again and again, the prophets of Israel spoke this word of judgment against the people's religion. It is one of the most prominent themes in the Old Testament. Here is another example from Isaiah: "This people . . . honor me with their lips, while their hearts are far from me" (Isaiah 29:13). A third example is this famous passages from Amos:

> I hate, I despise your feasts, and I take no delight in your solemn assemblies. . . . Take away from me the noise of your songs; to the melody of your harps I will not listen. But let justice roll down like waters, and righteousness like an ever-flowing stream. (Amos 5:21-24)

In Micah, God's judgment falls especially heavily on the clergy of the house of Israel:

Its priests teach for hire,
   its prophets divine for money;
yet they lean upon the LORD and say,
   "Is not the LORD in the midst of us?
     No evil shall come upon us."

                            (Micah 3:11)

The second feature of this part of the prophetic tradition is that God is not simply opposed to this perversion of his worship from a distance. He is going to do something about it.

Jeremiah, for example, preached that God would tear down the great Jerusalem temple and cast the people out of his sight (Jeremiah 7:14-15). And Micah wrote:

For behold, the LORD is coming forth out of his place . . . ,
And the mountains will melt under him
   and the valleys will be cleft,
like wax before the fire . . . ,
All this is for the transgression of Jacob
   and for the sins of the house of Israel.

                          (Micah 1:3-5)

These passages make me very nervous. I know that I stand under judgment for the superficiality of much of my ministry. If you think I am just saying that for effect, you are very much mistaken. The passage about the priests from Micah (3:12) ends this way: "Because of you [the clergy] . . . Jerusalem shall become a heap of ruins." There are those who are saying that the Episcopal church is going to become a heap of ruins. The trouble is, the people saying that often appear to think that they are going to be standing safely off on the side watching while others get plowed under. Well, all of us do things like that at one time or another; we push these prophecies back into the past, or off onto some other group. When we do that, we miss our calling as Christians. The first thing Christians do is to step forward to admit that we are *all* under this judgment. That's exactly what we do on Ash Wednesday. As the First Epistle of Peter

puts it, "The time has come for judgment to begin with the household of God" (1 Peter 4:17). Not with somebody else's household,
but *our* household.

Human nature being what it is, this prophetic theme got
pushed into the background. It wasn't lost, though. There were a
few faithful souls who treasured these prophecies and copied them
and handed them down, and they continued to be read in the worship of the synagogues, and people heard them. Gradually there
grew up a new belief around the older tradition. A time was coming
when God actually would "come down out of his place," sending his
agent into the world, and this agent of the Lord would be God's
Messiah — later referred to as the "Son of Man" (Daniel 7:13). The
Son of Man would appear on the great future day of God's visitation. He would be the one to clean up the worship of the Lord.[18]

Was this good news or bad news? What do you think? Most
people don't want to hear any bad news, for understandable reasons
— unless it is bad news for someone else. That unattractive human
trait — feeling pleasure at the misfortune of others — is called
Schadenfreude, and its ubiquity is a good example of original sin. We
push bad news off on others whenever we can. Most good Jews of
first-century Palestine believed that the Messiah would come to
overthrow the hated Roman occupation and restore them to their
rightful place of moral and religious superiority. Isn't that what you
and I would think? Don't we all think, secretly or not so secretly,
that our ways are the best ways? Of course we *say* that we respect
the ways of others, but as soon as we are genuinely threatened, tolerance goes out the window. The Episcopal church is a classic example. I know many congregations who are virtually at war because of
issues related to worship style. Lay leaders will obtain permission to
have a new service with "praise music," guitars, and overhead pro-
jectors to keep that constituency happy, but when the new "renewal
service" gets really big and starts drawing people away from the traditional service, that's threatening, and people start sharpening
their knives against one another.[19] Whichever side we are on, whatever the issue is, we are programmed by Sin to dig in our heels and
refuse to believe that we, too, might need to repent. We are con-

vinced that the Messiah will approve of us and whatever it is that we are committed to. It is inconceivable to us that God would make us, whoever we are, a "heap of ruins"; he must have meant somebody else.

One of the last of the Old Testament prophets is known to us as Malachi.[20] Like the others, he fiercely attacks the corruption of the religion of his day, and like the others he foretells a time when God will actually arrive in the temple to set things straight. He wrote a magnificent passage which was unforgettably set to music by Handel in *Messiah*. Here it is:

> The Lord whom you seek will suddenly come to his temple; the messenger of the covenant in whom you delight, behold, he is coming, saith the LORD of hosts. (Malachi 3:1)

Good news, surely; the Lord "whom you seek" is promised. If he is the one we seek, then it stands to reason that he will be just what we hoped for and counted on.

But Malachi has more to say:

> The Lord whom you seek shall suddenly come to his temple. . . . But who may abide the day of his coming? and who shall stand when he appeareth? for he *is* like a refiner's fire. . . . And he shall sit *as* a refiner and purifier of silver: and he shall purify the sons of Levi, and purge them as gold and silver, that they may offer unto the LORD an offering in righteousness. (Malachi 3:2-3)

Those of you who love the Handel oratorio will remember the notes leaping up like flames in this portion. Sometimes, though, the beauty of familiar music conceals from us the depth of the meaning. This passage means that when the Messiah comes it is going to hurt. It's going to be like being melted down in a furnace. This text is, in fact, so very uncomfortable that it is a wonder the Levite priests didn't suppress it.[21]

Now, with this Old Testament background in mind, let us imagine that we are in the capital city of Jerusalem in 33 A.D. It's not like this town; Jerusalem has only one church and everybody goes there. It's Passover Week, and it's a mob scene. The temple is tourist attraction #1, religion at its apex. Here are all the religious instincts of humanity on display. There's liturgical dance in the sanctuary, performance art in the courtyard, and a rock mass in the nave. You can buy a tour guide in the narthex, a cookbook in the transept, and bumper stickers in the parish hall. Weight Watchers meets in the Sunday School wing, yoga in the gym, AA in the audio-visual room. There's a prayer group in the basement, a flower show in the courtyard, and group therapy in the reception room. And you can get your money changed at five convenient ATM locations. What a temple! What a church! God must be very pleased.

But what is this uproar all of a sudden? People shouting and running in all directions, animals underfoot, loud crashes, splintering wood, coins rolling across the floor, tables upset, food all over the place, utter chaos and confusion. What in God's name is going on? We look around for the source of the uproar. Our eyes are drawn to the figure in the center — a man with a strong physical presence, obviously; a man whose face is flushed with anger, still breathing rapidly from the sudden exertion, holding a crude whip of cords lashed together. We are told by witnesses that this one man, walking into the temple precincts like any other ordinary sightseer or worshipper, suddenly stooped over, took some rushes from the ground and twisted them into a whip (for of course no one is allowed to bring a sword or club into the temple) and began to lash out at all the perfectly innocent tradespeople. This mess is the result.

No one is able to explain why this person has not been arrested. He acted as though he had every right to behave in this extraordinary way. He even said something about it being his father's house: "You shall not make my Father's house a house of trade" (John 2:16). There is apparently an imperial manner about the man, an air of unapproachability, a corona of sovereignty that makes one think twice. "The Lord whom you seek shall suddenly come to his temple . . . but who shall stand when he appears? For he is like a refiner's fire."

The religious authorities go up to him. They do not lay a hand on him; instead, they seem to be asking him questions. Let us go nearer and listen to what they say. Their main concern seems to be probing for the source of his strange authority: "What sign have you to show us for doing this?" they say — almost as if they really want to know. They seem to be thinking that maybe a man with so much power can be useful to them. Jesus' reply cuts off any such speculation: "Destroy this temple, and in three days I will raise it up" (John 2:18-19).

And with this enigmatic rejoinder, the stranger passes unhindered through the crowd and continues on his way, while the temple authorities are left muttering to themselves, "It has taken forty-six years to build this temple, and will [he] raise it up in three days?" (John 2:20).

You see, what Jesus did on that famous day in the temple in Jerusalem was not to lose his temper. You often hear the "Cleansing of the Temple" story interpreted that way — "See how human Jesus is? He gets angry just like everybody else" — but that isn't it at all. On that day, Jesus announced in an unmistakable way that he was Lord of the temple.[22] That's what unnerved the religious leaders even more than the actions themselves. When he threw over the tables of the moneychangers, he was saying, *I AM the messenger of the covenant, of whom the prophet spoke.*[23]

Jesus was also saying, in his action, *I have come to purify the worship of my Father.* This was the prophet's announcement: "He will purify the sons of Levi and refine them like gold and silver, till they present right offerings to the LORD . . ." (Malachi 3:3). Ouch! You and I don't like this sort of thing any more than the people of Jesus' time did. We don't think we are in need of any refiner's fire. Oh, sure, we need some polishing, some buffing; maybe we need some rough edges smoothed and some dents straightened to make us flawless, but we don't need any blast furnaces. We don't want Jesus in here turning over the pews — or, to put it more accurately, he can turn over somebody else's pew, but not mine! We have worked hard to make our worship just the way we want it, and we don't want anybody — not even the Son of God — messing around with it.

What is left for us, then? Where can we stand? Is it all bad

Rembrandt: Christ Driving the Money Changers from the Temple

With his usual striking realism, Rembrandt depicts the chaos and turbulence in the Temple as Jesus moves into action. Notice how the movement in the lower half of the picture is all toward the left, as the weighty figure of Christ, swinging his cords, strides across the picture plane sweeping all before him. We see the table at the moment of its overturning; it is just now striking the floor as dogs bark, barrels roll, people are thrown down helter-skelter from their seats, and a calf tramples the fallen in panic. High above this scene of turmoil, however, the religious authorities look down from their seats of power; their posture of detached superiority is hardening into implacable hostility. We can easily imagine that if any of them were not opposed to Jesus before, they will be from now on. "Let him create his little disturbance now," they seem to be thinking. "It will be a different story tomorrow."

news for us today? Are we going to be abandoned in this state of unease, knowing that if we had been there in Jerusalem that day we
would have been part of the groups conspiring to get rid of this disruptive person who seemed to think he was the Messiah? Is this the
news for today, that God is angry with us, that we do not and cannot please him, that there is no pure worship in the land?

It is not a coincidence that the church reads this hard lesson in
the middle of Holy Week. This "messenger of the covenant" has
thrown over all the pews of all of us who love our church fairs and
our favorite hymns and our big endowment and our social position
in this elegant suburb more than we love the Lord our God. On Ash
Wednesday, we committed ourselves to keep a "holy Lent." How are
we doing? I don't know about you, but I have flunked Lent. I flunk
it every year. I *know* I need to go through the refiner's fire. But now
hear this. This same Jesus who has turned over my prayer desk is
also the one who is on his way this very week to betrayal, condemnation, humiliation, abandonment, and death *on my behalf.* The
prophet Micah spoke more truly than he knew when he said, "Behold, the Lord is coming forth out of his place . . . for the sins of the
house of Israel." The Son of God has come down out of his place,
down from heaven, down from his glory, down from his place of untouchable majesty on high to take our corrupted nature upon himself, that the whole world might be raised to new life on the third
day. In place of the polluted worship of the temples and churches
Jesus goes to lay down his own life, his own self, his own body, as
the true pure worship of the Father. For this is what we read in John
the evangelist:

> The Jews said to him, "What sign have you to show us for doing
> this?"
>
> Jesus answered them, "Destroy this temple, and in three days I
> will raise it up."
>
> The Jews then said, "It has taken forty-six years to build this
> temple, and will you raise it up in three days?"
>
> But he spoke of the temple of his body. When therefore he was
> raised from the dead, his disciples remembered that he had said

this; and they believed the scripture and the word which Jesus had spoken. (John 2:18-22)

And so it is even now, this evening, that the Messiah comes to his temple. Jesus himself — his Incarnation, his Crucifixion, his Resurrection — *Jesus himself* becomes the pure worship of the Father. The refiner's fire is the one he passes through himself.

Yes, my pew will be thrown over — my pretensions, my props, my defenses, my masks, and, especially, my idols will all be stripped away. God is not going to let any of us continue indefinitely keeping him on the margins while we pursue our own idolatrous interests. But the good news, the joyous news, the liberating news is that the Messiah with the whip is "the Lamb of God, who takes away the sin of the world" (John 1:29). He has come to his temple, and in his blazing light we see ourselves as the guilty creatures that we are; but his coming in judgment is at one and the same time his offering of his body and blood for our true worship. The submission of the Christian community to the purifying and refining of the Messiah is our testimony to the world that Jesus is Lord, that he will not let us go until we are as righteous and holy as he is himself. Even now at this moment the summons goes out to you, that you join with the first disciples and make your confession. Let it be said of us this very evening that "they believed the scripture and the word which Jesus had spoken" (John 2:22).

The Lamb of God

—⚬⚬⚬—

The next day {John the Baptist} saw Jesus coming toward him, and said, "Behold, the Lamb of God, who takes away the sin of the world."

(JOHN 1:29)

God himself will provide the lamb for a burnt offering, my son.

(GENESIS 22:8)

Without the shedding of blood there is no forgiveness of sins.

(HEBREWS 9:22)

Around the world, wherever there has been Christian art, there have been lambs. Lambs standing up with flags, lambs lying down with flags, lambs lying on books. The Latin name for this symbol is *Agnus Dei,* the Lamb of God. *Agnus Dei* is also the name of the ancient hymn that we often sing during the Eucharist. The words of this *Agnus Dei* form part of all the Masses by the great composers — Bach, Haydn, Mozart, Verdi, and so forth.

O Lamb of God, that takest away the sin of the world,
    have mercy upon us.

O Lamb of God, that takest away the sin of the world,
    have mercy upon us.
O Lamb of God, that takest away the sin of the world,
    receive our prayer.

A famous nineteenth-century preacher, Alexander Maclaren, wrote:

> [This] text ("the Lamb of God which taketh away the sin of the world") is the sum of all Christian preaching. . . . My task, and that of all preachers, if we understand it aright, is but to repeat the same message, and to concentrate attention on [it]. . . . There is no reason for our being gathered together now, except that I may beseech you to behold for yourselves the Lamb of God which takes away the world's sin.[24]

But how many of us "understand it aright"? Many of us have heard and said "O Lamb of God, etc." so many times that we never think about it one way or the other. We are not even aware that it is open to multiple interpretations, some of them very wide of the mark. During the sentimental Victorian era, for example, it was popular to imagine Jesus as a lamb because he was supposedly mild, meek, and gentle. This sort of cultural bias can take us a long way off course. Today, perhaps, our cultural problem is not so much sentimentality as it is lack of Biblical knowledge. My own informal polls of faithful churchgoers reveals that very few know what the Lamb of God image signifies. A person of today, hearing the phrase "Lamb of God," thinks of nothing particular. A person of New Testament times, however, would immediately have been flooded with associations, vividly engaging his mind and heart on the deepest level.

Here's what the people of John's time knew that we don't know today:

First, they knew that a Messiah was expected, a figure of divine power and authority who would bring God's salvation to the entire world and who would destroy all evil forever. That's no surprise;

that much we all could have guessed. But what we are not likely to know is that there were various books known to the people of that time depicting this Messiah as a victorious, triumphant, conquering Lamb. This seems very peculiar to us; why would they use such a whimsical little animal to represent conquest and victory?

If you look up the book of Enoch, part of the Jewish apocalyptic literature of the time, it becomes clear. It's rather exciting reading, as a matter of fact, if we use our imaginations and think of ourselves as beleaguered and endangered, like the Jews of that time. In Enoch, the people of God are allegorically depicted, in good Old Testament tradition, as a flock of sheep requiring care and protection.[25] Lambs are born to the sheep, which of course suggest new generations; this hope is threatened, however, by onslaughts from wild beasts who kill and destroy the lambs. The lambs cry pitifully to the sheep to protect them, but the sheep are unable to do so. Then one of the lambs begins to grow horns. (In the Bible, when you see something about horns, that means power and dominion.) A sword is then given to this great horned Lamb, now an adult, and it vanquishes and destroys all the enemies of God's sheepfold.

We're not accustomed to this kind of story, but to the people of that era, close to the time of Jesus, it was second nature. If you know your book of Revelation, you will recognize the conquering Lamb, triumphant over Satan and every form of evil and sin and death. That's why the Lamb in Christian symbolism carries a flag; it's a battle flag. The winner carries away the banner of the loser; the Messiah has "captured the flag."[26]

Second, the book of Revelation gives us a number of clues to a second, deeper meaning. The victorious Lamb of God in Revelation still bears the marks of having been slaughtered. What would a slaughtered lamb mean to a New Testament Christian?

Although many mainline churchgoers today seem to be squeamish about the theme of blood, the Epistle to the Hebrews makes a great point of saying that "without the shedding of blood, there is no forgiveness of sins" (Hebrews 9:22). For a thousand years and more, the children of Israel had offered animal sacrifices to God as expiation for sin. Blood was poured on the altar and on the ground, and climactically it was sprinkled on the mercy-seat of the Ark of the Covenant, as a means of atonement.[27] In addition, lambs were offered in the temple, morning and evening, every day of the year; this was the chief duty of the priests. The idea of a lamb slaughtered as a sin offering was as familiar to the people of Jesus' time as TV commercials are to us. "The Lamb of God who takes away the sin of the world" would therefore require no interpretation; the question would be whether Jesus of Nazareth could possibly be such a Lamb.

Third, more dramatic still is the imagery of the Passover Lamb. Imagine yourself part of the whole company of the children of Israel, enslaved in Egypt, on the night of their flight to the shore of the Red Sea.[28] Imagine the excitement, the preparations, the apprehension — the packing of what little they had and what could be carried, the baking of unleavened bread for the journey, the hushing of the children, the anticipation of freedom, the fear of the unknown — and all the while, the knowledge that the angel of death was about to pass over their heads and the heads of the Egyptians.[29] And what was to protect them, while they waited, from the angel of death? *The blood of a lamb,* that's what. Doesn't that give you a little shiver of recognition? Here's the story from the book of Exodus:

> Then Moses called all the elders of Israel, and said to them, "Select lambs for yourselves according to your families, and kill the passover lamb. Take a bunch of hyssop and dip it in the blood which is in the basin, and touch the lintel and the two doorposts with the blood which is in the basin; and none of you shall go out of the door of his house until the morning. For the LORD will pass through to slay the Egyptians; and when he sees the blood on the lintel and on the two doorposts, the LORD will pass over the door, and will not allow the destroyer to enter your houses to slay you. . . .
>
> And when you come to the land which the LORD will give you, as he has promised, you shall keep this service. And when your children say to you, 'What do you mean by this service?' you shall say, 'It is the sacrifice of the LORD's passover, for he passed

over the houses of the people of Israel in Egypt, when he slew the Egyptians but spared our houses.'" And the people bowed their heads and worshiped. (Exodus 12:21-27)[30]

So you may be sure, there was no human being within earshot of John the Baptist (or the reading of the Fourth Gospel) who did not know that the Passover Lamb was a sacrifice for deliverance.[31] The description of Jesus as the Lamb of God who takes away the sin of the world is therefore a *combination* of the blood sacrifice for sin and the Passover Lamb for deliverance "out of bondage into freedom."[32] "Christ our Passover [lamb] is sacrificed for us; therefore let us keep the feast" (1 Corinthians 5:7-8).[33]

Even this is not all, however. We may note a fourth theme. In Isaiah 53, one of the most celebrated passages in the entire Bible, we read of a mysterious figure, a suffering servant of God who is despised and rejected, a man of sorrows and acquainted with grief, a man who goes like a lamb to the slaughter, a man who bears in his own body the sin of others. In this famous image, the early Christians saw their Lord, and felt that they understood for the first time what Isaiah saw by revelation and faith. "Behold, the Lamb of God, who takes away the sin of the world."

A major theme of Holy Scripture is the incapacity of human beings to extricate ourselves from our own worst tendencies. The more the external things change, the more they remain the same. Such things as the sexual revolution, the changing role of women, and the advent of cybertechnology have undoubtedly changed society in major ways that we do not yet understand; but if the twentieth century taught us anything, it taught us that civilized humanity is capable of bottomless depths of wickedness hitherto unsuspected. The myth of human moral progress died in Auschwitz. The best thinkers among us know that optimism about human nature is, as Ecclesiastes says, the "sacrifice of fools" (Ecclesiastes 5:1). The Biblical witness is that humanity left to itself is caught in a downward spiral of self-destruction. The first eleven chapters of Genesis depict this, and St. Paul describes it graphically in Romans 1–3. In John's Gospel, Jesus says, "That which is born of

Matthias Grünewald: Crucifixion Scene
from the Isenheim Altarpiece

This masterpiece is recognized the world over for its unique combination of extreme, grotesque horror and intense religious devotion. Even in strictly formal terms it is singular, for several reasons. The size of the figures relative to their placement is deliberately distorted, so that the massive, tormented body of Jesus is oversized and appears to be hanging closer to the viewer than the anguished Mary Magdalen. The Virgin is extraordinary: young, beautiful though ghastly pale, wrapped from head to toe in stark white, she and the beloved disciple would unbalance the canvas were it not for the great originality of the figure of John the Baptist on the right side. He is oversized to match the man on the Cross, he stands almost at the edge of the picture plane, and his pointing finger is enlarged. Holding a book of prophecy, he speaks the words from John's Gospel: "He must increase, I must decrease." Many Christian preachers over the centuries have seen their vocation in these terms, always to point away from themselves to the Crucified One. The Lamb of God accompanies John, bleeding into a communion chalice and reminding us in unmistakable terms that the excruciating suffering that we see on the Cross is *to take away the sin of the world.*

the flesh is flesh" (John 3:6). We cannot produce our own salvation. Only the intervention of God can do it.

This is the background of the Incarnation and mission of Jesus, the Lamb of God. He comes into a world full of religion, full of sacrifice, full of ritual as old as the race itself. In all these sacrifices, even including the ones that were instituted by the Holy One of Israel himself, there was a built-in problem. The Epistle to the Hebrews describes this problem at length. Here is a sample from its argument:

> For since the law has but a shadow of the good things to come instead of the true form of these realities, it can never, by the same sacrifices which are continually offered year after year, make perfect those who draw near. Otherwise, would they not have ceased to be offered? If the worshipers had once been cleansed, they would no longer have any consciousness of sin. But in these sacrifices there is a reminder of sin year after year. For it is impossible that the blood of bulls and goats should take away sins. (Hebrews 10:1-4)

In the sacrifices of the old covenant, precisely because they are offered over and over and over, there is a daily reminder that sin continues. All over the world, throughout the history of humankind, sacrifices of all conceivable kinds have been offered to the gods — everything from flowers thrown into the sea to the blood of animals to human flesh. All over the world, throughout the history of mankind, there has been a sense that something was not right, something was missing, somebody wanted more, further compensation or propitiation or expiation had to be attempted. And then it would have to be attempted again the week after, and the week after that. . . . What sort of sacrifice would be efficacious *once and for all?*

Day after tomorrow, on Good Friday, you will hear the reading of the story of the journey that Abraham took to sacrifice his son Isaac according to God's command (Genesis 22:1-19). This story has long been appointed to be read on the day commemorating Jesus' Crucifixion. We read that as the father and son went along, with God only knows what unspeakable thoughts besieging Abraham's mind, the uncomprehending youth said, "Father, here is the wood and the knife, but where is the lamb for the sacrifice?" Abraham, in his anguish, could not have known the full meaning of the reply so carefully crafted by him out of his own depths to calm his cherished son, but generations of Christians have known. "God will provide himself *the lamb* for a burnt offering, my son."

In Jesus Christ, God has provided his own sacrifice. He gives up his divine status and comes into the world to stand in our place, defenseless under the curse of sin — not his sin, but ours. He stepped into the place prepared for him from the beginning of the world, for *in Jesus, God* is acting, both to take sin upon himself and to take it away. The Son of God, unlike Isaac, is not uncomprehending. The Second Person of the Trinity is acting with a will identical to that of the Father. As the apocalyptic, conquering lamb he defeats sin, stamps it out, eradicates it. As the Paschal lamb he stands between us and the specter of Death.[34] As the sacrificial lamb he gives his own blood to be the *once-for-all* offering to cleanse his own from sin for ever. Yes, once for all: *ephapax* in Greek, a word repeated in Hebrews four times for emphasis.[35] The sheer, utter, final efficacy of Christ's self-offering is underlined by Thomas Cranmer's Eucharistic words: "his one oblation of himself once offered, a full, perfect and sufficient sacrifice. . . ."

> He has no need, like those high priests, to offer sacrifices daily, first for his own sins and then for those of the people; he did this *once for all* when he offered up himself. (Hebrews 7:27)

> For Christ has entered, not into a sanctuary made with hands, a copy of the true one, but into heaven itself, now to appear in the presence of God on our behalf. Nor was it to offer himself repeatedly, as the high priest enters the Holy Place yearly with blood not his own; for then he would have had to suffer repeatedly since the foundation of the world. But as it is, he has appeared *once for all* at the end of the age to put away sin by the sacrifice of himself. (Hebrews 9:24-26)

Many people will want to know how all of this actually works. How could someone's death two thousand years ago have anything to do with Sin and Death today? I have more than once been sneered at for proposing such a thing, especially in view of the fact that Sin seems to continue its sway unabated. Let the church be first to step forward to take this charge upon herself: sexual abusers among clergy, overt racism in congregations, blatant egomania and rivalry among factions, bishops as well as priests and nuns accused of abetting mass murder.[36] The efficacy of Christ's sacrifice cannot be proven by the behavior of Christians. The identification of Jesus as the Lamb of God can only be affirmed by faith — faith in the future of the Creator God who has promised us a completely recreated future. There are no satisfactory "answers" to the question about ongoing evil. We are not given an "answer"; we are given the Son of God himself. "Behold, the Lamb of God."[37] "Behold!" doesn't mean "Look!" It has a revelatory quality. It means "See and believe." To repeat Maclaren's words, "There is no reason for our being gathered together now, except that I may beseech you to behold for yourselves the Lamb of God which takes away the world's sin."

Preachers pray a lot about their sermons. We don't pray that the sermon will be good; we pray that Jesus Christ will make himself known. The point of the sermon is not compliments at the church door, much as the preacher may crave them. The point is that you behold and believe that you yourself are one for whom Christ died. In this Holy Week preaching, it is not the preacher that reaches out for you. It is the Word of God reaching out for you in Jesus Christ. It is your sin, not just someone else's, that is taken away in his sacrifice of himself. It is you who are "washed in the blood of the Lamb." It is you who, like Isaac, have been snatched back from the very brink of the grave by the One who has provided his own Lamb as a substitute. It is you who have heard, tonight, how God has made the Great Exchange, becoming an offering for sin so that you might receive new life and new righteousness in him. Behold: the Lamb of God.

AMEN.

PART THREE

Thursday of Holy Week: Commonly Called Maundy Thursday or Holy Thursday

———✸———

The God of revenges works freely, he punishes, he spares whom he will. And would he not spare himself? He would not. . . . He would not spare, nay he could not spare, himself. There was nothing more free, more voluntary, more spontaneous than the death of Christ. 'Tis true, he died voluntarily; but yet when we consider the contract that had passed between his Father and him, there was a kind of necessity upon him. All this Christ ought to suffer. And when shall we date this obligation, this necessity? When shall we say that began? Certainly this decree by which Christ was to suffer all this was an eternal decree, and was there anything before that that was eternal? Infinite love, eternal love; be pleased to follow this home.

JOHN DONNE

Note to the reader

———— ⚬⚭⚬ ————

It is customary, in Maundy Thursday services, to have the liturgy of the Word and Lord's Supper, sometimes accompanied by footwashing and sometimes not, and then to conclude with a dramatic service of Tenebrae (shadows). The church is stripped of all its finery, the lights are gradually extinguished, and the congregation leaves in darkness and silence.

The quaint name Maundy Thursday derives from Jesus' words at the Last Supper, "A new commandment I give to you, that you love one another, even as I have loved you." In Latin, "new commandment" is *mandatum novum,* the first words of the introit, or hymn, for this night. "Maundy" is a Middle English version of *mandatum.*

Lord, Not My Feet Only

———— ◆◇◆ ————

*Jesus, knowing that the Father had given all things into his
hands, and that he had come from God and was going to God,
rose from supper, laid aside his garments, and girded himself
with a towel. Then he poured water into a basin, and began to
wash the disciples' feet.*

(JOHN 13:3-4)

This is a good crowd here tonight, considering the fact that it is
a weeknight, but it isn't as large as the Palm Sunday or Easter
congregations. That's all right. There wasn't a big crowd at the first
Maundy Thursday service either. Rest assured that there is no better
night to be in church than this night. Think of yourselves as Jesus'
very own beloved disciples, drawn — not just *invited,* but actually
drawn, pulled in, because he wants *you* — "You did not choose me,"
he says in John's Gospel; "I chose you" (15:16). On the surface, you
may think that you came tonight from duty, or habit, or curiosity,
but those are not the real reasons. The real reason is that Christ
himself has brought you here to be with him at the meal that he has
arranged and set, to eat the food and drink the wine that he himself
gives to us. It is particularly heartwarming to see young people at
the Maundy Thursday service. To each of you, a very special welcome from the Lord Jesus Christ himself, for he is here. He is living

and present with us, as he promised, by the power of the Holy Spirit. Tonight, the Lord brings us close around his table as he brought his disciples to the Upper Room at the Last Supper. This is the foretaste of what it will be like when we are at table with him in the kingdom of God.

But you know, in the real world that we inhabit, there are certain problems associated with dinner parties. Who gets to sit next to whom? Does the twelve-year-old get to sit at the grown-up table or the children's table? If the dinner is in a restaurant, who gets to sit at the good tables and who gets stuck next to the kitchen? If it's a banquet, there's going to be a head table; who sits there? And if it's a really big affair, there's going to be an A list and a B list. Human dinners almost always have this built-in competition. Jesus' disciples were not free from this sort of thing; the Gospels tell us that two of them came to him privately and asked him to seat them on his right and left. They were competing with the other ten for the privileged position.

Now to be sure, some people care more about status and privilege than others, but no one, absolutely no one, is free from anxiety at some level about having a place at the table. Because of this unease we feel, we make up rules about it so that we can be assured of our position. How can we be certain of a good seat? Maybe it's giving an extra amount of money, maybe it's putting in the prescribed number of hours, maybe it's serving on the right committees. Sometimes looks and fashionable dress are the criteria; other times it's just who you know and what access to power you have. We heard plenty about access to power during the recent uproar about presidential pardons, didn't we? Those who had the access got the pardons.[1]

Within the Christian community, we often try to be more subtle about these gradations of worthiness, but it doesn't always work very well, human nature being what it is. In the New York City parish where I used to serve, there were a number of pecking orders: those who were in prayer groups and those who weren't, those who gave blood and those who didn't, those who were socially adept and those who weren't. I remember the first time we had footwashing

Fra Angelico: The Last Supper

This serene depiction of the Last Supper does not attempt to re-create the atmosphere of the original event. Rather, it is meant to inspire awe and devotion in the viewer, who understands that the Lord gives the bread directly to the faithful as he shared it with his disciples "on the night he was betrayed."

on Maundy Thursday; it caused some disturbance. Some people liked it and others emphatically did not. Some people rushed up to the front to volunteer and others refused to do it at all. It was pretty funny, actually. People got really anxious about it, especially the ones who didn't want to do it. They felt they were being made to look like second-class citizens. Similarly with the passing of the Peace when it was first introduced. Maybe you have forgotten about the problems the church had with the Peace years ago. Quite a few people absolutely hated it. It threatened to become an occasion for war instead of peace. Those who liked passing the Peace felt that they were among the righteous, and many were annoyingly self-congratulatory. Those who didn't want to pass it knew that they were regarded by the others as sub-Christian, lacking in the proper feelings, uptight, rigid, and stuffy.

Some of this was superficial, but some of it had to do with theological issues. In the final analysis the real issue was that of worthiness before God. When I was a young married woman in Richmond, Virginia, I used to be a volunteer at a home for severely disabled people. I visited patients once a week. There was one woman who had a great deal of trouble with her feet. When I visited her, I gave her a foot bath. It was not at all unpleasant for me; her feet were perfectly clean, and bathing them seemed to give her some relief. Then my husband's company transferred us to another town and I have never washed anyone's feet since. This raises the question of worth. When the roll is called up yonder, will I get any points for having washed feet forty years ago, or had I better look around for some way to do it again? How dirty do the person's feet have to be to count? You can see the mess we can get into with these kinds of questions.

Because of these problems, the footwashing story has always seemed like bad news to some people. Jesus said to his disciples, "If I then, your Lord and Teacher, have washed your feet, you also ought to wash one another's feet. For I have given you an example, that you also should do as I have done to you" (John 13:14-15). That alarms me. I know it doesn't mean literally go out and wash feet, but I also know that it means doing things for other people that really might be unpleasant and difficult. How many of those things do I have to do? How long do I have to keep on doing them? Does picking up a sick person's prescription count as footwashing, or do you have to do something more grungy? The story burdened me. I found it easier just to pass it by.

But there is wonderful news tonight. Biblical interpreters over the centuries almost unanimously agree that the *first message* of the footwashing story is that it is an interpretation of the death of Jesus. When the Lord gets up from the table, puts on the loincloth of a slave, and kneels at the feet of his disciples, he does it first and foremost to teach his disciples the meaning of his death. It is indeed significant that, after he has finished washing their feet, he sits down with them again at the table and says, "I have given you an example, that you also should do as I have done to you," and I am not trying to cast that into the background; however, all interpreters seem to agree that it is *the secondary, not the primary* meaning of his action. The *primary* meaning is that the Son of God is stooping down from his heavenly throne to wash us clean from our transgressions. The primary meaning is that the Lord of the Universe is preparing to undergo utmost humiliation in order to purify us from the contamination of sin. The primary meaning is that the Eternal Word which was in the beginning with God has become flesh, not only "to dwell among us, full of grace and truth" (John 1:14), but also to love us and to serve us to the outermost limit, even to death on the Cross. And so the evangelist John begins the story by telling us, "Now before the feast of the Passover . . . Jesus knew that his hour had come to depart out of this world to the Father" (13:1). In this way, you see, John places the story in its proper context before he tells it.

There are many other Biblical texts that say the same thing in other words. On Palm Sunday you heard a reading from St. Paul: "Christ Jesus . . . was in the form of God, [but] did not count equality with God a thing to be clutched at, but emptied himself, taking the form of a slave. . . . And being found in human form he humbled himself and became obedient unto death, even death on a cross" (Philippians 2:6-8). The parallel use of words is important:

[73]

he was in the form (Greek *morphe*) of God; he took the form *(morphe)* of a slave. Nowhere in the Gospels is Paul's teaching more dramatically enacted than it is tonight as Jesus performs the service of a slave. And here are Jesus' own words in the Passion narrative of the Gospel of Luke which we also read on Palm Sunday: "Which is the greater, one who sits at table, or one who serves? Is it not the one who sits at table? But I am among you as one who serves" (Luke 22:27). All of this is acted out by our Lord in the footwashing. His action shows forth the meaning of his death.

Now let's turn our attention to the conversation Jesus has with Peter. We all know Peter — always the first one to speak and the first one to regret it. "He came to Simon Peter; and Peter said to him, 'Lord, do *you* wash *my* feet?' Jesus answered him, 'What I am doing you do not know now, but afterward you will understand.'" We can see from this exchange that there is a lot more to the footwashing than Jesus just telling them to go and do likewise. If that was all he was doing, the disciples wouldn't have had any trouble understanding it. The primary meaning of the action, however — its relation to Jesus' self-offering — will not become clear until after his death and Resurrection. So Peter, misunderstanding completely as usual, says, "You shall *never* wash my feet." Greek scholars point out that this is a very strong negation. Peter vehemently refuses the service of the Lord, just as you and I would probably do. But Jesus answers him, "If I do not wash you, you have no part in me." Here the symbolic significance of the action becomes more apparent. We are taken back to John the Baptist's name for Jesus: "The Lamb of God, who takes away the sin of the world" (John 1:29). Peter, quickly realizing he has made a mistake, says, "Lord, not my feet only but also my hands and my head!" (Peter never says anything by halves. He wants to build three booths on the Mount of Transfiguration; he says he would die before he would deny Jesus and then denies him three times; he wants to be washed all over even though he doesn't know what the washing is for.) Jesus says to Peter, "He who has bathed [been cleansed by me] does not need to wash . . . he is clean all over."[2]

So, brothers and sisters in the family of our Lord Jesus, before we start talking about the service we owe to one another, we need to enter more deeply into the meaning of the service that Jesus renders to us. The footwashing is "a parable of the humiliation of the Son of God."[3] The cleansing of the feet represents the cleansing by blood and water to come on Good Friday.[4] Jesus' glory is shown in his humiliation. The laying down of his garments foreshadows the laying down of his life.[5] Remember, this is the very last action of Jesus toward his disciples in his earthly life. John says it is the demonstration that "he loved them to the end" — to the end of his earthly strength, to the end of his earthly capacity, to the end of his earthly life. But far more, to the end of the world, to the outermost boundaries of time, and beyond his own Second Coming into the time that is beyond time, *he loves us to the end.*

Tonight we are gathered around the Lord's table just as the disciples were on that last night. There is no other night quite like it. Here before us is the most precious of all opportunities: we are invited to participate in what Jesus has done for us. Tonight we can be stubborn, like Peter before he understood — nobody's going to wash me, I already gave at the office, I don't want my leader down on his knees, if there's going to be any washing it's going to be on my terms[6] — or we can humbly receive the Lord into our hearts at the Eucharist as he has humbly given himself for us. Let us listen again to the words of the choir anthem that was sung just now:

> Alone to sacrifice thou goest, O Lord. . . .
> [We] know that for our sins this is thy pain.
> For they are ours, O Lord, our deeds, our deeds;
> Why must thou suffer torture for our sin?

Tonight as the lights go out we will remember how the Lord *loved us to the end,* loved us so much that he took our sin upon himself. You will find yourself being drawn into the story of how he entered the darkness in our place, and you will discover how that makes you more willing to enter other people's darkness, to serve them as Jesus has taken the form of a servant — indeed, the form of a slave — to free us and purify us and bring us into his family for

Dirck Bouts: The Lord's Supper

This painting is the dominant central panel of the altarpiece of St. Peter's Church in Leuven, Belgium. The worshippers, looking up as they received Communion, would be moved to recall that they were in the presence of Christ himself just as he gave the bread and wine to his disciples at that first Communion.

ever. Maundy Thursday and Good Friday will hold no terrors for you, because you know that at their heart lies a greater promise than the world has ever known. We all need washing tonight. No one of us is less in need of his cleansing than another. When we come to his table we are not divided into an A list and a B list. It is one table, one gift, one Lord, one faith, one baptism. Do not go away without opening your heart to his love for you, his service to you, his purifying grace so freely offered, and his transforming power for your new life, beginning at this very moment.

AMEN.

Night of Shame, Night of Glory

∞

And he came out, and went, as was his custom, to the Mount of Olives . . . and knelt down and prayed, "Father, if thou art willing, remove this cup from me; nevertheless not my will, but thine, be done." {And there appeared to him an angel from heaven, strengthening him. And being in an agony he prayed more earnestly; and his sweat became like great drops of blood falling down upon the ground.}

(LUKE 22:39-44)

This night is one of the three greatest nights of the Christian year, but it doesn't generally attract the hordes of Christmas Eve, or even the Easter vigil crowd. It's a good bet that most people who make the effort to come to church on Maundy Thursday — that's you — are already committed Christians in one form or another. The preacher can dispense with crowd-pleasing warm-ups and go directly to the heart of the matter. There is no better night to be in church than this night. On that night in the Upper Room in Jerusalem when Jesus sat at table, no one was present but his inner circle. I do not think it is wrong for you to think of yourselves as the inner circle tonight — not because you are worthier than others, but simply because in the mystery of his will and purpose he has chosen you to be here. This is the supreme night of love, this night in which the Son of God declares himself ready to lay down his life for you and for me. That makes us brothers and sisters at the deepest level, each of us drawing near to one another as Jesus draws us very close to himself. Perhaps tonight more than any other night we see into his heart.

This is family night. John the evangelist tells us that on this night Jesus said to his little adopted family, "A new commandment I give to you, that you love one another; even as I have loved you" (John 13:34).[7] When families are working the way they are supposed to, the parents' love for the children is self-sacrificing and unconditional. I remember reading a book when I was barely a teenager, called *Three Came Home.* It was about a mother and two children who survived several years in a Japanese prison camp. I remember only one thing about it, but that part I recall with great vividness. The mother had managed to smuggle a bottle of vitamin pills into the camp. Obviously there was only a limited number of pills. The mother doled out the pills one by one to the children. She did not take a single one of the pills herself. That impressed me so deeply that I still remember it fifty years later. This is what human parents will do for their children; *how much more* does our Father in heaven offer his own life to us in the person of his Son![8] We are not commanded to love one another in order to win our way into God's favor; we are already in his favor because of his perfect love. "Love one another," he said, *"even as I have loved you."* The last half of the verse is the operative part that makes the first part work. "We love, *because he first loved us"* (1 John 4:19). A new family is coming into being on this night, a family in which there will be no unfaithfulness, no betrayal, no failure of love — a family of brothers and sisters with one Father in heaven and a Brother who loves us so dearly that he is preparing, tonight, to give us all the vitamins tomorrow. "This is how we know love," writes John, "that he laid down his life for us" (1 John 3:16).

Tonight's liturgy, more than any other in the Christian year, focuses directly on the new relationships that God brings into being through the blood of Jesus. Everybody here tonight is your brother, and your sister. The meaning of the Christian gospel is not private religious experience, but a new community in Christ's blood. All of our ways of understanding human relationships are reordered tonight. It is described by the Lord very specifically in the Gospel reading that you just heard. "Kings and others in authority exercise lordship," he says. Powerful people act in ways that the world recognizes and rewards. We all know that; it's the way the world works. "But it is not so among you," says the Lord; "rather, let the greatest among you become as the [least], and the leader [become] as one who serves. For which is the greater, one who sits at table, or one who serves? Is it not the one who sits at table? But I am among you as one who serves." Those words are from Luke's Gospel (22:25-27). In Mark's Gospel, however, we read the same story but with something more; Jesus utters a mysterious and revelatory saying that has attracted attention for two thousand years. He says, "Whoever would be great among you must be your servant, and whoever would be first among you must be slave of all. For the Son of man also came not to be served but to serve, and *to give his life as a ransom for many*" (Mark 10:43-45).

To give his life as a ransom for many — what does it mean?[9] Please understand that our Lord doesn't say "many" meaning *less than all;* he says "many" meaning *more than few.* His disciples are *few,* but those saved by his blood will be *many.* Very many. Those who are ransomed will include those that belong to him who were not there on that night two thousand years ago; they will include — wonder of wonders — we ourselves, we who are here on *this* night. Those who are ransomed include you and me. How do we know this? We know it because we are shortly going to participate in his Body and Blood, the pledge of his eternal life given to us. He gave them the cup that night — he gives us the cup this night — saying, "This cup which is poured out for you is the new covenant in my blood" (Luke 22:20).

Now let us turn our attention to what occurs immediately after the Last Supper. Moving on in the Gospel of Luke, we read that Jesus went out to the Mount of Olives "as was his custom," and the disciples trudged along after him, with — by now — considerable amounts of fear and foreboding. The Master comes to the place he

Daniele Crespi: The Last Supper

This fine composition is particularly effective in showing Jesus' isolation at his own party. The disciples turn to one another in varying degrees of self-absorbed perplexity ("Is it I?"). Even the beloved disciple leaning his head on Jesus seems bemused and unresponsive to Jesus' increasing withdrawal into his solitary destiny. Two faces strike the viewer: that of Christ as he thinks of what lies before him, and that of Judas, who turns to face the viewer directly as though to confirm his intentions. The scroll at the top refers to a verse from the Psalms: "Men ate the bread of angels."

seeks and asks the disciples to wait and pray while he goes some distance further.

> He withdrew from them about a stone's throw, and knelt down and prayed, "Father, if thou art willing, remove this cup from me; nevertheless not my will, but thine, be done." [And there appeared to him an angel from heaven, strengthening him. And being in an agony he prayed more earnestly; and his sweat became like great drops of blood falling down upon the ground.][10]

Why did Jesus struggle and suffer like this before his death?[11] Matthew, Mark, Luke, and the Epistle to the Hebrews all testify about this great agony that he endured. According to one translation of St. Mark (J. B. Phillips), he "began to be horror-stricken and desperately depressed"; the Greek is very strong here. In Hebrews we read: "In the days of his flesh, Jesus offered up prayers and supplications, with loud cries and tears, to him who was able to save him from death. . . . Although he was a Son, he learned obedience through what he suffered" (Hebrews 5:7-8). Why do you think Jesus is suffering like this? It can't be just fear of death; many people have gone stoically and fearlessly to their deaths, even vile criminals. Why have the New Testament writers preserved this memory of Jesus agonizing? They could have just omitted it. Instead, they have put special emphasis on it.

Yesterday morning, the Bible study group discussed this question. Some wonderful insights were offered. One person said, "When we face our trials, we have him; but he had no one" — he had no Savior. Another observed that Jesus gave up more than anyone else has ever given up; Jesus gave up his divinity — his divine privileges and power — to come among us; as St. Paul wrote, "He was in the form of God . . . he took the form of a slave" (Philippians 2:6-7). A third person remarked that Jesus' death would mean the cancellation of everything that had been successful about his ministry. This led to a discussion of the nature of crucifixion itself. Most of us don't know much about crucifixion as a method. We will speak further about this tomorrow [Good Friday] at noon, but for now let us just be aware that, perhaps more than any other form of execution that has ever been devised, this method was designed to degrade. It was done in public places so that everyone could participate in the shaming of the crucified person. That was its purpose: to shame, to humiliate, and finally *to dehumanize.* What irony! Jesus was the one truly perfect human being, yet the crucifixion method was arranged for the purpose of announcing to the passersby that this object on this cross *is not even human.* Crucifixion shows us the ultimate cruelty that lurks in the human heart. This is the way that we managed to put the Son of God to death. Without doubt, from the point of view of the disciples, his crucifixion would mean the total obliteration of his teaching and, more striking still, it would mean the extermination of his memory. It can't be said too strongly: this is not the path that religious figures are supposed to travel. This is not an enlightened passage into the higher consciousness; this is not a serene yielding to a warmly enveloping spirit; this is not a radiant light-filled translation to a higher realm. This is an unspeakable ordeal of blood and spittle and mockery and excrement and utmost degradation. Why? *Why?*[12]

The answer has never been easy to encompass, and theologians have taken many positions, but the Bible study group yesterday was getting close to the center. One person said that if sin was separation from God (as it is often defined), then Jesus, as he prayed and agonized in the garden that night, was preparing to be separated from the Father. The mystery of the Crucifixion can never be entirely grasped by us, but the New Testament witnesses repeatedly testify that it was *for sin.* The meaning of this terrible method surely lies in the correspondence between the ugliness of the Cross and the ugliness of human sin.

Sin is a very unfashionable topic, and sometimes it seems as if the church is bending over backwards to avoid talking about it or even mentioning it. When we do mention it, we skip over it as lightly as possible and move on to more pleasant things. On this night, however, I think we can talk about it because the group that comes out for Maundy Thursday can take it, and here's the reason. Sin is a meaningless concept to those who do not know God. It cannot be defined apart from the holiness and righteousness of the God of Abraham, Isaac, and Jacob, the God and Father of our Lord Jesus Christ. Sin is not disobedience in general, rebellion in general, bad behavior in general. It is disobedience, rebellion, and bad behavior *in the sight of God,* the God who has made his covenant with us in holiness and righteousness. Therefore — listen carefully to this great truth — to know sin is to be already in a state of grace.

Let us say that again. To know that one is a sinner in God's sight is to be already in a state of grace. Episcopalians over sixty will remember how, in a strange way, it was *good* to be able to say the General Confession and refer to ourselves as "miserable offenders." I had a dear friend who said fervently, "I *love* to confess my sins!" That's because he knew God, and he knew the gift of God in Jesus Christ. Listen to these words from Psalm 51, the Ash Wednesday Psalm: "I know my transgressions, and my sin is ever before me. Against thee, thee only, have I sinned, and done that which is evil in thy sight, so that thou art justified in thy sentence and blameless in thy judgment." Only a person who really knows God, as King David knew God, can say those words.[13]

Justified in thy sentence and blameless in thy judgment. . . . We will hear more about this tomorrow. Tonight we ask, Why is Jesus down on his knees in the garden, sweating blood and pleading with his Father? It is because he is preparing to take God's judgment against Sin upon himself. In an important verse, St. Paul says in Romans 8:3 that God, "sending his own Son in the likeness of sinful flesh and for sin . . . condemned sin in the flesh." We are not able to understand entirely what that means — *God condemned sin in the flesh* — but it is surely related to what our Lord is facing *in his flesh* as he agonizes in the Garden of Gethsemane. This is not going to be just a crucifixion, horrible as that is. Incomparably more horrible is the separation from the Father that Jesus will undergo. The Son of God is going to receive in his own body the condemnation of God against Sin, and in so doing, he takes that condemnation away from us. "There is," St. Paul writes, "therefore now no condemnation for those who are in Christ Jesus" (Romans 8:1).[14]

Tonight, then, you see, we are brought together as new people, remade by the sacrifice of Christ. God has condemned sin in the flesh of Jesus and we are free. Our overwhelming response, the motive power behind all Christian action, is *gratitude.* Gratitude is a very personal motivation. Gratitude arises out of the Holy Week vision of Jesus, not soaring unscathed into realms of light above us and beyond us, untouched by human pain, but down on his knees on the ground, weeping, abandoned, sweating blood, beseeching his Father, preparing to meet Sin and Death disarmed and unprotected, gathering himself for his climactic battle against your Enemy and mine. We cannot achieve freedom from sin and death through our own spiritual striving. The victory is given to us as a present, the free gift achieved for us through the suffering and death of Jesus Christ the only-begotten Son of God.[15]

As an act of grateful worship, responding to this news of what our Lord has done for us, we are now going to sing together a communion hymn. Think about the words as you sing them. They tell the story of what he has done for us, and they give us the words to say back to him. This will be our prayerful refrain: "Thou didst give thyself for me/Now I give myself to thee." Don't worry about *how* you are going to give yourself to him; he will show you in his own time. The most important thing tonight is to focus on him, on his "love unfailing," on his ultimate gift, on his finished work for us and for our salvation. We will be aware also of our closeness to one another as we sing, for this is not an action of solitary individuals, but an action of the whole family together. We cannot remain the same after he has drawn us together. The love you show to one another is a direct reflection of the love he has shown to us.

Let thy Blood in mercy poured, let thy gracious Body broken,
Be to me, O gracious Lord, of thy boundless love the token.
Thou didst give thyself for me, now I give myself to thee.

Thou didst die that I might live; blessed Lord, thou cam'st
  to save me;
All that love of God could give Jesus by his sorrows gave me.
Thou didst give thyself for me, now I give myself to thee.

By the thorns that crowned thy brow, by the spear-wound
    and the nailing,
By thy pain and death, I now claim, O Christ,
    thy love unfailing.
  Thou didst give thyself for me, now I give myself to thee.[16]

AMEN.

The Lord Looked at Peter

—∞∞∞—

And after an interval of about an hour still another insisted, saying, "Certainly this man also was with him; for he is a Galilean." But Peter said, "Man, I do not know what you are saying." And immediately, while he was still speaking, the cock crowed. And the Lord turned and looked at Peter. And Peter remembered the word of the Lord, how he had said to him, "Before the cock crows today, you will deny me three times." And he went out and wept bitterly.

(LUKE 22:59-62)

I am a stranger among you tonight. I have never been in this parish before. And yet I am not a stranger to you, nor you to me, because tonight, more than any other night of the whole year, we are family. Well might we say with our Jewish neighbors, "Why is this night different from all other nights?" This is the night in which Jesus first invited his family to sit at table with him in the kingdom of God. This is the supreme night of love, this night in which the Son of God declares himself ready to lay down his life for you and for me. That makes us brothers and sisters at the deepest level, each of us drawing near to one another around the table as Jesus draws us very close to himself. That is the way we come to know him. Jesus Christ is on the covers of all the newsmagazines this week, but you cannot find the real Jesus by reading about him in *Time* and *Newsweek* and *U.S. News and World Report*. We come to know Jesus as we draw together in his living presence, known to us in the Word and the Sacrament. Tonight we see the meaning of true humanity and true divinity, matured and perfected in the one unique person Jesus of Nazareth, the Son of Man and Son of God.

Tonight is indeed a night different from all other nights. Nowhere else in the history of religion do we see a scene like this, the Almighty Lord from heaven kneeling on the ground in the loincloth of a slave, washing the dirty feet of mere human beings, a task performed only by the lowest persons in the society. Do you understand that? This was a slave's job. Yet Jesus did it. "When he had washed their feet, and taken his garments, and resumed his place, he said to them, 'Do you know what I have done to you? . . . If I then, your Lord and Teacher, have washed your feet, you also ought to wash one another's feet. For I have given you an example, that you also should do as I have done to you'" (John 13:12-15). And he said to them, "A new commandment I give to you, that you love one another; even as I have loved you" (John 13:34).

Truly, it is family night. When families are working the way they are supposed to, the parents' love for the children is self-sacrificing and unconditional. A father will jump in front of a train to save his daughter, a mother will shield a son from gunfire with her own body, a sister will give her bone marrow for her brother. How much more does our Father in heaven offer his own life to us in the person of his Son! Jesus washes his disciples' feet as a token of the extent and depth of his love. A new family is coming into being on this night, a family of brothers and sisters with one Father in heaven and a Brother whose love for every one of us is greater and more unconditional than any love the world has ever seen.

The sermon text tonight is just one Biblical sentence, from the story of what happens to a member of Jesus' family that evening after the Lord's Supper. Let us come further together into the story of Maundy Thursday, the night in which Jesus was betrayed. My text, from Luke's Gospel, is "The Lord looked at Peter."

Jesus' family was not an impressive group of people on that

Lorenzo Ghiberti: The Last Supper
(panel from the bronze gilt doors
of the Baptistry, Florence)

Ghiberti's magnificent doors depicting the life of Christ in a series of panels use limited space to excellent advantage. Here he shows the disciples crowded together so that their intimacy with one another in fellowship with Jesus is emphasized, thereby lending more poignancy to their subsequent desertion of the Master.

last night of the Master's life. The lamentable tale of the disciples' failure is distilled in the story of Peter. All four evangelists tell it. Here is Luke's version:

> Then they seized [Jesus] and led him away, bringing him into the high priest's house. Peter followed at a distance; and when they had kindled a fire in the middle of the courtyard and sat down together, Peter sat among them. Then a maid, seeing him as he sat in the light and gazing at him, said, "This man also was with him." But he denied it, saying, "Woman, I do not know him." And a little later some one else saw him and said, "You also are one of them." But Peter said, "Man, I am not." And after an interval of about an hour still another insisted, saying, "Certainly this man also was with him; for he is a Galilean." [Matthew says that Peter began to curse and swear at this point.] Peter said, "Man, I do not know what you are saying." And immediately, while he was still speaking, the cock crowed. And the Lord turned and looked at Peter. And Peter remembered the word of the Lord, how he had said to him, "Before the cock crows today, you will deny me three times." And he went out and wept bitterly. (Luke 22:52-62)

And the Lord turned and looked at Peter. Here is the archetypal unmasking of the guilty human being. Let us recall what happened after the Last Supper:

> When they had sung a hymn, they went out to the Mount of Olives. Then Jesus said to them, "You will all fall away because of me this night . . ." [But] Peter declared to him, "Though they all fall away because of you, I will never fall away." Jesus said to him, "Truly, I say to you, this very night, before the cock crows, you will deny me three times." Peter said to him, "Even if I must die with you, I will not deny you." (Matthew 26:30-35)

Have you ever said anything as foolish as that? Of course you have. It isn't just politicians that say, "I will never lie to the American people." You and I have all said our versions of "Read my lips; no new taxes." Ask your children about the promises you've made to them and not kept. Half of the people who have said, "For better, for worse, for richer for poorer, in sickness and health . . . until death us do part," are now divorced. Think of all the men who have said, fervently, "I love you!" to women they can't even remember the next morning. I was trying to think of an illustration for this sermon of all the bad things I have said I would never do and then gone ahead and done. The problem is that I couldn't think of anything that I was willing to tell you.

So what happens to Peter, with all his best intentions? Only a few hours after making his extravagant promises of fidelity, Peter, faced with the threat of being hauled off to prison along with his Master, turns tail and disgraces himself, just as the Lord had predicted. We should note that Peter's reactions were complex that night. When the motley crew of conspirators first appears on the Mount of Olives to arrest Jesus in the dark, at first Peter seems to have made a spunky attempt to resist them. His feisty, impetuous nature is appealing to us; that's one reason he's such a popular Biblical character. Clearly he thinks of himself, at least on some level, as a macho, stand-up kind of guy. He was probably his mother's favorite. We've all known people like Peter, basically good guys with gung-ho natures and leadership abilities, but very tiresome after a while to their wives. This is the man who stood outside the house of the high priest and lied three times, the third time with vehement curses: "I've never had anything to do with this man Jesus." *And the Lord turned and looked at Peter.* I ask you to imagine that look and the way it pierced the soul of this feckless disciple. Do you remember anyone looking at you like that? That look needs no words. That look says, "Peter, now you know, and you know that I know, what a fraud and a traitor you are." That look strips away the covers from the various defenses that you and I use with greater and lesser success to deceive ourselves into thinking what nice people we are.

My father had a look. He didn't use it very often, but it was scary. It was all the more scary because my father was loved and respected by everyone, certainly by me. It was not possible to shrug off his look or to return it in kind. It went to the heart because it was the look of disappointed love. My father has been dead many years, but to this day I am motivated by my wish not to disappoint him.

But this is only a feeble approximation of what happened when Jesus looked at Peter. The look of Jesus comes from the depths of the Holy Trinity that was in the beginning before the world was made. The look of our Lord is lit from within by the uncreated light of the incarnate Word. It is the look that goes along with the prayer that we said at the beginning of this service: "O God to whom all hearts are open, all desires known, *and from whom no secrets are hid.* . . ." Do you ever think about those words that we say so often? Can you focus for a moment on what this really means, *no secrets hid from God?* There is a sense in which we spend our whole lives hiding secrets not only from one another but from ourselves. There is no hiding from God, however. Peter tried to hide, but the Lord found him with that look. Jesus' look penetrated through Peter like the "two-edged sword" in the Epistle to the Hebrews, "piercing to the division of soul and spirit, of joints and marrow, and discerning the thoughts and intentions of the heart. And before him no creature is hidden, but all are open and laid bare to the eyes of the One with whom we have to do" (Hebrews 4:12-13).

How can we survive this piercing look? The answer is, we can't, any more than Peter could. *Something has to happen* to us, something that we do not deserve, cannot earn, and have no right to expect. That is what we have been learning during these forty days and forty nights of Lent. Beginning with that long confession of sin that we said on our knees on Ash Wednesday, we have examined ourselves before the searching gaze of the Lord and we have repented in dust and ashes. I hope that many of you recognize this Lenten movement in your own lives. It puts us in the right frame of mind for this evening at our Lord's table.

This is family night. Families are crucibles in which failure and sin must be worked out. At the very heart of family life lies the need for forgiveness. Family life can only be healthy when husbands and wives seek one another's forgiveness, when parents forgive children, and parents model forgiveness so that the children will learn how to do it. Alas for those parents who have not taught their children, by word and example, to confess and seek forgiveness, for the time will inevitably come when our children must forgive us. This is a good night to think about these things and to offer them up to the Lord, for in his Cross we see the height, breadth, and depth of his mercy for the forgiveness of sins.

Forgiveness is not cheap. Let us never forget that. Even in our mundane lives, forgiveness always costs the forgiver. It all depends on how much there is to be forgiven. It is not difficult to forgive a child for some little error. I don't have any trouble forgiving my husband for forgetting to leave me the car keys; the irritation is only momentary. But when the offense is major, it is a different matter. It is not so easy to forgive adultery, or alcoholism, or abuse. It is not so easy to forgive decades of neglect or indifference or cruelty. Forgiveness in these cases is costly indeed. Even with these reflections, we can only have an approximate understanding of what Jesus underwent in order that we might be forgiven. Only by looking at him on the Cross can we see the price that was paid for our failure. It is indeed the greatest price ever paid. That is what Peter's redemption, our redemption was worth to him.

Think, tonight, of how Jesus looks at you and me. He sees the worst things that we have ever done, and the worst that we are. He sees us far more clearly than we see ourselves, because most people live in a state of perpetual denial about their own faults. This is the night to give up that denial. The look of Jesus conveys truth — the truth about our feeble attempts to pretend that we are able to stand in our own moral superiority. In that one look, the Judge of all the earth exposes us as the frauds we are.

But Jesus' look is not a look of pure judgment. If it were, we could not bear it. It is also and at the same time a look of restitution, of reconstitution, of rectification. The transmission of this story, which must have been approved by Peter himself, is the living testimony that the moment of Peter's humiliation is also the beginning of his rehabilitation. Being judged and found wanting by God is, believe it or not, the very fabric of our salvation. It is in this

The Last Supper
(painted stone carving, Naumburg Cathedral)

This vigorous rendering of the Last Supper shows the disciples devoting themselves with gusto to the business of eating and drinking. Judas, however (looking much older than he usually does), betrays his agitation by clutching the tablecloth as he dips the bread in the common dish.

judgment that we are redeemed. The Judge himself, at the very moment of Peter's betrayal, is taking the judgment upon himself.

As we gather tonight at the altar to receive communion, let this sink into your consciousness: The Lord Jesus Christ has drawn us here together on the night before his sacrifice. He has drawn us as surely as he drew those very human and flawed disciples to his table for his Last Supper. He looks at us, he sees everything that there is to see, and he says, Come; this is my body, this is my blood, poured out for you for the remission of sin. To him all hearts are open, all desires known, and from him no secrets are hid. In Christ our masks come off as the Lord turns his gaze upon us. In that penetrating look is the discovery that saves, the exposure that purifies, the judgment that redeems. In that look is Peter's salvation and ours. That is why it is our joy to repent and confess our sins. That is why we use white tonight, the color of purity and celebration. Our robes are washed to dazzling brightness in the blood of the Lamb. That is why we say, "Thanks be to God."

AMEN.

PART FOUR

Good Friday

———⊶⊷———

*Towards noon Pilate gave judgment, and they made such haste
to execution as that by noon he was upon the cross. There now
hangs that sacred body upon the cross, rebaptized in his own
tears and sweat, and embalmed in his own blood, alive. There
are those bowels of compassion, which are so conspicuous, so manifested, as that you may see them through his wounds. Then those
glorious eyes grew faint in their light, so as the sun, ashamed to
survive them, departed with his light too. And then that Son of
God, who was never from us, and yet had now come a new way
unto us in assuming our nature, delivers that soul (which was
never out of his Father's hands) by a new way, a voluntary
emission of it into his Father's hands . . . emisit, he gave up the
ghost; and as God breathed a soul into the first Adam, so this
second Adam breathed his soul into God, into the hands of God.*

JOHN DONNE

Note to the reader

———∞∞∞———

This Good Friday section is divided into four parts.

The first two, "Seven Meditations" and "Six Meditations," were written to be delivered in sequence, with pauses for prayers, hymns, and choir anthems, at traditional three-hour noontime services. The three hours, noon to three, represent the time that Jesus hung on the Cross.

The third section, "Three Meditations: The Three Signs on Calvary," was prepared to be delivered at a shorter noontime service.

These three sections are best read as three distinct sequences — in other words, each sequence read straight through in order, but separate from the others — because for most readers it would be too strong a dose to read more than one of the three sequences at a sitting. Indeed, it is recommended that a reading of a sequence of the Good Friday sermons be followed by an Easter sermon.

The fourth section, "More Sermons for Good Friday," consists of three full sermons, each independent of the others and designed to be delivered at one-hour services.

SEVEN MEDITATIONS

—⁂—

I determined to know nothing among you except Jesus Christ and him crucified.

(1 CORINTHIANS 2:2)

First Meditation:
The Man with No Trousers

———⦿———

You have chosen the better way by being here at this noontide hour. There is no other day like today. There has been no other day like it in history and never will be again. Millions of people have been prematurely put to death; but of this death alone can it be said that it has to do with the salvation of the whole world. By your presence here today, you demonstrate your commitment to the possibility that this claim just might be true.

Most people, of course, are not here. They are out doing what they do on an ordinary day — working, shopping, eating, working out at the gym, standing in line at the bank. It has always been like this. When Jesus was crucified, most people did not even notice; they were preoccupied with their own concerns. Crucified people were of no account; we do not know the name of a single crucified person except this One.[1] What is it, then, about *this* death, *this* execution, that continues to draw a chosen few away from their daily routines on this Friday every year? What message is there in this event that will make it worth your while?

The New Testament uses a formula to explain Christ's death which has become so familiar that we do not stop to think what it means. We say that Christ died *for our sins*. The connection between Christ's death and sin is so permanently and emphatically fixed in the Bible that it seems right to begin our inquiry there. And yet we do not begin there, because the Christian gospel does not start with us, certainly not with our sin, but with God and his goodness. Sin is not the first word, nor is it the last. The first and last words are that "The LORD is gracious, and full of compassion; slow to anger, and of great mercy. . . . O give thanks unto the LORD; for he is good: for his mercy endureth for ever" — and please note, these wondrous verses are from the *Old* Testament (Psalms 145:8; 136:1). We begin at the beginning, with God being gracious. Only from there do we move into the story of human rebellion against God.

The subject of sin is not a popular one in our time. We have drifted a long way from the days when sin was widely understood to be revolt against God, disobedience of his good commandments, violation of his covenant, and an offense to our relationships with other inhabitants of God's creation. We are losing a concept of sin because we are losing the knowledge of God. Ted Koppel made a remarkable statement in a commencement address; he noted that the Ten Commandments were not the Ten Suggestions. Our current cultural concept of God is so malleable, diminutive, and vague that he or she wouldn't have any right to issue commandments. To be honest, most people nowadays probably wouldn't sit still to listen to these thoughts, but you are different. People who come to church on Good Friday are aware that something is wrong and needs to be put right. You wouldn't be here if you didn't have a sense of that.

Many well-meaning Christians, observing the trend away from a robust understanding of sin, have tried to make it more palatable by watering down the definition. A favorite way of defining sin in the church recently has been "not living up to one's potential." That is a classic definition for our time, isn't it? It's the flip side of "Be all that you can be." But is this possible? Who will decide whether you have lived up to your potential or not? Are you ultimately going to be the one to decide this yourself? When we talk about living up to our potential and being all that we can be, we are already making mental allowances for loopholes, for exceptions, for escape hatches. If something comes up that doesn't fit our plans for ourselves, we say, "I can't deal with it." In order to fend off nagging doubts, we say, "Nobody's perfect." I remember a woman on her deathbed who said, "I did the best I could." It seemed clear enough to me that she was not at all sure that this was an effective defense against the awful possibility that she had *not* done her best, or that her best was *not good enough.*

The Holy Scriptures of the Christian church put forth a very different view of human nature. There is a sense in which we are offered no loopholes, no escape hatches whatsoever. Jesus did not teach us to pray, "Lord, I did my best"; he taught us to pray, "God, be merciful to me a sinner" (Luke 18:13). St. Paul wrote, "There is no one righteous, no, not one," and St. John says, "If we say we have no sin, we deceive ourselves, and the truth is not in us" (Romans 3:10; 1 John 1:8). Most pithy of all is Paul's statement, "There is no distinction; . . . all have sinned and fall short of the glory of God" (Romans 3:22-23). There's the key, right there. If we know God, we aren't going to be using human potential as the benchmark, but the glory of God — which is specifically and concretely made known to us in Jesus Christ: "We have beheld his glory, glory as of the only-begotten from the Father, . . . full of grace and truth" (John 1:14).

One of the most arresting short statements about sin in Scripture is to be found in Isaiah 53, a traditional reading for Good Friday which you will hear in a few moments. "All of us, like sheep, have gone astray; each of us has turned aside to his own way."[2] Each of us wants to pursue his own course. We are driven by self-will. Even in our relationships with others, our motives are contaminated by the ever-present sneaky reminder that we are seeking a payoff for ourselves. Personally, I have found it impossible, humanly speaking, to avoid this component of self-involvement in everything I do. Perhaps that is why Isaiah says in another chapter that even "our righteous deeds are like filthy rags" (64:6).

And so, in addition to each person going his own way, we have here also a picture of drastic estrangement on a *communal* level. Not only are we estranged from our best selves; we are alienated from one another and, most important, from God. The image of sheep going astray is one of creatures who have lost their bearings altogether, who have gone off the path and cannot find their way back.

It is customary in sermons to talk about the stupidity of sheep; however, the Bible does not say that sheep are stupid. It says that sheep are *lost*.

What are the possibilities of real human fellowship? New Yorkers like me are accustomed to going our own way most of the time, often quite rudely. It has been discovered, however, that a spark of fellow-feeling can be ignited when a whole group of people are lifted out of themselves to serve a larger cause, as in England during the Blitz, or in New York after the attack on the World Trade Center. But let us ask this: once the emergency is past, what will hold us together? What common thread is there that unites all of humanity, even groups that hate each other? The world has seldom seen so much goodness in one place as in New York in the aftermath of September 11. Within weeks, however, firemen and police officers were scuffling, and serious allegations about the misuse of donated funds were dividing the non-profit community.

The Biblical testimony is that the common thread is our human need. We are each of us distinguished by our failure to embody human potential and to mirror the glory of God. The greatest saints, the ones whom we admire the most, are the first to admit this. We are in desperate straits, all of us, in spite of appearances. Even if we have managed to convince ourselves that we're just fine, and a lot of us do that, God looks at us and sees otherwise. I overheard a fascinating scrap of dialogue: one upper-crust, three-piece-suited man said to another, angrily, "My son-in-law is an emotional cripple!" The other man said, quietly, "We're all emotional cripples." I was astonished by this wisdom. The second speaker had hit on the common thread. We're all cripples of one sort or another. We're all using crutches. One of my professors at seminary was attacked in a college lecture by a cocky student who accused him of using religion as "a crutch." With a quickness that still amazes me, the professor said, "You're absolutely right. What's yours?"

If we were attending church services today in certain other neighborhoods, certain other societies, we would be able to tell at a glance that everybody was leaning on crutches. Here in this affluent parish, our weaknesses are very well concealed. I don't see any con-

Andrea Mantegna: Calvary

This fifteenth-century Italian painter depicts Golgotha specifically "outside the city wall," with the Temple Mount in the distant background like an unattainable heaven, definitively separated from the vile place of execution by a colossal wall. Golgotha is shown as a place designed to dispatch crucified victims regularly and as a matter of course; note the pile of skulls on the left and the holes in the pavement designed specifically to hold crosses. Mantegna is known for his attention to historical detail, especially in the rendering of architecture and costume; the efficiency of the Roman Empire is on display here in its most brutal form. For the group of soldiers on the right, crucifixion is just another day's work; they are portrayed as glamorous military figures decked out in all their imperial panoply. Their heedless lounging about is effectively contrasted with the suffering of the helpless friends of Jesus on the left. Although Mantegna could not have been thinking in today's terms, this is a striking portrayal of the oppressor flaunting its power over the oppressed.

The crucified figures loom into the sky; one thief is tense with agony while the other one struggles, but Jesus, already dead, seems to embrace the universe with his tortured arms. "I, if I be lifted up from the earth, will draw all men unto myself" (John 12:23).

spicuously needy-looking people here today. But you know, one of the dangers in coming to church is that you can't fool your clergy. They know what lies under the glossy surface, because all clergy worthy of their calling have looked into their own souls and have seen the "heart of darkness" there.

During the Persian Gulf War, one of the *New Yorker* writers was reminded of an incident described by George Orwell during the Spanish Civil War. Orwell wrote from the front lines that he saw a man from the opposing, Fascist forces jump out of the trench and run along the parapet in full view, presumably carrying a message to an officer. He had nothing on but a pair of ill-fitting trousers, which he held up with one hand as he ran. Orwell wrote, "I refrained from shooting him. . . . I had come here to shoot at 'fascists,' but a man who is holding up his trousers isn't a 'fascist,' he is visibly a fellow-creature, similar to yourself, and you don't feel like shooting him."

When God looks at us, he does not see titles, bank accounts, club memberships, vacation homes, net worth. He sees frail, vulnerable creatures trying to cover up our spiritual nakedness. When Jesus came down from heaven to live among us, he lived among us at that level. The Son of God gave up all his divine prerogatives and came into the world to be a fellow-creature with us in our deepest need. We were God's enemies, deserving of death; but he looked at us trying to hold up our trousers with one hand and declared that we were not enemies but friends.

And, Isaiah continues, "The LORD has laid on him the iniquity of us all." As Jesus goes to the Cross today, even his trousers are taken away from him. He is denied even this last shred of decency. He enters the world of dereliction and disgrace, the man with no trousers, and he does it for love of his enemies — that is to say, he does it for love of us.

Second Meditation: Shame and Spitting

A few years ago, *Newsweek* magazine did a cover story on Shame. The cover photo showed a little child, looking utterly miserable, wearing a dunce cap. The picture was distressing. The basic premise of the story itself was a good one, and I will return to that in a minute, but nothing good can come of shaming a child in such a way. Parents and teachers who shame and humiliate children are doing a monstrous thing. Making a public spectacle of a child is harmful to the emerging personality. It was an attention-getting cover, but it worked against the point that many people wish to make nowadays, namely, that we need to recover a sense of shame in our society.

Let's see if we can keep two ideas of shame in our minds for a moment: 1) shame that crushes the spirit, which is clearly a bad thing, and 2) shame that instructs and edifies. It is the second kind of shame that writers such as Russell Baker miss in a culture where white-collar criminals can come out of prison and make very big dollars for lecturing and writing books without showing so much as a hint that they are sorry for what they did. Being ashamed of one's conduct and admitting it is a sign of strength and character. It is a step toward growth and maturity. This is the kind of shame that works. It is not imposed from outside, like the dunce cap. It is chosen by the person who has offended; he or she steps forward and, as we used to say, takes his punishment like a man. These two kinds of shame, the punitive and destructive kind that is thrust upon a person by a more powerful figure, and the constructive shame that comes as an honest reflection upon misdeeds, are both important for understanding the death of Jesus.

When I was young, the authority figures in my life — my mother and father, my grandmother, my aunt — would say to me on certain well-chosen occasions, "You ought to be ashamed of yourself." With me, I think this worked. I think the context was right. For a child to be ashamed in a positive way, certain factors have to be present. The child needs to know that his family members love him and that they are trustworthy people, not capricious or violent. The family's shared values need to be strong and lived out daily. The child's ego, or self, should be healthy and developing toward maturity. I distinctly remember that, when I was told that I should be ashamed, I knew what my elders meant and I thought that there was truth in what they said. This kind of family or community consensus is necessary in order for a healthy understanding of shame to develop. When this happens, admitting in public that one is ashamed of oneself can be an act of courage. It means saying goodbye to self-pity and self-justification. At its best it is a major step toward transformation. To put it in Biblical terms, it means praying the prayer that was warmly commended by Jesus in the parable of the Pharisee and the publican — "God, be merciful to me a sinner." The man who prayed that prayer, said our Lord, "went down to his house justified" (Luke 18:14).

In spite of these positive images of shame, however, we find ourselves in a cultural predicament. We have inherited several decades of drift away from a healthy sense of sin and guilt. We feel that it is bad for our self-esteem to be ashamed of anything. This attitude is not only harmful for society but also destructive for personal and family relationships. One of the most fatuous sentences ever written was, "Love means never having to say you're sorry." (That's from *Love Story,* by Eric Segal.) On the contrary, love often requires being sorry, being ashamed, and seeking forgiveness. Human relationships can't flourish without confession and forgiveness, because we are forever disappointing one another.

Shame in its truest and best sense has to do with our standing before God. When a person feels shame before God, it is a sure sign of growth in grace. King David demonstrated this in an unforgettable way when he was confronted by the prophet Nathan about his conduct with Bathsheba. David confessed his sin and shame instantly, without dissembling, without excuses, without self-pity. Robert McNamara gave us another example of confession in his memoir about the Vietnam War.[3] At any rate, it takes a strong person to say, "I am ashamed of myself and I want to be held accountable."

Now let's look at some key passages from the Bible and Prayer Book that have to do with the Crucifixion of Jesus. First, from the letter to the Hebrews: "Let us fix our eyes on Jesus . . . who . . . endured the cross, scorning the shame" (12:2). Then, from Isaiah 50:6 (these words were set to music by Handel in *Messiah*): "I gave my back to the smiters, . . . I hid not my face from shame and spitting." And from our Prayer Book, one of the Collects for Holy Week calls the Cross an instrument of *shameful* death.

It is important to understand what crucifixion was as a means of putting people to death. This is not a pleasant subject, but this is the day to think about it. Consider the various means of executing people, a preoccupation that unfortunately seems to be returning to a central place in our country. The electric chair, the firing squad, the hangman's noose, the lethal injection — these are noted for their supposed efficiency. The Elizabethan penalty of being hanged, drawn, and quartered was designed to inflict suffering but also as a warning to the population. Other means of execution over the centuries have been devised to cause pain, and to prolong agony. The particular peculiarity of crucifixion was that it was meant not just as a deterrent but also, specifically, to degrade. No other method has ever matched it in terms of public disgust; that was its express purpose.[4] Ancient Roman writers could hardly bring themselves to mention it, and it was considered too revolting to discuss in polite Roman company. As for the Jews, death by crucifixion was nothing less than accursed and Godforsaken (more of that later in these three hours).[5]

When I was a young woman living in Richmond, Virginia, I used to have regular discussions with a skeptical friend who said that she didn't get the point of the Crucifixion of Jesus. Many people, she pointed out, died even more horrible deaths, with more protracted suffering. Three hours, she said, was not so long compared to others who live in agony for many days. That is quite true, and at the time I was not well enough informed to argue it with her. What I know now that I wish I had known then was the significance of the Cross as a sign of utter contempt. Being hung up by the roadside on a cross, completely exposed and powerless, was to be displayed as publicly as possible as an object of the most extreme scorn and revulsion. It was impossible for a crucified victim to be dignified or heroic. That was the nature of the method — to reduce the convicted person to subhuman status. You have perhaps noticed that the New Testament writers have nothing to say about the physical details of the Crucifixion — not a single word about the pain, the breathlessness, the nakedness, the wrenching of the joints, or any of the other horrible aspects of death on a cross. What they do call attention to is the *shame* — the spitting and mocking, the location outside the city, the carrying of the cross, the placement between two scummy, low-life thieves, the degradation, the Godforsakenness.[6] The placard over Jesus' head might just as well have said, "Not fit to live." That is what is important for us to understand about the Crucifixion. Jesus consciously, deliberately, voluntarily stepped into the place of utmost humiliation. He *scorned the shame,* that is, he went into it with full knowledge of what he was facing. In one sense it was not imposed on him from outside ("I lay down [my life] of my own accord," he said; John 10:18), but in going willingly to this particular form of death, he took upon himself a sentence that he in no way deserved, and became a victim of what others would do to him.

So Jesus experienced the bad kind of shame, the kind that is inflicted upon the powerless by the powerful. "He hid not himself from shame and spitting." He is the only person who in his whole life never had anything to be ashamed of, yet he made himself helpless in order to undergo this worst form of disgrace and abandonment. As St. Paul writes, "He was in the form of God, but . . . took upon himself the form of a slave and became obedient to death, even the death of the cross." It is impossible not to see Jesus, in this event, making some sort of exchange with us. Pay very close attention to the words of the next hymn when we sing it, because of all our hymns it says it best: "The slave hath sinned and the son hath suffered." The slave (that's you and me); the Son (that's Jesus). The shame belonged to us; the effects fell upon him. "Surely he has borne our griefs and carried our sorrows." And here is the wonderful thing. Because he has taken our place under the ultimate burden of shame, shame is no longer a burden for us, but almost a badge of honor. We may now wear shame as King David did, as the colors of the One who overcomes. Because he was willing, and because he alone was able to take on himself the shame of the whole world, we are now able to stand upright and say, "I'm sorry," and, "I am ashamed of myself," without being crushed. Indeed, far from being crushed, we are now able to rejoice and find new life and freedom as we confess our faults before God and our fellow humans. Because our precious Lord *hid not his face from shame and spitting,* you and I will never have to wear a dunce cap again.

Third Meditation:
Scapegoat and Sacrifice

———— ⊗⊗⊗ ————

A few years ago when the Metropolitan Museum had an important show of Caravaggio's works, a valuable insight was available to Christian museumgoers. One of the paintings depicted the crucifixion of St. Andrew. Except for the fact that Andrew appeared to be older than Jesus and his cross was in the shape of an X, you really couldn't tell the difference between one crucifixion and another. The picture of St. Andrew left me essentially unmoved. Why did the paintings of the death of Jesus have so much more significance for me? The external details were more or less the same. It was the *meaning* of the two deaths that was different. Only the death of Jesus in all world history has had saving significance for the entire human race. Ultimately no painting, no movie, no television program can explain this to us; we have to hear the words of the Bible in faith.

In the Gospel of John we read the famous assertion of St. John the Baptist: "Behold the Lamb of God, which taketh away the sin of the world" (John 1:29, 36). Every Christian will recognize these words, yet few nowadays will know how to appropriate them in their full Biblical context. Likewise most Christians will be familiar with the words of St. Paul used in the Eucharist: "Christ our Passover [lamb] is sacrificed for us" (1 Corinthians 5:7), but many would not be able to explain them. What a lot we are missing! Those fortunate ones among us who are Bible readers will recognize at this point the Old Testament background that is so crucial for understanding the death of Jesus.[7] You see, the whole sacrificial system of Hebrew worship, which went on for thousands of years B.C., prepared God's people to understand two vital things:

> *First,* that the innocent must die for the guilty;
> *Second,* that there is no sacrifice for sin without the shedding of blood.

There are three motifs in the Old Testament that fill out the picture:

The first motif is that of the blood sacrifice for sin. It is described in Leviticus 4. If anyone sins unintentionally (notice that "unintentionally"! "I didn't mean to" and "I didn't know" are no excuses), an animal is killed and the blood of the animal is poured out by the priest to make atonement. That is the way the sin is erased. The blood of the sacrificial animal is an offering for sin.

The second motif is that of the scapegoat. We find this in Leviticus 16; the events described there are sometimes referred to as "the Good Friday of the Old Testament." A live goat is brought to the priest. "And Aaron shall lay both his hands upon the head of the live goat, and confess over him all the iniquities of the people of Israel, and all their transgressions, all their sins; and he shall put them upon the head of the goat, and send him away into the wilderness. . . . The goat shall bear all their iniquities upon him to a solitary land" (Leviticus 16:21-22). And then, in a fascinating and prophetic way, the first and second motifs — the blood sacrifice and the scapegoat — seem to blend into one another. We read that the concluding act of the ceremony of atonement is the carrying of the carcasses of the sacrificial animals outside the camp to be burned, as the scapegoat is driven out into the wilderness (Leviticus 16:27). These rituals are the backdrop for the assertion in the New Testament that Jesus suffered outside the gate in order to sanctify the people through his own blood (Hebrews 13:12).

Crucifixion in twelfth-century glass, Chartres Cathedral

The masters of Chartres Cathedral, knowing that their work had to be seen from a distance, were able to convey a message through these strong forms. The drooping head and wrenched torso of Christ, together with the expressions and gestures of the Virgin and the beloved disciple, make an impression even from a great height.

The third motif is that of the Passover lamb, or Paschal lamb
(*pascha* is Greek for Passover). We read all about this in Exodus 12:

> Tell all the congregation of Israel that on the tenth day of this
> month they shall take every man a lamb, . . . a lamb for a house-
> hold; [and on] the fourteenth day of this month . . . the whole as-
> sembly of the congregation of Israel shall kill their lambs in the
> evening. Then they shall take some of the blood, and put it on
> [their] doorposts. . . . The blood shall be a sign for you, upon the
> houses where you are; and when I see the blood, I will pass over
> you, and no plague shall fall upon you to destroy you, when I
> smite the land of Egypt.

In the New Testament, all these motifs are combined in a wonderful way. The shedding of blood, the innocent victim offered for
the guilty perpetrators, the bearing away of the people's sin into the
wilderness outside the camp, and the blood of the Passover lamb as
the sign of deliverance from slavery and death — all of this explains
what we mean when we say "Behold the Lamb of God, who takes
away the sin of the world" and when we say "Christ our Passover
(lamb) is sacrificed for us" (1 Corinthians 5:7).

And so the One who said of himself, "I am the good shepherd"
is now laying down his life for the sheep. The words of the hymn
that we just sang celebrate it: "Lo, the Good Shepherd for the sheep
is offered." The innocent One dies in the place of the guilty many
— the "one oblation of himself once offered."[8]

And so these words from the Epistle to the Hebrews are appointed for Good Friday:

> We have been sanctified through the offering of the body of Jesus
> Christ once for all. . . . When Christ had offered for all time a sin-
> gle sacrifice for sins, he sat down at the right hand of God. . . . By a
> single offering he has perfected for all time those who are sancti-
> fied. . . . Therefore, brethren, since we have confidence to enter the
> sanctuary by the blood of Jesus . . . let us draw near with a true
> heart in full assurance of faith. (Hebrews 10:10, 12, 14, 19, 22)

Fourth Meditation:
The Common Criminal

―――◦ΩΩ◦―――

When John the Baptist was languishing in prison, he sent a message to Jesus asking him to explain himself.[9] Apparently John could not understand why Jesus had not begun to exercise his Messianic authority and power in the way John had thought he would. Jesus replied with a definition of his ministry and then said, "Blessed is he who takes no offense at me" (Matthew 11:6). Yet, we are repeatedly told throughout the four Gospels, people did just that. Here is the story of two women who took offense at him.

The first woman (let's call her Sally) told me that she was having trouble finding an Episcopal church that she liked. I suggested that she try St. Such and Such. "Oh, no," she exclaimed. "I could never go there." "Why not?" I asked. To my amazement she said, "I would have to look at that big cross they have behind the altar with that figure of Christ hanging on it. It would upset me terribly!"[10]

The second woman (let's call her Jane) is a woman whose husband and children I used to know pretty well. Although Jane appeared to be a very agreeable person to those who saw her socially at the club or the church, I knew it to be a fact that she made life difficult for her family. She was manipulative, domineering, willful, and unforgiving. The fact that she had a pleasing personality on the surface just made it worse, because she was used to getting her own way with blandishments. It was almost impossible to get hold of her to help her see what she was doing; she considered herself a person of superior virtue.

During Holy Week several years ago she said something that, from my point of view, was deeply revealing. First I should explain that, although many churches have been doing dramatic readings of the Passion narrative for many years, the church she belonged to had not done it before. On one Palm Sunday, she participated in such a dramatized version for the first time. As a member of the congregation, representing the crowd, she was supposed to shout "Let him be crucified!" This part of the reading is often a significant moment for those who take part; in fact, I know people whose faith has been kindled, or rekindled, at that moment. After the service was over, several of us were standing around at the coffee hour talking about how moving the service had been. People were especially talking about how they had felt when they shouted "Let him be crucified!" At this point Jane said, with considerable energy, "I couldn't do it! I just couldn't say it! I just couldn't say such an awful thing!"

I have often thought, since, how terribly sad that was. In her stubborn blindness, Jane could not identify herself as a sinner like all the rest of us. She could not admit that she, too, was capable of evil thoughts and malicious deeds. She was preoccupied with her own virtue and her own religiousness. Because of this, she could not see who Jesus is or who she is. A wise Benedictine monk once said, "If you can't handle the violence in the Psalms, you can't come to terms with the violence in yourself." This is even more true of the Cross. If we can't look at the Cross, then we can't look at ourselves either.

I have one more little story to tell. This is another story about Sally, the woman who didn't want to look at the figure of Jesus on the crucifix. She told some of her friends about an experience she'd had in a department store. In order to appreciate this, you have to picture the department store and you have to picture Sally. The store in question is fashionable and elegant. Sally herself is fashionable and elegant, the epitome of aristocratic dignity. She bought an expensive blouse at the store and took it with her in a shopping bag.

Unfortunately, the saleswoman had forgotten to remove the white plastic device that was attached to the blouse. When Sally tried to go through the door, the alarms went off and the security forces pounced upon her. "Oh, my dear, how horrible for you!" cried her friends, listening to the story. "It must have been so distressing! Did you call your husband? Did you have your identification? Did you call your lawyer? Did you ask to see the president of the store?"

"Oh," said Sally, "That wasn't a problem. I didn't have any trouble establishing who I was. That wasn't the bad part. The really bad part was the feeling of being treated like a common criminal!"

Those were her exact words. Like a common criminal. This is the woman who won't go to the church in her neighborhood because it has a figure of Jesus on the cross and she doesn't want to look at it.

Sally was able to tell the department store police who she was; and yet the truth is that she does not know who she is. I tried to explain to Sally that the feeling of shame that she felt was a clue to the meaning of the death of Jesus, who was arrested like a common criminal, exhibited to the public like a common criminal, executed like a common criminal. I was unable to put this across. She does not believe herself to be guilty of anything. Wronged, yes; misunderstood, yes; undervalued, yes; imperfect, perhaps; but not guilty, certainly not sinful. Because she believes herself to be one of the "good" people, because she could never, never commit a small sin like shoplifting, she cannot see the connection between Jesus' death as a common criminal and herself.

Sally could not hear the message of Good Friday, Jane could not hear it, but perhaps you can hear it today, on their behalf as well as your own. When you reflect upon Jesus Christ hanging on the cross of shame, you understand the depth and weight of human sin. How do we measure the size of a fire? By the number of firefighters and fire engines sent to fight against it. How do we measure the seriousness of a medical condition? By the amount of risk the doctors take in prescribing dangerous antibiotics or surgical procedures. How do we measure the gravity of sin and the incomparable vastness of God's love for us? By looking at the magnitude of what God

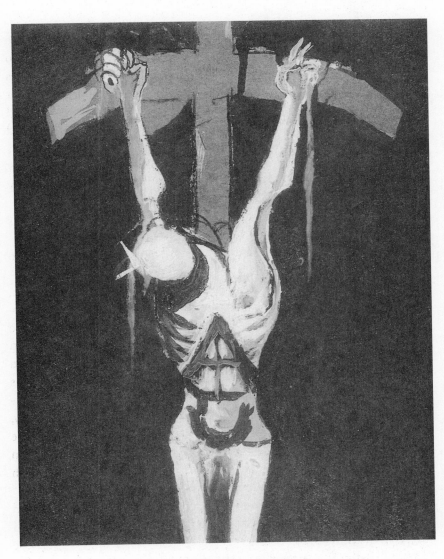

Graham Sutherland: Crucifixion

Like many other painters since World War II, Sutherland has abandoned all sacred references, identifying the crucified one with all nameless, tortured victims.

has done for us in Jesus, who *became like a common criminal* for our sake and in our place.

When you really come to know the unconditional love and forgiveness of Jesus, then you will also come to know the depth of your own participation in sin. And *at the very same moment* (this is the glory of Good Friday) you will come to know the true reality, the true joy and gladness, of the good news of salvation in Jesus Christ our Lord.

Fifth Meditation:
Somebody Has Got to Pay

O n Good Friday, all the Biblical motifs come together, and
there are a great many of them. We retell the story of the Passover and the Exodus, the primary Biblical event of deliverance from
bondage, recapitulated in the theme of the conquering Christ. We
hear of atonement in the Old Testament and the way it is achieved
through the blood of the sacrificial offering. We hear of the ark of
the covenant, the mercy seat, and the sprinkled blood. We reenact
in our imaginations the Lord's submission to the kingdom of death,
over which God alone can be victorious. We hold up the image of
the Passover lamb, the sacrifice of the only son, the self-offering of
the Suffering Servant, and climactically, the motif of substitution,
as Jesus bows his head under the weight of the world's sin and absorbs the ancient curse into himself. Let us try to bring some of
these images into a sharper focus. To this end, I call your attention
to a single verse from Paul's Second Epistle to the Corinthians:

> For our sake God made him to be sin who knew no sin, so that in
> him we might become the righteousness of God. (2 Corinthians
> 5:21)

In this extraordinarily important verse we learn what it was that
happened to Jesus on the Cross. We might wish that Paul had ex-

pressed himself in a clearer way, or that his syntax was less tortured ("there are some things in [Paul's letters] that are hard to understand" — 2 Peter 3:16), but this single verse has always been recognized as having a special significance in the interpretation of the Crucifixion.

God made him to be sin who knew no sin. Three things — the fact of sin, the fact of Jesus' sinlessness, and the fact of Jesus' death by crucifixion — are inextricably tied together. You may ask what this verse has to do with the Cross, since the Cross is not mentioned specifically. To that we reply that there is no other point in Jesus' life that we can identify as the point when God made him "to be sin" *except the moment* when he cried out "My God, my God, why hast thou forsaken me?"

Even the so-called "Jesus Seminar," which has identified about 90 percent of Jesus' Gospel sayings as "nonhistorical," admits that Jesus really did utter the Cry of Dereliction. It is very unlikely that anyone would have imagined this, and even more unlikely that it would be saved and treasured by the church if it hadn't been really uttered. "My God, my God, why hast thou forsaken me?" Why did the Lord say that?

The only answer that has ever satisfied me is that, in that moment, the Son of God "became sin." The hideousness of it overwhelmed him. In that moment, he experienced separation from the Father for the first and only time. The condemnation that we deserved was absorbed by him.

This idea has always caused offense. Some of that offense will reappear in every generation, because we do not like to believe that we deserve condemnation. (Someone else, perhaps, but *not me.*) Another aspect, though, of the atonement has caused offense because there has been a huge misunderstanding. Some preachers and teachers have pictured, in repugnant terms, a wrathful Father piling condemnation on an innocent, victimized Son. This mistake must be strenuously resisted.[11] At the heart of the mystery of the atoning sacrifice of the Son of God is the fact that the Father's will and the Son's will are one. This is an action that the Father and the Son are taking *together.* "Father, if it be thy will, let this cup pass from me; yet not my will, but thine, be done. . . . No one takes my life from me; I lay it down of my own accord. . . . The Good Shepherd lays down his life for the sheep. I have power to lay it down, and I have power to take it again" (Luke 22:42; John 10:11-18).

The various Biblical writers give us this story from different perspectives. One of these perspectives is reflected in the famous eucharistic prayer of Thomas Cranmer in the Episcopal Prayer Book: Christ made "a full, perfect, and sufficient sacrifice, oblation, and *satisfaction,* for the sins of the whole world." Many teachers avoid this idea of satisfaction today, and to be sure it has often been made overly abstract and formal, but there is great truth in it. In order to understand the Cross of Christ, Cranmer is suggesting, we need to consider the gravity of sin.[12] In the time of the Old Testament, the guilt offering had to be weighed so that a value could be given to it. We need to weigh the Cross, the price paid. Looking at Jesus Christ crucified, we see the degradation and Godforsakenness of it and we see the true nature of sin.[13]

Something had to be done about sin. Some sort of satisfaction had to be made. This is not some medieval abstraction; it is a basic perception in human existence. In the early 1990s a young black boy in Teaneck, New Jersey, was shot by the police when his hands were raised in surrender. His anguished father cried, "Somebody has got to pay!" Justice must be done and must be *seen* to be done. Anselm of Canterbury long ago wrote, "God's justice must be satisfied" — not "must" in the sense of rigid logic, but "must" as an event of the moral order. In the Cross of Christ, justice is *actually done;* it is not a "legal fiction" as some have charged over the years. In the Cross, God has not declared a general amnesty. No one except a criminal is going to be satisfied with a general amnesty. Something more is happening here.

Even without reference to God's justice, our own human sense of justice demands that reparations be made, that sentences be served, that satisfaction be given when there is great offense. We speak today of "closure"; it is a way of acknowledging the heart's need for some step to be taken from outside the self to make healing possible. Even human beings demand this; how much more so the God of justice and righteousness! For there to be satisfaction "for the sins of the whole world," there had to be an intervention from outside the structures of sin. Somebody *had to pay* the price for sin.

It has always been the case, as far as I can tell, that communities of poor people and people of color who suffer from systemic injustice all their lives seem to understand that Jesus is paying the price for sin better than more affluent people do. Suburban congregations tend to be struggling largely with personal issues — illness, divorce, addictions, intergenerational conflict, financial problems, that sort of thing — so that we think more in terms of finding support and healing than we do overcoming injustice and oppression. It is amazing how so many African-Americans continue to speak of their hope for justice in specifically Christian terms. I have noticed this all my life. The hymn that we will soon sing, "Were you there when they crucified my Lord?" comes out of their community. The refrain "sometimes it causes me to tremble" does not refer simply to the suffering of crucifixion. The line in the song evokes layers upon layers of meaning: the connection of his suffering to their suffering, the similarity of the evil done to him to the evil of slavery done to them, the forgiveness of his enemies reflected in their forgiveness of whites so often demonstrated. But most of all, in the context of this particular meditation on the paying of the price is the extraordinary Biblical theology of the Civil Rights movement articulated by Dr. King and many, many others.[14] In the vision of justice that they continually held forth, there was a deep sense that in the moral order, God had already done something so powerful and definitive that it could not be stopped. When Dr. King kept saying, "the arc of the universe is long, but it bends toward justice," he wasn't just mouthing a pretty thought. The faith that nourished him in the nonviolent struggle was the faith that God had already made the down payment.[15] Therefore "we shall overcome some day."

"Somebody has got to pay." This is the thought that lies behind the arguments for the death penalty. It is the emotion that drives us when we retaliate against someone when our lives have been disrupted. It is the factor that keeps Israelis killing Palestinians and Palestinians killing Israelis world without end.

But it is not world without end.[16] The cycle of violence, the cycle of injustice, the cycle of retaliation was stopped in the body of Jesus. The old world of Sin and Death came to an end on the Cross. That is the Christian proclamation. God has paid. If you or I were God, we would have arranged for *somebody else* to pay that price, someone who we figured was deserving of condemnation. God arranged for his own self to pay the price; Jesus, the one person who did *not* deserve condemnation, stood forward to take the weight of sin upon himself, instead of us. "For our sake God made him to be sin who knew no sin, so that in him we might become the righteousness of God."

But where, O Lord? And how long? Where is that righteousness? "Bring in the day of truth and love and end the night of wrong!"[17] It is a long time coming. This is where our faith is tested most severely. But in the lives and in the witness of Dr. King and the Freedom Marchers, Bishop Oscar Romero and the martyred nuns of El Salvador, Bishop Tutu and the women of the Black Sash in South Africa, we have seen the downpayment at work.[18] May God grant grace to each of us in the measure that he sees fit, that we may be enabled to bear witness in both words and deeds that the cycle of wrong came to its appointed end in the crucified body of Jesus, and that we will embody that truth in our lives until the great Day when the night of wrong will at last be obliterated by the light of the One who comes.

Sixth Meditation:
The Accursed Messiah

—&—

This meditation is based on the third chapter of Galatians which was just read to you. It is rarely heard in the church, and rarely preached upon — because of its complexity? Or because it is tough to take? At any rate, it is one of the central texts for understanding the Crucifixion.[19] Like so many of the passages in Paul's letters, it is a conception of great originality and penetrates to the heart of what is happening on Good Friday. Let us hear the central portion again:

> All who rely on works of the law are under a curse, for it is written, "Cursed be every one who does not abide by all things written in the book of the law, and do them." . . . Christ redeemed us from the curse of the law, having become a curse for us — for it is written, "Cursed be every one who hangs on a tree."

Focus for a moment on just one sentence. *All those who are seeking justification by works of the law are under a curse.* What are works of the law? Basically, works of the law are works that are commanded by God — godly works, moral works, righteous works, the best works that we can think of — good deeds, as we say. Now listen to Paul's words again: "All those who are seeking justification by works of the law are under a curse." That is the most radical utterance ever uttered — I'm quite serious — and the Epistle to the Galatians is the most radical writing ever produced. Perhaps you can sense why. If St. Paul is truly saying that to rely on God's own commandments is to be under a curse, what becomes of morality? What becomes of godliness? Indeed, what becomes of religion?

Now in the congregation at Galatia there were many who were preaching and teaching that justification was available only through works of the law. What is the meaning of this word *justification?*[20] It may sound technical and forbidding, but it isn't really. We readily use it today in a question like, How are you going to *justify* what you just did? That is, how are you going to demonstrate that you are in the right? That's what's at stake, for the Galatian Christians and for us. Think about yourself for a minute. What do you rely on in order to prove to yourself and others that you are a worthy human being? What do you count on to clear yourself from judgment, whether the judgment of your own conscience or the judgment of those parental voices that still lie in the back of our psyche even though our parents have been dead for decades, or the judgment of our peers and our families and our grown children, or, for that matter, the final judgment of God? What do you count on to clear yourself from judgment? How do you *justify* yourself?

Some rely on status and rank achieved in a career. Some rely on the successful raising of children (that's a particularly undependable one). Some of us justify ourselves by the number of people we control, whether in the workplace or at home. We justify ourselves by our reputation, our good name. Or maybe we rely on our "life style" — we think of ourselves as being in better shape, or more healthy, or slimmer, going to more fashionable places, eating in the best restaurants and talking about it afterwards. Most telling of all, we seek to justify ourselves by the kinds of people that we think we are. You justify yourself, I justify myself by convincing myself that I am a certain kind of person: more moral, more sensitive, more loving, smarter, more thoughtful of others, more patriotic, more community-minded, more socially aware, whatever. Or, to take the reverse of that, more martyred, more put-upon, more misunderstood, more long-suffering than anybody else. We can sum all of this up by say-

Rembrandt: Christ on the Cross

In the fourteenth and fifteenth centuries, artists usually painted Crucifixion scenes with elaborate landscapes and a full cast of characters. These two later images by different painters both seem to depict Our Lord at the moment of his anguished cry, "My God, my God, why hast thou forsaken me?"

Francesco Goya: Crucifixion

ing that we justify ourselves, subtly or not so subtly, by elevating ourselves above others.

But what about God? How do we justify ourselves before God? Well, by keeping his commandments, right? But what are they? Here are two of them: "Thou shalt love the Lord thy God with all thy heart and with all thy soul and with all thy mind, and thou shalt love thy neighbor as thyself." How are we doing on those? Can we justify ourselves before the throne of God by saying, "Well, I kept some of the commandments some of the time"? I once had a woman from our local community help me with choosing some fabrics. When we were talking about colors and patterns we did all right, but I had a hard time keeping her off the subject of religion. She wanted me to know that she had no use for the church. "What is religion?" she said. "It's 'do unto others,' that's what it is. I don't have to go to church for that." I wish I had had the nerve to look her in the eye and ask her how she could say that with such confidence, because the fact is that, far from "doing unto others," she had a reputation in town for being unusually self-centered and bent on having her own way.

St. Paul quotes from the Book of the Law, the Torah itself, to make his point. From Deuteronomy 27:26, "Cursed be every one who does not do everything that is written in the book of the law." That certainly puts our ostentatious efforts at self-justification into perspective. How can we live, then, under the threat of this judgment by almighty God? According to Paul, we can't. It really doesn't matter what we seek to justify ourselves by, because it's no use. Using an old expression, I once said to my husband in a jocular way that someone we knew was "living in sin" with a woman. My husband said, "We're all living in sin." That's the point. We are under a curse because we are in bondage to the power of Sin and we can't do the right thing all the time even if we want to; as Paul says unforgettably in Romans 7: "The evil I do not want to do, that is what I do."

Now comes the critical verse in our text. "Christ has redeemed us from the curse of the law by becoming a curse on our behalf." "What is a curse?" asked a young woman in a Bible class I was teaching; "A curse is a swear word. I don't understand how Christ became a swear word." But that isn't what *curse* means in the Biblical sense. Cursing and blessing, in the Bible, means the power of God to accomplish his ultimate purpose, and so, the power of God to bless or the power of God to condemn. If we were living under the rule of the law, we would all be condemned.

Christ became a curse for us. You know that St. Paul, before he became a Christian, was zealous and even vehement in his persecution of Christians. Why? The reason Paul was so enraged against Christianity is that he, a highly trained rabbinical Jew, could not tolerate the idea that the Messiah of God, long promised and long expected, had died under the condemnation of God.[21] And why did Paul the Pharisee think such a thing? Here is the key: in Deuteronomy there is a verse that says, "Cursed be every one who is hanged on a tree." A dead body publicly displayed was anathema to good religious people, a Godforsaken object.[22] And so the claim of the Christians was that the Messiah had died under the curse of God. That was intolerable for the zealous Paul. He went to Damascus to root out Christianity wherever he could find it. And you know what happened; he was knocked off his horse, blinded for three days, and utterly transformed by his vision of the risen Lord Jesus Christ.

So Paul had to go back into the Bible and find out: Why? Why did the Messiah of God die a Godforsaken, God-accursed death? Why did the Messiah die by crucifixion, the most shameful of all methods of execution? When St. Paul read the passage in Deuteronomy with Jesus in mind, he must have seen fireworks. Now he understood: Jesus was taking upon himself the curse that would have been ours because of our inbred nature as rebels against God's righteous commandments.

Now what this means for you and me is that there is no condemnation in heaven or earth that can touch us any more. "Christ has redeemed us from the curse of the law by becoming a curse for us." We deserved the condemnation, but he stepped into our place. Therefore, as Paul writes in Romans, "There is now no condemnation for those who are in Christ Jesus."

A woman close to me lives tormented by her memories of her mother. Her mother wanted to spend her last years under her daughter's roof, but her daughter, my friend, did not feel up to it. She arranged for her mother to have good care, and she visited her very often, but she cannot shake off her sense that she failed her mother. She feels condemned. Once she was telling me about this and she said, using the present tense, "I wonder if my mother forgives me." Then she said, "I guess she does." I was struck by this, "I guess she does." It was so uncertain, so unconvinced. It was clear that my friend could not really believe it, that she continued to labor under the thought of that condemnation. How I pray for my friend that she will come to know the merciful action of Jesus on the Cross, where he took our condemnation upon himself so that we should not have to bear it. My friend's mother's forgiveness is something that will not be known to us until the resurrection; but *Jesus forgives us right now.* We do not "guess" it; we know it. What is more, he not only forgives us, he *justifies* us. When a printer lines up a margin, he says he is "justifying" the margin. We cannot see it fully now, but in forgiving us God is also justifying us, making us not bent, but straight. That is what is happening on the Cross. We cannot do it for ourselves. He alone can do it for us; he alone has done it for us. In the words of the hymn, "Rock of Ages,"

> Should my tears for ever flow,
> Should my zeal no languor know,
> All for sin could not atone:
> Thou must save, and thou alone.[23]

Seventh Meditation:
The Heart That Broke

⸏⸏⸏⸏⸏

I direct your attention now to one final verse of Scripture: "My soul is deeply grieved to the point of death; remain here and keep watch" (Mark 14:34). These are the words of Jesus to his disciples as he goes into the Garden of Gethsemane on the last night of his life. These words are very strong in the original Greek and they have been variously translated:

> My soul is very sorrowful, even unto death.
> My soul is overwhelmed with sorrow to the point of death.
> My heart is nearly breaking.

and we might add, from the Psalms, "thy rebuke hath broken his heart" (69:20).

We need to let our imaginations work on these verses so as to approach more closely to the meaning of the sorrow of Jesus. Think of how you would feel if the person you love most in all the world were to say, "My heart is nearly breaking." I think it would make our hearts break too. But the heartbreak of Jesus is almost indescribable, for it is unique.

Was Jesus' heart breaking because he knew he was going to die? We can answer that with an unqualified NO. It has often been noted that even the most ordinary human beings frequently go to their deaths quite bravely and stoically. Why would the Son of God be more heartbroken about dying than Thomas More or Marie Antoinette or Dietrich Bonhoeffer or even criminals who go calmly to their lethal injections? The evangelists, in their accounts of Gethsemane, put a lot of emphasis on the agony of Jesus in the garden. Why?

The answer is a simple one, but simple as it is, it requires faith to understand it — faith and the imagination of faith. Every single person in this church today has been given at least a small glimmering of faith, or you would not be here. However tiny your seed of faith may be, it is enough. Your faith is a mustard seed that Jesus promised would grow into a great tree. If you are new to all this, let your seed of faith begin to sprout and grow today.

Jesus' heart was breaking in the garden not because he was going to die, but because he knew that, on the Cross, he would assume the burden of the sin of the world. Jesus had never experienced personally the weight of sin before. He had seen it, grieved over it, and forgiven it — but he had never succumbed to it, had never himself been personally overwhelmed by it, because he alone among all the human beings who ever lived was not a sinner. Now he was about to take upon himself the entire accumulated mass of the whole world's sin, and what that must have been like we can only imagine, for no other human being has ever been through anything like it.

It is bad enough to watch someone we love suffer. It is unendurable to think of someone we love suffering because of what we have done. There are not words enough in the world to say what was going on when Jesus suffered on account of the sin of everybody that ever lived. The evangelists don't even try. Matthew and Mark simply report that Jesus cried out, "My God, my God, why hast thou forsaken me?" and that Cry of Dereliction from the Cross, as it is called, has rung down the ages as Jesus' own expression of what was happening as he voluntarily bowed his head and became accursed for our sake, and in our place. "For our sake God made him to be sin who knew no sin, so that in him we might become the righteousness of God" (2 Corinthians 5:21).

It is important that we understand what this "rebuke" is. The "rebuke" is not the Father rebuking the Son. Rather, it is the rebuke of Sin, the sentence pronounced on Death and the condemnation of the works of the Devil, that Jesus undergoes today. The Bible makes it very clear that this Father and this Son are accomplishing this work together, that their two wills are one will. It is the will of them both that Jesus should absorb into himself the rightful wrath of God against sin. God the Father and Son together love us so much that it was their one will that we not be destroyed by it.

A few weeks ago I heard a sermon by a priest who had just returned from the fiftieth reunion of the veterans of the battle of Iwo Jima. He used as a Lenten illustration the example of soldiers who threw themselves on hand grenades, absorbing the explosion in their own bodies, offering themselves to certain death in order to save others. It was a very moving sermon and the illustration works, up to a point, but it is not sufficient. Jesus has done still more. The sort of death he suffered was not heroic or glorious, but shameful and degrading. The death Jesus died was not so much to save his comrades, for they all forsook him; it was to save not only his friends but also and most especially *his enemies,* and indeed in the end his friends became his enemies — such is the depth of our disgrace. And finally, Jesus was broken, not only by Death, but also by the consequences of Sin, as he took our place on the Cross on the first Good Friday.[24]

We do not understand value until we see what the price is. Only by looking at the price — the Cross of Christ — do we learn the weight of God's judgment against Sin and the value that we have for him. It just isn't enough to say that Jesus died for us. We need to understand the many-times-repeated statements in the New Testament that he died *for our sin.* That is his heartbreak. That is what makes his death different from other deaths, his agony different from other agonies, his sorrow . . . well, let Scripture speak: "Behold, and see if there be any sorrow like unto his sorrow" (Lamentations 1:12). The answer is, no, there isn't any other sorrow like unto his sorrow. We did not know how great was the burden of Sin until we saw what Jesus had to endure in order to save us from it. Jesus bowed his head

Rembrandt: Descent from the Cross

No other image of the Passion and death of Jesus communicates more directly his descent into the finality of the grave and the death of human hopes. The long diagonal begun in the upper left corner with the white sheet used to lower the body continues remorselessly down across the grouping of faces, punctuated by a single torchlit hand, then down into the darkness surrounded by shadowy faces and forms where the grave awaits. We might truly call this the Descent into Hell.

under the condemnation that went along with captivity to Sin. That is what you and I are worth to him. Jesus did that for you. That is why you cannot go out from here today and be the same ever again.

The service last night dramatized it for us. The altar was stripped, the candles were put out, the lights were slowly extinguished, and then there was a horrific crash upon the organ that made it seem as if the world was coming to an end. "The underlying intention of this dramatic action [symbolizes] the apparent victory of the powers of darkness and the seeming failure of the divine plan of redemption at the [time of] the crucifixion."[25]

Put yourself in the place of the disciples. I encourage you, today, to try to imagine their situation. If we can do so, we will understand and celebrate Easter as never before. It is three o'clock on Good Friday. Capture this moment. This is the space between Good Friday and Easter. Jesus is dead. All is blackness and despair. Can you feel the magnitude of what he has done? Christ has descended into hell for us. Satan has had his way. There is no human hope left. The long-awaited Messiah has died the despised death of the lowest criminal class. Nothing we can do will bring him back. All the spring flowers and sunshine and Easter eggs and greeting cards and positive thinking in the world will not bring him back. We are left in the wreckage, in the darkness, in the silence. There is nothing — *nothing* — that can rebuild this wreckage, nothing that can lighten this darkness, nothing that can break this silence — except an act of God.

SIX MEDITATIONS

Author's note

Many years ago I was privileged to hear Theodore P. Ferris, the re-
nowned preacher of Trinity Church, Copley Square, Boston, at a
three-hour Good Friday service. One of the features of his preaching
of the Cross was the intense emphasis he placed upon the words of
the Good Friday hymns and the importance of our singing them at-
tentively and devotionally. Clearly he thought this was a particularly valuable way for us, the congregation, to receive the Word of
the Cross into our hearts and lives. I have never forgotten this and
have sought in my own way to carry forward his conviction.

First Meditation:
Despised and Rejected

⸺∞⸺

I wonder if you would agree with me that we live in a time when it has become popular to be one of two things in America: either generically religious or completely secular. From where I sit, orthodox, Biblical Christianity is not considered cool. As members of Christian churches drift further and further away from knowledge of the Bible and historic doctrine, it is therefore becoming more and more difficult to help people understand that Christianity is not just one of many religions, that it can't be blended together with yoga and Tarot cards and self-help and angel worship to make a bigger and better religious hybrid.

Why not?

There is one definitive answer to that question and it is the Crucifixion of Jesus Christ. I believe that all of you here today know that already. I don't think you would be here if you didn't have at least a glimmer of an idea that the Crucifixion is an event unique in the history of religion and that it demands our awed and undivided attention. It is my prayer today that the crucified Lord himself would be present during these three hours by his Holy Spirit, in my words and in your hearts, for in his risen glory he is indeed able to make the message of the Cross a living and breathing power — power for radically reoriented living.

Reflect with me for a moment on the Scripture that you just heard. Many of you know that Handel set these words to music so affecting that singers all around the world, of whatever faith, consider it a rare privilege and responsibility to sing them: "He was despised and rejected of men; a man of sorrows, and acquainted with grief"; and, the prophet continues, "he was as one from whom men hide their faces" — meaning that he was so disfigured that we could not bear to look at him: "His appearance was marred beyond human semblance" (Isaiah 53:3; 52:14).

Despised and rejected. Those are very strong words. Do you think any of us know, really know in our gut, what those words refer to? I am trying to think of examples. Many older women in our culture, for example, speak of being rejected when their husbands leave them and marry younger women. Men and women alike speak of being rejected when they apply for positions they want and are turned away ("Don't call us; we'll call you"). No one likes to be rejected for membership in a co-op or club. Writers speak ruefully of the pain of receiving numbers of rejection slips. Rejection is especially painful for younger people; we often hear of adolescents who become despondent, or even commit suicide, if they are rejected by a girlfriend, or a sorority. Even in churches, I am sorry to say, these things happen; look around you at any church gathering and you will see that there are people hanging around on the fringes; no one is talking to them, no one is sitting next to them. These are images of rejection that are familiar to us all. But *despised* and rejected? How many of us can speak of being not only rejected but also despised? We would have to look much harder to come up with that combination. The prophet depicts the Servant suffering at the extreme frontier of human experience.

Religious figures are not usually associated with disgrace and rejection. We want our objects of worship to be radiant, dazzling avatars offering the potential of transcendent happiness. The most compelling argument — I will say this again during these three hours because it bears repeating — the most compelling argument for the truth of Christianity is the Cross at its center. Humankind's religious imagination could never have produced such an image.

Jean Poyet: Road to Calvary

This page from an illuminated manuscript illustrates the Passion of Christ with stunning emotional depth. No image more effectively portrays Jesus' utter isolation and humiliation. He sits, bound (as though he had a means of escape or resisting!), waiting as his instrument of torture is prepared, entirely alone and surrounded by enemies.

Wishful thinking never projected a despised and rejected Messiah. There is a contradiction at the very heart of our faith that demands our attention. We need to put a sign on it, though, like the signs on trucks carrying chemicals: Hazardous material, highly inflammatory cargo. Handle at your own risk.

The March 29, 1999, issue of *Newsweek* has Jesus on the cover. "2000 Years Of Jesus," it says. The article is by the estimable Kenneth Woodward, a believing Christian who has written much to spread the faith during his long tenure at the magazine. There are a couple of disappointments in the way his story has been packaged, though. A caption says that the "agony of crucifixion" is "a symbol of the redemptive power of suffering." That won't do, for a number of reasons. As Flannery O'Connor famously said to Mary McCarthy, "If it's a symbol, I say to hell with it."[26] The Crucifixion was not a symbol; it was an actual event. The "redemptive power of suffering" was a phrase frequently invoked by Martin Luther King, Jr., and there is deep truth in it, but the phrase taken by itself fails to indicate that we are speaking here not of just any suffering, but the unique, world-transforming suffering of the Son of God. As Dr. King knew as well as anyone, the suffering of Christ's servants is redemptive because it is a participation in his own. Moreover, it is not the physical suffering that reveals the meaning of the Cross. He was *despised and rejected* by humanity; that is what we need to understand.

We will enter into this more deeply as the three hours progress, but in this first section of our Good Friday service, let us begin by reflecting that Jesus, hanging on the Cross, not only suffered a depth of rejection that none of us can even imagine, but also seems to have experienced something even worse, indeed, something of ultimate horror. The only saying from the Cross recorded by *two* evangelists is the Cry of Dereliction: "My God, my God, why hast thou forsaken me?" This suggests that something actually *happened* to Jesus as he was crucified. Something from another dimension was occurring. The cosmic drama of God and man came to its climax outside Jerusalem at Golgotha. What was it? Why was the Son of God abandoned, despised, rejected? What dreadful onslaught was he experiencing?

I don't mean to be suggesting that we can understand, in this life, the full dimensions of what happened on Good Friday. The Bible gives us images and metaphors, not scientific descriptions. One thing we know, however. Over and over again, all of the New Testament writers in one way or another tell us that Jesus' death was *for sin.* He underwent the ultimate disgrace, the uttermost humiliation. He interposed himself between us and Sin's fatal power. That is why his death was uniquely terrible. The shameful nature of crucifixion as a method of execution is directly related to the shameful conduct of the human race. As Jesus goes to the Cross, he is denied even the last scrap of charity. We don't grasp this easily. Reflect on it for a moment. He is not permitted a mask, or clothing, or a final meal, or the prayers of a chaplain. Crucifixion was specifically designed to strip away every shred of decency, privacy, or humanity. None of this is an accident. It is all connected to the depravity of the human condition that lies just under the surface. Perhaps it was possible to avoid this conclusion once upon a time, but if there is one thing high technology and mass communications revealed to us in the twentieth century it is the capacity of the human race for evil. The torturing and tormenting of the Son of God — for that is what it was — displays the truth about what the human race can do. The despising and rejecting of the Messiah is a portrait of what we are really like.

And so the death of Christ is an event that separates the Christian gospel from religion in general. The Cross is the innermost criterion of our faith. Without it, not only do we not have Easter, we do not even have Christianity. If we do not grapple with the despised and rejected Messiah's last hours, the irreligious and ungodly aspect of his Passion, the inhuman and godforsaken nature of his death, we simply cannot understand what it is that makes the story of Jesus different from any other story.

We began this meditation with Isaiah 53 and we end with it. No Biblical passage has attracted more attention or been more difficult to pin down. On Good Friday we read it because for two thousand years the Christian church has believed that the prophet was given this vision five hundred years before Christ to show us how it was all in the mind of the triune God from the beginning:

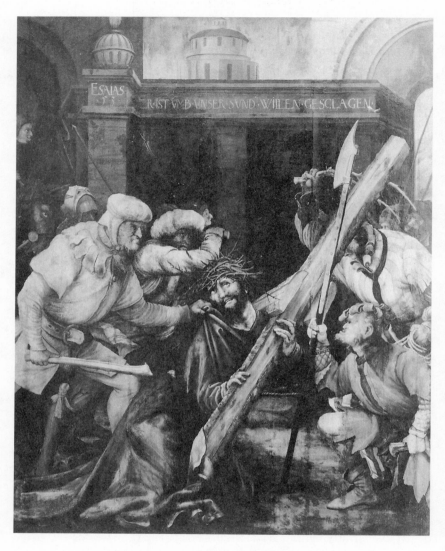

Matthias Grünewald: Christ Carrying the Cross

This painter goes to extraordinary lengths to emphasize the revolting inhumanity of the treatment Jesus receives as he endures his Passion. The contorted facial expressions and violent gestures of Christ's tormentors convey a powerful sense of human depravity.

He was despised and rejected by men;
   a man of sorrows, and acquainted with grief;
and as one from whom men hide their faces
   he was despised, and we esteemed him not. . . .
But he was wounded for our transgressions,
   he was bruised for our iniquities;
upon him was the chastisement that made us whole,
   and with his stripes we are healed.
All we like sheep have gone astray;
   we have turned every one to his own way;
and the LORD has laid on him the iniquity of us all.

                            (Isaiah 53:3-6)

This section closes with the singing of a hymn. Think about these words as you sing them, and make them your own, today:

Alone thou goest forth, O Lord, in sacrifice to die;
Is this thy sorrow nought to us who pass unheeding by?

Our sins, not thine, thou bearest, Lord; make us
   thy sorrow feel,
Till through our pity and our shame love answers love's appeal.

Grant us with thee to suffer pain that, as we share this hour,
Thy cross may bring us to thy joy and Resurrection power.[27]

Second Meditation:
God Made Jesus to Be Sin

At the very end of this service we will be reading Psalm 22 together. It begins with these words, "My God, my God, why hast thou forsaken me?" Those of you who stay to the end of these three hours will see that this Psalm written hundreds of years before Christ contains a startling number of details about the Crucifixion of Jesus. Reading it on Good Friday brings us close to the experience of the early church immediately after the Resurrection. Imagine yourself as one of the disciples trying to make sense of the stupendous thing that has happened to you. Wouldn't you be tempted to set the Crucifixion aside as a nightmarish episode that had now been cancelled out by the Resurrection? Wouldn't you want to set aside the terrible thing that had happened and concentrate on the happy ending? Human nature being what it is, we would have expected the Biblical writers to say as little as possible about the Crucifixion, passing right over it to the glory of Easter. Instead (and the significance of this can't be emphasized too strongly), they made the Passion narrative the centerpiece of all four Gospels.

One of the first things that happened to the disciples after the Resurrection was the discovery that the Crucifixion was in the Old Testament. We in the church today need to recover the intimacy with the Psalms that was common in former times. Even today we have Psalms in all our services because we are following ancient Jewish and Christian practice. Jesus and his friends would have prayed from the Psalms every day, several times a day. It would have been a deeply ingrained habit with them. Imagine the disciples returning to the Psalms after the Resurrection and discovering that the Crucifixion is right there in them. Wouldn't that blow your mind? As the early Christians prayed the Psalms in the light of the Resurrection, they saw that the exposed and tortured death of Jesus was part of God's plan from the beginning. Everything that happened that day on Calvary, it seemed, was foreshadowed in the Psalms. The Crucifixion had not been a horrible mistake after all. Their Master hadn't been humiliated, degraded and treated like "the filth of the world, the offscouring of all things" for nothing.[28] His suffering had a meaning, a meaning held in the mind of God as part of his purpose for salvation. It was all a fulfillment of what the prophets had said. Imagine what a thrilling discovery it must have been as they pored over the familiar words of Scripture with completely new eyes!

Psalm 22 was one of the most amazing of all the texts. Imagine yourself as one of the disciples trying to get a grip on the stupendous thing that has happened to you. How are you going to explain the fact that the Lord Jesus, now raised from the dead and ruling over your transformed life, had been a derelict on a cross along with the criminal scum of the land? How, in particular, are you going to live with the Cry of Dereliction? Did Jesus really think that God had abandoned him? If so, how could he have been the divine Son of God?

The Psalms were Jesus' prayer book. Even in an extremity of pain and suffering greater than anything you or I will ever know, the words of the Psalms were on his lips. Mark's Greek indicates that he cried out on the Cross with a desperate kind of scream. Still, his words were addressed to God, as though even in this farthest reach of despair Jesus continued to place his trust in God. There is a Psalm, number 88, which I often recommend to people who are so angry at God that they cannot pray. It is one long outburst of anger and hopelessness. There is not a word of comfort or encouragement in the whole of Psalm 88. But there is one remarkable thing about it. It is addressed to God. It begins, "O LORD, my God, I call for help by day; I cry out in the night before thee." We all need to know of this Psalm. It teaches us that we can still pray even when we can't pray. No matter how dark and terrible your thoughts may be, you can still offer them to God. In a very real sense, God is there ahead of us. We know he is, because of what the Bible tells us about Jesus' death.

"My God, my God, why hast thou forsaken me?" I have pondered these words for many years, and I have read many interpretations of them. I have often been disappointed in these interpretations. It often seems to me that they are trying to avoid what Matthew and Mark do not avoid, trying to soften what they do not soften. There are other places in the New Testament where we can check our reactions. The Epistle to the Hebrews and the letters of the Apostle Paul are similar to Matthew and Mark in their insistence that Jesus drank the dregs of abandonment and despair on the Cross.

In the second letter of Paul to the Corinthians, there is a sentence of great importance. "For our sake God made him [Jesus] to be sin who knew no sin, so that in him we might become the righteousness of God" (2 Corinthians 5:21).[29] This single verse has always been recognized as having a special significance in the interpretation of the Crucifixion. Here, we find a key to the Cry of Dereliction. For our sake God made Jesus, who knew no sin, *to be sin.* Even grammatically, it is a strange formulation. There are depths upon depths here.

In order to understand the Cross of Christ we need to consider the gravity of sin. In the time of the Old Testament, a guilt offering had to be weighed so that a value could be given to it. This is described in the book of Leviticus (5:15-16). We need to weigh the Cross, the price that Jesus paid. The higher the price, the greater the sin. If Jesus suffered abandonment by God on the Cross, then that is an indication to us of the enormity of sin. Paul was making this connection when he wrote to the Corinthians. Looking at the Cross of Jesus Christ, we see the degradation and Godforsakenness of it, we see how "he was despised and rejected by men," and we see the gravity, the weight, of sin. The price paid by the Lord is commensurate with the depth of human wickedness. I don't know if I can do justice to this or not. I feel very inadequate to the task. If Jesus was despised and rejected on the Cross it is because he took upon himself the burden of all that was despised and rejected by God. He took it for our sake. He took it so that it would be removed from us. And when he took it, he experienced something that perhaps even in the Garden of Gethsemane he had not foreseen. When Jesus rose from his knees in the garden, he had overcome his fear; he had engaged in the second stage of his lifelong battle with the evil Power and he had accepted the will of the Father. Surely, however, he did not fully even then know what it would be like, for *he knew no sin.* Jesus was not like you and me. He lived in unbroken fellowship with the Father every moment of his life. Never once had he been distracted by the selfishness that afflicts you and me. He had been the Man for God and the Man for Others all of his life.[30] Now for the first time his communion with his Father in heaven is broken, not just broken in the sense of God being *absent,* but — infinitely more dreadful than anything you or I will ever know — it was broken as he took into himself the full weight of God's *condemnation and judgment* on the unholy triumvirate of Sin, Death, and the Devil.

There is a portion of another Psalm that will help us here:

> There is no soundness in my flesh because of thy indignation;
>> there is no health in my bones because of my sin.
> For my iniquities have gone over my head;
>> they weigh like a burden too heavy for me.
>
> (Psalm 38:3-4)

Now perhaps we can see. The voice of the speaker in that Psalm as it was originally written and sung was the voice of a human being. It was my voice, your voice, saying as in the old General Confession, "The burden of them [our sins] is intolerable." "There is no health in us," we used to say, echoing the Psalm: "There is no health in my bones because of my sin."[31] This person who is speaking is the person whom God in Christ looks upon. He looked upon us, not from afar, but from within our midst. He did not remain above our struggle, but came down into it. He looked upon us with our sins overwhelming us, crushing us, drowning us; and he entered into our condition until he began, on the Cross, to speak along with us, indeed to speak *instead of* us: "My iniquities have gone over my head." Our Lord Jesus Christ loved us with such an unrivalled love that he determined to step into our place and take our unbearable burden upon himself as though it had been his own. He bowed his head and became subject to the dark Powers, and for that one soul-destroying, earth-stopping, light-quenching moment it overwhelmed him too. "My God, my God, why hast thou forsaken me?" *God made him to be sin who knew no sin, so that in him we might become the righteousness of God.*

> Therefore, kind Jesus, since I cannot pay thee,
> I do adore thee, and will ever pray thee,
> Think on thy pity, and thy love unswerving,
> Not my deserving.[32]

Third Meditation:
Outside the Camp

———∞∞∞———

A few years ago my husband and I were away from home and we attended Palm Sunday services at a church in the town where we were staying. We are always gripped by the dramatic reading of the Passion narrative. It is one of the most solemn moments in the church year. In particular, the involvement of the congregation in the reading never fails to make an impression. When you hear yourself shouting "Crucify him," you know that something momentous is taking place in your own soul.

The reading ended and we sat down in our pew, feeling somewhat stunned. We were grateful for the silence that followed. Then the rector went up into the pulpit. We expected words of equal gravity, something worthy of the occasion. Such was not to be the case. He began to talk about the high school football game that he had attended the day before. He tried to make it funny. Maybe it was funny. No doubt the local congregation was able to relate to it better than we were. Still, I thought the laughter was forced, thin, as though the people really didn't want to laugh but were trying to be polite. I think he was trying to connect the football team's loss with the loss that the disciples were feeling when Jesus was on the Cross. It did not seem adequate to the moment, to say the least.

The first funeral I ever went to was for my mother's best

friend, Louise, a woman I adored. She died young, of cancer, in her fifties. I was bereft, almost as upset as my mother was. After the service we went back to the family's house for a gathering of family and friends. Lavish refreshments were served, as is the custom in the South, and there were quite a few people present. No one was talking about the person who had died. They were talking about everything else in the world, including football. I was greatly distressed. I wanted to hear someone talk about Louise, her vivacity and intelligence, her high spirits, her keen interest in young people like me. No one even mentioned her. It was a conspiracy of silence. That was my first close encounter with avoidance.

I was in a church bookstore last week looking for Easter cards. A young woman came in with a friend. She was apparently a teacher's aide in the church school. She was complaining to her friend that she had been called in by the head teacher, who disapproved of the way she was telling the Easter story to the children. She was told that she absolutely could not mention the fact that Jesus had died, because it would upset the children. The clerk behind the counter said she wasn't so sure about that; she had taught Sunday School, she recalled, and the children didn't seem to be upset, just curious. This clerk was a wise person. She said, "This worry about mentioning death is a grown-up concern, not a child's."

I have studied Easter cards over the years. They never, ever mention death. You can find nice Christian Easter cards if you try hard, with crosses on them and the words "Christ is risen," but you won't find any that say anything about death. I read an article about the people who compose the messages for Hallmark cards. They had been instructed that the word "death" was never to appear, not even on sympathy cards.

You get the point. Avoidance and denial are typical human responses to unpleasant situations. Many people honestly believe that if you don't talk about something, that will help. People who have grown up in families where difficult subjects are not discussed have to be retrained in order to cope better with their lives. I once attended a workshop on how to be helpful to suicidal people. I will never forget what the leader said. He said, "Steer toward the pain."

Most of us think we are supposed to do exactly the opposite. If you want to help, he said, "Steer *toward* the pain."

Two weeks ago, I found an Easter card that amazed me. I was visiting my mother in the small Virginia town where I grew up, a town with a large population of churchgoing African-Americans. There was a special rack of cards in the supermarket, produced by a company called Baobab, after the famous African baobab tree. They were wonderful cards and I bought quite a few of them even though they were not designed for white people. Here is what was printed on one of them:

> May the goodness of His gospel of love, the remembrance of how He suffered to help us live more abundantly, and the joyful promise of His Resurrection live in your heart at Easter and always.[33]

"He suffered." The card actually referred, explicitly, to Jesus' suffering! I was thunderstruck. I had never, ever seen it on any "white" card. Why, do you think, was that word there? The answer, surely, is that suffering has been a way of life for black people as far back as they can remember. Avoidance and denial has not been an option for them. As I reflect on the way that "the blood" is a term readily used in the African-American church to evoke the Crucifixion and all that it means for us, another memory comes to mind. Twenty-five years ago when I was a young preacher, I went to a Florida parish to do the Good Friday three hours. Shortly before the service the rector said to me, "I hope you aren't going to say anything about 'the blood.'" I was too unsure and inexperienced then to protest, but I remembered it recently when my sister and I attended a service at a black Baptist church in South Carolina. The gospel choir sang a joyous hymn, "There to my heart was the blood applied, glory to his Name!"

We just read the lesson from Hebrews. "Jesus suffered outside the city gate in order to sanctify the people by his own blood" (Hebrews 13:12). Our Lord's Passion was the ultimate example of nonavoidance. He went straight into his suffering, straight to his betrayal, scourging, mocking, crucifixion, and death. Instead of avoiding pain, he entered into it. He "suffered outside the city gate." You know what that means. He was an outcast. He had no protection. He was denied the identity of citizen, the privileges of a godly Jew, the status of decent human being. The writer of Hebrews continues, "Let us then go to him outside the camp and bear the abuse he endured. For here we have no lasting city, but we are looking for the city that is to come." The path to the city that is to come, the route to the Kingdom of God, the way to eternal life in Christ is the way *through* suffering, not a detour around it. Therefore, says Hebrews, through him we now offer our sacrifices to God. Through him, we can do things that we thought we could never do. Very often, when I visit a particularly sick patient and feel a little frightened, I stop in the hallway before I go into the room. I ask the Lord to be with me, to help me not to avoid the suffering but to identify with it, the way he did.

The United States is full of walled communities now. Greenwich, Connecticut, the town next to ours, is being referred to as "the walled city." When you drive along the back roads, instead of lush greenery you see eight-foot million-dollar stone walls. Many Americans now live in "gated communities." Maybe some of you do. Even if not, however, those of us who are affluent are able to live our whole lives protected from the deprivations and struggles of our fellow human beings. Jesus did not do this. He went outside the camp, outside the city wall, outside the protective gates. He steered into the pain. Because he did this, we are now new, free people. Through him, we can live lives of sacrifice. We can do small things to share the pain of others, and as we share it, we can give comfort. In the life of another human being, very little can be very much.[34] In the words of Hebrews, "Let us continually offer a sacrifice of praise to God . . . . Do not neglect to do good and to share what you have, for such sacrifices are pleasing to God" (Hebrews 13:15-16).

May the goodness of his gospel of love, the remembrance of how he suffered to help us live more abundantly, and the joyful promise of his Resurrection live in your heart at Easter and always.

There to my heart was the blood applied; Glory to his Name!

Fourth Meditation:
Not Bad But Good

⸺⸙⸺

Good Friday is not for the faint of heart. It is brave of you to be here today. A few years ago when I was teaching at the Kanuga Conference Center in Hendersonville, North Carolina, I noticed that there was a new object there, located by the path that everybody uses to go down to the lake and the boathouse. It is a wood-carving of Jesus on the Cross. As soon as I saw it, I thought to myself, this is going to be trouble. Sure enough, a couple of days later I heard that there had been quite a few complaints. One person said that the sculpture was depressing to her and she didn't go down to the lake to be depressed.[35]

There is nothing new about this. It has been a problem ever since the Crucifixion of Christ took place. St. Paul had plenty of problems with people thinking that the Crucifixion was too depressing. The Christians in Corinth thought it was too depressing. They didn't want to hear about it. Paul wrote some words to them that mean a great deal to the Good Friday preacher: "I determined to know nothing among you except Jesus Christ and him crucified" (1 Corinthians 2:2). A minister of the gospel could not ask for a better motto than that. Paul was a straight shooter; he knew that the Cross was "a stumbling block to Jews and foolishness to Gentiles," but for those who believe, he wrote, the Cross is "the power of God and the wisdom of God" (1 Corinthians 1:24). So I do not hesitate to congratulate you for being here today. The world is going heedlessly by, doing its errands, but you are in the right place. Today, we come together, putting aside our usual preoccupations, to give our undivided attention to the most important event of all time. That is the Christian claim.

Not everyone sees the meaning of the Cross. They find it depressing. Many people are unclear about why this is called "Good Friday." As we say nowadays, they "just don't get it." In order to "get it," we need to see things from a Biblical perspective. First and foremost, we need to see *ourselves* from a Biblical perspective. Scripture says, "The LORD sees not as man sees; man looks on the outward appearance, but the LORD looks on the heart" (1 Samuel 16:7). How does "man" see, that is, how do we see one another? Why do you think the spin doctors stay so busy? Why are the plastic surgeons making so much money? What are the commercials and advertisements selling — youth and good looks, or well-earned wrinkles? Self-indulgence and conspicuous consumption, or compassion and generosity? What sells a political figure today — substance or image? All of us, and I include myself, are affected by the obsession of our culture with image. This is what "man" sees.

What do the Hebrew prophets see when they look at us? This is what Jeremiah sees: "Every man's . . . images are false, and there is no breath in them. They are worthless, a work of delusion" (10:14-15). This is what Isaiah sees: "My people go into exile for want of knowledge; their honored men are dying of hunger . . . the nobility of Jerusalem and her multitude go down . . . and the eyes of the haughty are humbled" (5:13, 15). Make no mistake, that's about you and me. "Let any one who thinks that he stands take heed lest he fall" (1 Corinthians 10:12).

Most people will identify this as a negative, offensive message and will reject it. But if it is truly bad news through and through, then why do we confess our sins when we come into church? Why do grown-up, strong men and women get down on their knees and say, "We have followed too much the devices and desires of our own hearts; we have offended against thy holy laws"? Why do we say,

"We have left undone those things which we ought to have done, and we have done those things which we ought not to have done"?³⁶ Why would we say that if it was bad news? Why would we come to church today if it was Bad Friday? The amazing thing about Christian faith is that the bad news is part of the good news. I once knew a man, a highly successful man as the world counts such things, who told me, "I love to confess my sins." How well I understand that. What did Jesus say? "I have not come to call the righteous, but sinners to repentance" (Luke 5:32).

What does the Lord see when he looks at us? He doesn't see us the way we try to present ourselves to others. When God looks at us, he does not see titles, bank accounts, club memberships, vacation homes, net worth. He sees a pathetic bunch of sinners trying to pretend that we are powerful and successful and masters of all we survey. He sees us perpetually trying to divide up the world into good people and bad people, with ourselves on the good side, of course. The typical human being, and maybe especially those of us who go to church, have certain techniques for getting ourselves off the hook. We may agree that we are sinners of a sort, but not really. We think of a dividing line between slightly blemished people and *really bad* people. The really bad people are deserving of death, right? That's one reason that the death penalty is so popular in America. We think of ourselves as being on the right side of that dividing line between the moderately bad and the *really* bad.

Let us be very clear here. When Jesus was put to death, it was as one of the *really bad people,* one of those who are loathed and despised, the scum of the earth. We have to put in a little extra effort to understand this. When people try to explain how grotesque the Cross is as a religious symbol, they often come up with the electric chair as an analogy. It isn't a very good analogy because electrocutions were at least theoretically supposed to be quick, and they were not public. But there is one similarity: both methods were used to dispatch the lowest of the low, and both were used by the state to get rid of people who were deemed unfit for human society. When Jesus came down from heaven to live among us, he lived among us at that level. The Son of God gave up all his divine prerogatives and entered the world to be executed alongside criminals in the same manner as they.

I know from the nature of this subject that it is not easy for everybody. There are those who, like the Christians in Corinth, will turn away from the Cross. There are those who will be upset by a picture or statue of the Crucifixion. There are those who will not come to church on Good Friday. There are those who think they don't need any help from God, because they are safely on the right side of that wall they've put up between themselves and those they deem unfit. Most telling of all, there are many who call themselves Christians who can not or will not come alongside others in their pain — which, after all, is the real point, to suffer shame and loss for Christ's sake. St. Paul wrote that "Christ crucified is a stumbling block to Jews and foolishness to Gentiles . . . but to those who believe, [the Cross] is the power of God and the wisdom of God" (1 Corinthians 1:23-24). You are here today because the Holy Spirit has drawn you into the circle of that power and wisdom of God.

Perhaps for some of you it is the first time. Perhaps you have not been sure until now whether this message of Christ crucified has anything to do with you or not. This is the day to let go of our carefully constructed "images." The Lord looks right through those flimsy defenses and he sees the real person; to him, "all hearts are open, all desires known, and from [him] no secrets are hid."[37] He sees us as we really are. And what does the Lord see when he looks at us without our masks on?

I will tell you. He sees a person that he loves. He sees a person that he loves more than life, more than glory, more than power, more than riches, more than divinity itself. As Paul wrote to the Corinthians, "For you know the grace of our Lord Jesus Christ, that though he was rich, yet for your sake he became poor, so that by his poverty you might become rich" (2 Corinthians 8:9). And why did he do that?

Because he loves you. Because he loves me. He sees us in the midst of our deceptions and failures. He sees us in the full dimensions of our weakness and mortality, our material pretensions and our spiritual poverty, our vulnerability and our hypocrisy, and he loves us. He sees through our masks and our makeup, our devious words and our self-serving actions, and he loves us. He looks at us and he sees our cowardice and our failures and our fraudulence, and he loves us. St. Paul writes to the Romans, "God shows his love for us in that while we were still sinners Christ died for us" (Romans 5:8). What is Jesus doing on that Cross? Is it depressing? Is it frightening? Is it sad? Is it ugly? Yes, it is all of those things, but is it not also the greatest story ever told? That is why this awe-ful day is called Good.

> What language shall I borrow to thank thee, dearest friend,
> For this thy dying sorrow, thy pity without end?
> Oh make me thine forever! and should I fainting be,
> Lord, let me never, never outlive my love for thee.[38]

Fifth Meditation:
The Curse and the Substitution

———— ✺ ————

As you know, the ethnic Albanians of Kosovo are mostly Muslims.[41] It was reported in the news media that Serbian Orthodox paramilitary personnel were threatening some of these Muslim Kosovars with death if they did not make the sign of the cross. We need to take this very deeply to heart. There cannot be anything more blasphemous than this. This sort of action is the exact opposite of what Jesus was doing when he sacrificed himself on the Cross.

A great deal of attention was paid on television when three American soldiers were held captive in Yugoslavia. There was much outrage because in violation of the Geneva Conventions, they were exhibited on camera. There weren't any Geneva Conventions in Jesus' time, but consider, if you will, the sweeping violations of every conceivable human consideration in his case. His so-called "trial" was a farce, the "evidence" brought against him was nonexistent, there was nothing remotely resembling a defense. The whole thing was a foregone conclusion, a conspiracy between church and state, with the religious authorities — the good church people — happily handing him over to the Roman governor. No one wore yellow ribbons for the Son of God. His hometown did not have a prayer vigil for him. The President did not call his mother. There was no diplomatic intervention: all the people who might have done an intervention had voted to kill him. Jesus was alone, and there was no one to fight for him. Even God his Father, it seemed, had abandoned him.

I ask you now to pay very close attention to the words of the hymn that we will sing after this fifth meditation. Of all our Holy Week hymns, this one is perhaps the best.

> Ah, holy Jesus, how hast thou offended,
> That man to judge thee hath in hate pretended?
> By foes derided, by thine own rejected,
> O most afflicted.
>
> Who was the guilty? Who brought this upon thee?
> Alas, my treason, Jesus, hath undone thee.
> 'Twas I, Lord Jesus, I it was denied thee,
> I crucified thee.
>
> Lo, the Good Shepherd for the sheep is offered;
> The slave hath sinned, and the Son hath suffered;
> For our atonement, while we nothing heeded,
> God interceded.[40]

"The slave hath sinned, and the Son hath suffered." The slave (that's you and me); the Son (that's Jesus). The shame belonged to us; the effects fell upon him. "The LORD has laid on him the iniquity of us all" (Isaiah 53). Last night the choir sang an anthem that went to the very heart of this divine action. The words are remarkable. I can't do full justice to their complexity here, but I will quote a portion:

> Alone to sacrifice thou goest, O Lord,
> Giving thyself to death. . . .
> [We] know that for our sins this is thy pain.
> For they are ours, O Lord, our deeds, our deeds.
> Why must thou suffer torture for our sin?[41]

In the Passion according to Matthew that we read on Palm Sunday, the high priest says to the people: "You have heard his blasphemy. What is your judgment?" You will remember that the people (that's you and me) shout, "He is deserving of death." This is extraordinarily important because our participation in this drama is the definitive liturgical refutation of the idea that "the Jews" killed Jesus. "We know that for our sins this is thy pain; for they are ours, O Lord, our deeds." *Our* deeds. Jesus is not on the Cross because of "the Jews." He is there because of *us all.*

Let us turn our attention again to the section of Galatians that was read just now (Galatians 3:10-14).[42] The passage is short but complicated and not easy to understand. It begins, "All who rely on works of the law are under a curse." In brief, the meaning is this: In the book of Deuteronomy, which Paul is quoting, God promises blessings to those who keep his holy and righteous commandments but warns that those who do not will come under his curse. All humankind is therefore threatened, because we do not and, indeed, cannot obey or fulfil God's commandments. That's not a self-evident statement, though. Many people think they keep God's commandments reasonably well, or else they are not concerned about God's commandments at all. If you are aware that you do not measure up in this regard, then you are already God's person. If you know that you are a "miserable offender" against God's goodness, then you are already in a state of grace. I think that is why you are here today.

Now let's try to get inside Paul's mind for a moment. He has been thinking about the Old Testament, which is the only Bible he has (Paul didn't know he was writing the New Testament). He has been thinking about the Crucifixion of Jesus, its horror and strangeness. He has been rereading a passage in Deuteronomy that said a dead body should not be displayed publicly, that such a body was accursed. If a body hanged on a tree was accursed by God, Paul reasoned, and Jesus was hanged on a tree, then Jesus must have been under a curse. Yet he could not have been, for he among all men who ever lived was without sin. He must, therefore, have been taking upon himself the curse that belonged to someone else. This is the plain meaning of the Galatians passage: "All who rely on works of the law are under a curse," because we are constitutionally unable

Marc Chagall: White Crucifixion

Since World War II, the Church has come to the tragically belated recognition that many Christians over the centuries either have not known that Jesus was a Jew or have deliberately suppressed this essential fact. This 1939 painting by Chagall is a corrective. Christ, wearing a prayer shawl as a loincloth, is expressly identified with the suffering of the Jews across Europe in the 1930s.

to keep God's law. But *something has happened:* God has intervened by coming between us and his own decree. Verse 13: "Christ redeemed us from the curse of the law, having become a curse for us — for it is written, 'Cursed be every one who hangs on a tree.'" Here in this crabbed, ungainly sentence, for those who care to work through it, the meaning of the Cross is unveiled. I have been preaching and writing about the Cross ever since I can remember; I have been in the pulpit somewhere every Good Friday for more than two decades; with every passing year, I believe more and more that of all texts, this passage from Galatians gives us the most succinct and compelling view of what Jesus did on the Cross, on our behalf and in our place.

It is crucial that we understand that we do not have here a wrathful father doing something vengeful to his innocent son.[43] Unfortunately, some Good Friday preaching over the years has made it sound that way, reinforced by some hoary sermon illustrations making it sound as though the Son is totally unsuspecting.[44] There is nothing to suggest this in the New Testament. The Father and the Son are accomplishing our redemption together, with one will ("God was in Christ" — 2 Corinthians 5). When Jesus absorbs into himself the rightful wrath of God against Sin, it is because the love of the Father and Son *together* determined that we "should not perish, but have everlasting life" (John 3:16). This inner working of the Father and Son within the Trinity is evoked for us by Paul in a verse from 1 Thessalonians: "God has not destined us for wrath, but to obtain salvation through our Lord Jesus Christ" (1 Thessalonians 5:9).

When we truly understand this, when it sinks into our hearts, we will be overwhelmed with gratitude. If we truly understand what God has done for us this day, we will be seized by the desire to thank and praise him. That is our part, this Good Friday.

> Here the King of all the ages, throned in light ere
> worlds could be,
> Robed in mortal flesh is dying, crucified by sin for me.
> O mysterious condescending! O abandonment sublime!
> Very God himself is bearing all the sufferings of time.[45]

Sixth Meditation:
The Stealth Bomber

∞

During the NATO campaign to rescue the Kosovar Albanians from "ethnic cleansing," a very rare event occurred. The Pope, the Ecumenical Patriarch, the World Council of Churches, the Baptist Churches, global federations of Anglicans and other Protestant churches, and all eight of the American Roman Catholic cardinals got together to call for an Easter week pause in the NATO bombing and a halt to the "ethnic cleansing," along with a return to the negotiating table. Rarely do all these groups pull together for any cause. No one believed for a minute that Slobodan Milosevic would be impressed by this. The point is that there has been a growing consensus among Christians worldwide that the twenty-first century requires a more sophisticated, more multifaceted, more long-term solution than simply more and more bombing.[46]

Good Friday is relevant to this or it is relevant to nothing. Good Friday is not some private event that occurs in individual hearts alone without reference to the world at large. The Crucifixion of Christ was not a rogue action taking place back in the forest or up in the mountains where the commanding officers wouldn't bother to look. It wasn't part of a little "dirty war" that the State Department of the day could disown. On the contrary, it was a state-sponsored method of execution. As St. Paul says to King Agrippa in Acts,

[167]

"This thing was not done in a corner" (Acts 26:26). It was government-sanctioned. It came with the imprimatur of the Roman Empire, no less. What could be more legitimate than that?

Today, the world's ideas of legitimacy are overturned. Something happened on Good Friday that simply boggles the mind and escapes from our usual human categories. In order to understand this, it is important that we know where to put the emphasis. You know that all of us have a gruesome fascination with bloody events. Few of us are immune to the rubbernecking syndrome. I learned in my days as a youth minister that adolescent audiences will sit riveted to the spot if you give them an explicit description of the details of crucifixion. It is noteworthy, however, that the Passion narratives say almost nothing about these details. It is not the physical suffering that they want us to hold in our minds. The New Testament writers want us to focus on the shame.[47] When the prophet Isaiah wrote that God's Suffering Servant was "one from whom men hide their faces" (53:3), it was not the grisly physical phenomena that he had in mind, but the dehumanization: "his appearance was so marred, beyond human semblance" (52:14).[48] The Lord entered his Passion knowing that this was his destiny, to be one with us to the uttermost depths, not only of our physical condition, but more especially of our inner spiritual condition of shame and disgrace before God. In this last address of our Good Friday worship, let us seek to draw together all that Jesus accomplished in this total identification with us.

A recent article in *The Wall Street Journal* was called "God on Line." We have entered an age in which many people get most of their information from the Internet. Christians have entered this arena with notable enthusiasm and some remarkably sophisticated software is available which, for many of us, is a wonderful tool. Some of the truth about Jesus and his Cross can surely be found online in an introductory or supplementary fashion. With all due respect to the wonders of cyberspace, however, if Christian faith is to be worked out in real life, it must be in the context of actual, not virtual, human community.[49] We are brought into relationships of trust with each other because of the witnesses who tell us the story of Jesus, and because we trust them, we come ultimately to love them. A trusting relationship is not forged on the Internet, but in the context of the worshipping community. God is "on line" wherever two or three are gathered together in his Name. That is what we are doing, you and I, today. We are reaffirming our trust in the Biblical witnesses and in the power of Christian fellowship. We are, as Ephesians says, "fellow citizens with the saints and members of the household of God" (2:19). The fellowship that comes into being around the Holy Week and Easter proclamation is "built upon the foundation of the apostles and prophets, Christ Jesus himself being the cornerstone" (Ephesians 2:20). The very existence of the gospel message depends upon the trustworthiness of these witnesses. When St. Paul says, "The word of the cross is the power of God" (1 Corinthians 1:18), we may believe him. I have been teaching the letters of Paul for more than twenty years, and have learned that he can be trusted. I have loved the Gospel of John all my life, and I trust that too. I trust it far more than I trust the trendy scholars who are telling me that I am intellectually handicapped if I continue to rely on the Gospels.

Paul wrote to the Corinthians, "I determined to know nothing among you except Jesus Christ and him crucified" (1 Corinthians 2:2). He is giving them the ultimate criterion for faith and ministry. We should be careful about subscribing to any and all "religious" talk.[50] "Religion" arises out of human needs, longings, wishes. I do not believe that the idea of a crucified Messiah would ever have entered the unaided mind of Paul or John or anyone else. If the apostles were just making up the Cross and Resurrection out of some kind of religious delusion, then the whole history of Christianity is founded, whether consciously or unconsciously, on a fraud. I do not want any part of a religious fraud. The Cross is unique to Christianity. There has never been anything else like it in the history of religion. The Christian message proclaims, in a way never seen before or since, that God's purpose for the universe was revealed in the event of the death of Jesus Christ. Jesus came and died to reveal God's very self and the future of the human race.

We need to say more. The future of humanity and the whole of

God's creation does not belong to those who are accounted powerful and successful by the taste-makers and trend-setters. Paul wrote to remind the fashion-minded Corinthian church of this:

> Consider your call, brethren; not many of you were wise according to worldly standards, not many were powerful, not many were of noble birth; but God chose what is foolish in the world to shame the wise, God chose what is weak in the world to shame the strong, God chose what is low and despised in the world, even things that are not, to bring to nothing things that are, so that no human being might boast in the presence of God. (1 Corinthians 1:26-29)

When Paul refers to "what is low and despised in the world" he means the Cross of Christ first of all. In the Cross, everything that the world counts successful is stood on its head. This does not mean that God has no power. His way is a way of power, all right, make no mistake about that. When a disciple attempts to defend Jesus on the Mount of Olives on the night of his betrayal, the Lord says, "Do you think that I cannot appeal to my Father, and he will at once send me more than twelve legions of angels? But how then should the scriptures be fulfilled, that it must be so?" (Matthew 26:53-54). These are not the words of a weakling. Do you think that a 48-million-dollar Stealth bomber is powerful? It is nothing compared to God's power. And yet God's power makes itself known in ways the world does not understand. It is a way of power in humility, power in sacrifice, power in nonviolence, power in self-emptying love. In that sense the Incarnation of the Son of God is the true Stealth bomber; it is the might of the Creator himself in disguise. He has come in under the radar, as it were. The Cross of Christ reveals to us the power of God in a way that no one would have been able to predict, a way that no one understood, a way that is at odds with everything the world teaches. It reveals to us the power of suffering love. In the final analysis that is the only kind of love that counts. Love, as Paul writes, "beareth all things, believeth all things, hopeth all things, endureth all things" (1 Corinthians

13). Love that cuts and runs at the first or second or even third sign of trouble is not love at all. Real love persists, as Shakespeare wrote, even to the edge of doom.

In the midst of all the controversy and Jesus-bashing of recent times, we can confidently say one thing. No other human being has ever commanded such attention over a period of two thousand years. It is unavoidable, given human nature, that there will be varying interpretations of the meaning of his life. Yet the New Testament insists on these basic points:

1. In the Crucifixion of Jesus *the Scriptures are fulfilled,* that is to say, it was according to the plan and purpose of God from the beginning.
2. The Cross was *for sin,* that is, the atonement for sin and the overcoming of sin.
3. The Cross was *for us* — that is, on our behalf, in our place, and for our transformation.

"According to the Scriptures," "for sin," and "for us." These phrases hold the key to the meaning of the Cross. Why should we believe the latest here-today-and-gone-tomorrow academic theory?[51] These media-pleasing ideas are dressed up as though they were something new, but all of them have been sent around the ring before and have become tired and stale, whereas millions of people for two thousand years have put their trust in the Biblical witness and found it full of new life and new promise for every generation. Your presence here today attests — for those who have ears to hear — that Christ's Crucifixion was indeed the central event in the history of the world, unveiling as it does the very nature of the God who stands at the beginning and at the end, the Alpha and the Omega, who is and who was and who is to come (Revelation 1:8).

As the Gospel and Epistles of John emphasize, what our God accomplished for us in the Cross of Christ was the consummation of love. But this is not the soft, fuzzy sort of love that predominates in our sentimental culture ("Love is a warm puppy"). This is the love that goes to war. We understand from the New Testament that there is a war to be fought — a war against sin, a war against evil, a war against Satan, a war against death.[52] The war is fought by the love of God at work in the Crucifixion of Jesus. There has never been such a radical disclosure of anything whatsoever as what we see revealed at Golgotha. It seemed that day that there was an obliteration of love, an annihilation of life, an extermination of goodness, a total eclipse of God. In order to understand what Jesus has done, we really must try to put ourselves back into the place of those first disciples. No one anywhere at any time had ever put forth the idea that the Messiah of God would be put to death in a shameful fashion that was guaranteed to degrade, to disgust, and permanently to discredit. Even though Jesus himself had tried many times to warn them, they were totally unprepared, just as you and I would have been, to cope with the utter collapse of their Master's mission. God himself appeared to have withdrawn from the battlefield.

The ways of God are indeed strange. Listen to the words of the prophet Isaiah: "The LORD will rise up . . . to do his deed — strange is his deed! and to work his work — alien is his work!" (Isaiah 28:21). Martin Luther called this God's *opus alienum:* his alien work. The greatest challenges to Christian faith are those times when God seems to be either absent or, even worse, actively malevolent, sending one affliction after another to people and families without any apparent reason, piling on trouble where trouble has already made a seemingly permanent dwelling. The Old Testament is full of complaints about this. "O LORD, how long shall I cry for help, and thou wilt not hear?" (Habakkuk 1:2). There are no satisfactory answers to these questions about God's apparent failure to act. We do not offer "answers" today. God did not give us an "answer"; he gave his only Son. What we offer today is the divine drama: the King must die. All our stories are gathered up into the story of the humiliation of the Son of God. The paradox of the Crucifixion is *the enactment of the abandonment of God by God in the person of God himself* — "The Crucified God."[53] This makes no earthly sense, but it is this "strange work" which enables us to hold on in the dark. In the darkness at noon that descended on Calvary, God's hand was invisibly at work. This action of God is not made known in a blaze of light so that the whole world will be stunned into submission. It is made known in the darkness of the grave.

Here is the Lord's Word for all who have gathered at the foot of the Cross today. If you know what it is like to feel abandoned by God, if you have wondered if Christian faith isn't in fact a hoax and a sham, if you feel that pain and loneliness are a cruel joke on people who are fool enough to trust a God who doesn't appear to be around when you need him, Good Friday is for you. In this inconceivable action of submission to the very worst that "the world, the flesh and the Devil" can do, the Father and the Son together, in the power of the Holy Spirit, have completed the work of salvation. "It is finished" (John 19:30). Blessed are those who have eyes to see and ears to hear that Christ's completed work is accomplished precisely in the moment of seeming defeat. The weapon is his own body. The signs of victory are his wounds. "Worthy is the Lamb who was slain" (Revelation 5:12). In the darkness of the night of human pain, we are joined to him in his promise of everlasting day. "From henceforth," wrote St. Paul, "let no one make trouble for me; for I bear on my body the marks of the Lord Jesus" (Galatians 6:17).

AMEN.

THREE MEDITATIONS:
THE THREE SIGNS ON CALVARY

The First Sign:
Darkness at Noonday

———∝∞∾———

This week, you can read cover stories in any of three news-magazines about the Jesus Seminar and the Jesus-bashers, who delight in telling us every year at Easter time that most of the Gospel stories are fabrications and not to be believed. What this means, of course, is that we are being invited to trust instead in various modern scholars who, for one reason or another, prefer their own individual versions of Jesus to the living Lord of the church who makes himself known in Word and Sacrament Sunday by Sunday and day by day in the lives of believing Christians. It is in this context that the Biblical witness makes itself known and understood. The Holy Scriptures, almost without exception,[54] were written to be read aloud in the midst of the worshipping congregation, and it is in this context, faith speaking to faith, that the Lord reveals himself as the Way, the Truth, and the Life.

So when I ask you today to reflect with me on three signs from the Passion narratives, I am myself making a declaration of faith in the essential truth of those narratives. It is easy enough for scholars to poke holes in them by pointing out their dependence on Old Testament passages, their function in the early church, their scientific and textual impossibilities, and so forth. What is really challenging is to understand what these signs tell us as they reveal the meaning of the Cross and the purpose of God. Let us attend, then, to what Matthew, Mark, and Luke would teach us in the accounts of what happened on Calvary's hill as Jesus died. These three addresses today deal with the three signs that are said to have occurred as Jesus died.

St. Luke writes as follows: "It was about midday and there came a darkness over the whole land, which lasted until three in the afternoon; the sun was in eclipse" (Luke 23:44-45). Did such a thing really happen? If so, why do we have no records of it from any other sources? These are the wrong questions. In order to understand what the evangelists are trying to tell us, we must go back into the Hebrew Bible to search out the significance of darkness. We can identify at least three meanings.

First of all, we are reminded that before God created the universe, chaos and darkness was all there was. Before God brought light and order into being, there was only darkness and disorder. "In the beginning God created the heavens and the earth. The earth was without form and void, and darkness was upon the face of the deep . . . and God said, 'Let there be light,' and there was light" (Genesis 1:1-3). God is the creator of light. With his powerful Word he brought light into being where there had been only darkness. And light was the first thing of all that God created.

We just read the opening words of the book of Genesis. Now, listen to a kind of paraphrase of those verses written at the beginning of John's Gospel: "In the beginning was the Word, and the Word was with God, and the Word was God. He was in the beginning with God; all things were made through him. . . . In him was life, and the life was the light of men . . . the true light that gives light to every man was coming into the world" (John 1:1-4, 9). Later in that same Gospel of John, Jesus utters these famous words: "I am the light of the world; he who follows me will not walk in darkness, but will have the light of life" (John 8:12).

And so, putting all this together, we can say that when Jesus was dying on the Cross, the light of the world was going out. You are perhaps familiar with the famous Holman Hunt painting that hangs in St. Paul's in London, called "The Light of the World." It's very popular, but its depiction of a prettified Jesus with a glow

Eugene Delacroix: The Crucifixion

This picture conveys the sense of cosmic disturbance that the Biblical narratives emphasize. The soldier on the right seems to be having difficulty controlling his mount as the horse seeks to pull away from the man whose side has just been pierced. A wind has just come up, whipping Christ's drapery and the Magdalen's hair; this agitation is extended to the right side of the painting where the drapery of the Virgin is disturbed as she collapses. All around them a storm is rapidly approaching as dark clouds are driven forward toward the viewer by the wind. Because Christ's head is in shadow and the cross is shown very close to the picture plane, we feel that we, like Mary Magdalen, are being enveloped by the event and its consequences.

around his head is puny and sentimental compared to Scripture, which tells us that Jesus is the light of the world not because he has a glow but because he is the very source of its life. The creation came into being through him. When light itself came into being, piercing the darkness, *it originated with him,* St. John tells us. In the darkness on Golgotha, therefore, the creation goes into mourning for its Maker. The order of nature is reversed by the One who brought it into existence. This is not merely the death of an exemplary man. The eclipse over Calvary signifies the presence in human form of the Almighty Creator God himself, the Lord of the sun and moon, God the Son giving himself for the salvation of the world that he has made. When Jesus yields up his life, the light of the world is shut off.

The second meaning of the darkness can best be understood by going back to the Old Testament prophets. A common theme in all these prophets was that there would come a day of the wrath of the Lord, a time when God would deliver judgment against sin and evil for once and for all. Isaiah wrote:

The day of the LORD is coming — a cruel day with wrath and fierce anger — the rising sun will be darkened and the moon will not give its light. I will punish the world for its evil, the wicked for their sins. (Isaiah 13:9-11)

And here are the words of Jeremiah:

I will bring bereavement and destruction on my people, for they have not changed their ways. . . . At mid-day I will bring a destroyer. . . . The sun will set while it is still day. (Jeremiah 15:7-9)

And the prophet Amos says:

"In that day," declares the sovereign Lord, "I will make the sun go down at noon, and darken the earth in broad daylight. . . . I will make that time like mourning for an only son." (Amos 8:9-10)

And so the second meaning of the darkness over Golgotha is that, in the Cross, we see the promised judgment of God upon human sin. The eclipse signifies that God himself is acting here to pronounce sentence upon the wickedness of the world. The event is frightening, indeed. It is therefore our privilege, on Ash Wednesday and on Good Friday, and, indeed, whenever we confess our sins, to step forward in repentance on behalf of the whole world, as we read in the Epistle of Peter, "Now is the time for judgment to begin with the household of God" (1 Peter 4:17). It is our proper part, this day, to think of our own disobedience of God's holy commands, our faithlessness and chasing after false gods, our indifference to his sacrifice of unconditional love, our contempt of his righteous judgments upon the greed and injustices of our society. The prophets of old called the people of Israel to repentance; the eclipse over Calvary summons us, the people of God today, to confess our sins at the foot of the Cross.

The third meaning of the darkness can best be explained by using Jesus' own words. Earlier in St. Luke's version of the Passion we are told of Jesus' arrest in the garden:

> Turning to the chief priests, the officers . . . and the elders who had come to seize him, [Jesus] said, "Do you take me for a bandit, that you have come out with swords and cudgels to arrest me? . . . But this is your moment — the hour when darkness reigns." (Luke 22:52-53)

In the arrest, betrayal, suffering, and death of Jesus, all the powers of evil in the world are let loose. Chaos and night reign supreme. In one of our greatest Easter hymns, we find this line, "The powers of death have done their worst."[55] That is the third meaning of the darkness. The forces of evil are doing the very most that they can do. Satan is unleashed against the only-begotten Son of God. He comes back to Jesus in that black hour and whispers, "You see? I was right. You're a failure. You should have listened to me. I told you you weren't going to be able to convince anybody. Where are all your fine followers now? Where are all those people you healed and all those tax collectors and prostitutes and fishermen you spent so much time with? There isn't anybody left to carry your message. It's all over; you've failed. The world is in my power now; God has abandoned you."

In this final onslaught of Satan against God's anointed Messiah, we learn what is the outermost boundary and limit of the power of sin, darkness, and death.

The Second Sign:
The Temple Veil

———— ❦ ————

L ast summer I met a young woman named Holly who told me a story about her college days. When she was a freshman at a large university she went through the experience called "Rush," which, as you know, is a barbarous process designed, on the basis of utterly superficial criteria, to designate those who are deemed worthy of being members of sororities. Holly herself passed through Rush with flying colors and was elected to one of the high-status sororities. She was so disgusted with Rush, however, that she vowed not to sit in judgment on other women anymore and, instead, became a Rush counselor. In her senior year she was assigned eleven counsellees. Of the eleven, ten did not get into any sorority at all. All were devastated, and one was in such bad shape that Holly feared she might commit suicide.

This is sometimes called "making the cut," or not "making the cut" as the case may be. Human life is made up of such events. Without realizing what we are doing, we judge some people fit to associate with us and some not. Often the criteria that we use to make such determinations are entirely unrelated to the substance of the person. Some are "in" and some are "out" based on street address, blood lines, type of job, athletic prowess, fashions worn, color of skin, fraternity membership or lack thereof, and so on and so on.

Out in the Hamptons, on Long Island, New Yorkers are engaging in cutthroat activities as they try to get the right area code for their telephone so no one will know that they are (horrors!) brand-new arrivals.

One of the great problems of the Christian life is that, even though we know it is wrong to make these kinds of distinctions, we go on doing it anyway. We bow and scrape to the politically-correct altar of tolerance and inclusiveness, and then we go right back to our restricted clubs and our exclusive neighborhoods and our lily-white congregations. I don't know what the answer is to this problem. I participate in this system just as much as anyone else. If I go to a restaurant, I don't like to be put next to the kitchen. If I give money to some sort of benefit, I like to see my name in the highest category. When I ride on Amtrak, I surely do like the club car. When I get on an airplane, though, the situation is reversed, because I'm always in coach. I drag my carry-on past those first-class passengers sprawled out in their big seats drinking their drinks while I'm worrying about how to get my case into the bin. And then — the ultimate indignity — as soon as we all get settled *they draw that curtain.* That curtain announces to you that there is a superior class of people on this plane and you benighted masses are not allowed even to *look* at them.

Now let us turn to the second of the three signs that occurred at Golgotha when Jesus was crucified. This is what Mark's Gospel says: "Jesus uttered a loud cry, and breathed his last. And the curtain of the temple was torn in two, from top to bottom" (Mark 15:37-38). In order to understand the significance of this, we need to know something about the Jerusalem temple.

It was constructed as a series of courts within courts. First there was the Court of the Gentiles; anybody could go into that. If you were a Jewish woman, you could go through the Court of the Gentiles into the Women's Court, but no further; if you were a Jewish man, you could go through the Women's Court into the Men's Court. That was the limit for ordinary mortals. Beyond that, only the priests could venture. Within the Priests' Court was the temple itself, containing rooms within rooms. The innermost sanctuary was called the Holy of Holies. Inside the Holy of Holies was the Ark of the Covenant, covered by the mercy seat or throne of God, where the forgiveness of sins was to be found. No one, not Gentiles, not women, not men, not priests, not anybody could go in to the Holy of Holies at any time, with one single exception: once a year, on the Day of Atonement, also called Yom Kippur, the high priest went alone into the Holy of Holies carrying the blood of a sacrificial animal. As part of the rites on the Day of Atonement, the priest sprinkled this blood on the mercy seat and the people of Israel were cleansed of their sins for another year. But we have not mentioned the most important detail of all. In front of the Holy of Holies, the forbidden sanctuary of the mercy seat, there hung a large, thick, heavy curtain — the "veil of the temple" — beyond which no one could pass, except that high priest. There was no access for anyone through this curtain, this barrier, except through this intermediary, and that was only once a year.

So you see, there was a hierarchy of religious access. If you wanted to get close to God, if you wanted to be "in," if you wanted to be one of the chosen, if you wanted to be first class, you had to be the high priest, or at least a priest, or anything but a woman or a pagan. The whole setup was based on distinctions that separated groups from one another and restricted access to the mercy seat. In the moment that Jesus died on the Cross, all such distinctions came to an end. As the Son of God died, the Epistle to the Hebrews tells us that his blood was sprinkled, so to speak, on the heavenly mercy seat and "the veil of the temple was rent in twain from top to bottom." There was no longer any separation between the godly and the ungodly. There was no longer any curtain separating first class from second class. There was no longer a velvet rope dividing the supermodels, the agents, and the rock stars from the overweight, the unfashionable, and the uncool. All the fun of looking down on others as one passed through to the inner sanctum was wiped away. "There is no distinction," writes St. Paul to the Romans. "While we were still helpless, Christ died for the ungodly" (Romans 3:22; 5:6). That's the heart of the gospel, right there. It's the most radical utterance ever uttered, because it does away with religious attainment altogether. "While we were still helpless" — that puts the quietus on that beloved American scripture, "God helps those who help themselves." It's not in the Bible and never was. "While we were still *helpless,* Christ died for the *un*godly." This is so revolutionary that it is hard to describe. Everything we believe about religion and God would have led us to believe that Christ would die for the righteous, the godly, the upright. No, says the Lord himself, "I did not come to call the righteous, but sinners" (Mark 2:17). He died for those on the wrong side of the rope, the wrong end of the temple, the wrong side of the tracks. No wonder Paul could write, "There is neither Jew nor Greek, there is neither slave nor free, there is neither male nor female; all are one in Christ Jesus" (Galatians 3:28).

There is a sense in which this might be heard as bad news for us. What fun is it to be a Tri Delt if everybody is a Tri Delt?[56] What pleasure is there in travelling first class if there isn't going to be a curtain separating us from the unfortunates in the back?

Here's the reason it's good news, not bad. If God were going to make the cut based on godliness and righteousness and morality and piety and all those things, you and I might not make it. Somebody who never made it into a sorority at all might make it and we might not. When supermodel Cindy Crawford was twenty-three, in 1989, she made an amazingly astute remark. She said, "I'm sort of at the pinnacle of the model Cindy Crawford. A career should get better as time goes on. So, modeling is out. Everyone knows I'm gonna get old. That's their revenge."[57] This revealing comment reflects several things: the very small amount of room at the top, the impossibility of resting there peacefully, the need always to achieve more and more to stay there, the inevitability of the downturn, the jealousy and backstabbing that pursues successful people, the delight that others take in the decline of rivals. It's a precarious business, staying on the right side of that curtain.

I said earlier that I didn't know what the answer was to the problem we have with all this. But that's not really true. I do know, and so do many of you. We do know what the answer is. The answer is to keep telling the story. We keep in touch with the Christian community where the story is kept alive even though the community itself is full of hypocrites and sinners like you and me. We keep on telling the story: "the veil of the temple was rent in twain from top to bottom." The way to the mercy seat of the Lord is open for all human beings. "Christ died for the *ungodly*" — that's you and me. And maybe, just maybe, if we keep telling each other the story, we will quit specializing in exclusion and become Rush counsellors instead. Maybe we will make some progress toward more respect for people of other races and colors and customs and classes. And maybe we will start being happy, not because we have things that other people don't have, not because we have achieved a status in life that other people don't have, but because we see other people sharing in the riches of our Lord Jesus Christ, who gave his life for each and every one of us ungodly souls in order that the curtain might be torn down forever.

> Therefore, brethren, since we have confidence to enter the sanctuary by the blood of Jesus, by the new and living way which he opened for us *through the curtain* . . . let us consider how to stir up one another to love and good works. (Hebrews 10:19-20, 24)

The Third Sign:
The Open Tombs

———※———

The third sign that took place on the day that Jesus died is described for us in the Gospel of Matthew:

> And Jesus cried again with a loud voice and yielded up his spirit. And behold . . . the earth shook, and the rocks were split; the tombs also were opened, and many bodies of the saints who had fallen asleep were raised, and coming out of the tombs after his resurrection they went into the holy city and appeared to many. When the centurion and those who were with him, keeping watch over Jesus, saw the earthquake and what took place, they were filled with awe, and said, "Truly this was the Son of God!" (Matthew 27:50-54)

What is the meaning of these bizarre events? And why does Matthew say that the soldiers are moved to confess that Jesus is the Son of God precisely when they see the earthquake and the open tombs?

First we should notice the verbs in the account of the earthquake. In Greek there is a triple passive — it has even been called "the great triple passive" — the rocks *were split*, the graves *were opened*, and the bodies of the dead *were raised*. There is a powerful

Christ Knocking Open the Door of Hades

This unusual image shows a masterful Christ almost contemptuously kicking
open the door of Death and Hell, as if to say, see how easily I now defeat you!
But he has paid the price; his feet bear the marks of the nails.

sense here of a directing intelligence and a mighty arm at work in these phenomena. These rocks are not splitting by themselves. God is doing this. If Satan believed himself to be in control on that hill outside Jerusalem, his enjoyment must have been short-lived. God the Father and God the Son together are in charge of the entire operation; the amazing signs described in Matthew's Gospel are intended to demonstrate this fact.

The evangelist is telling us here in the most vivid and arresting way possible that the center of history is focused on Calvary's hill. A new book by the noted New Testament scholar Paul Minear makes this point. His title is, *The Golgotha Earthquake.*[58] The Crucifixion of Jesus of Nazareth is earthshaking in the truest sense of the word. The course of the world is interrupted here. Things will never again be as they were before, and in the eclipse as well as in the earthquake and the splitting of the rocks, God calls forth his whole creation as witness to his divine intervention. The universe is wrenched off its axis and sent spinning in another direction. The turn of the ages takes place today.

Fundamental to understanding the New Testament is the concept of the two ages, the Old Age and the Age to Come.[59] The Old Age is what we see all around us; the Old Age is the world of birth, death, politics, medicine, labor, money, success, failure, sports, war, taxes, elections, strikes, factories, newspapers, the State Department, the Supreme Court, the Congress, television, the Internet, life insurance, real estate. This is what we call the "real world." When we say that such-and-such a person is "not in touch with the real world," we have not paid him a compliment. One of the worst things that can be said about a preacher is, "She's not in touch with the real world." And yet it is this so-called "real world" which the New Testament describes as "old," as "evil," and above all, as "passing away." St. Paul writes, "The form of this world is passing away" (1 Corinthians 7:31), and St. John writes, "The world passes away, and the lust of it; but he who does the will of God abides for ever" (1 John 2:17).[60]

Over against this New Testament picture of the Old Age is the Age to Come. The Old Age is, by definition, that which passes away. The age of God, in sharpest contrast to it, is defined as *that which comes.* Think for a moment of your own life and history. Think of it the way you usually think about it; you had these parents and this childhood and you grew up to be this kind of a person and now you are older than you were and eventually you will be older still and sooner or later your life will draw to a close and you will die. Now, you will notice, in this kind of thinking the movement is always from the past through the present to the future. What I do today is influenced by what happened yesterday, and what I do today will have an effect on what will happen tomorrow. But what if that were changed? Suppose instead of looking at the future by way of the past and present, we began to judge and evaluate the past and present by the future, that is, *by what God will do in the future?*

This is exactly what is happening on the hill outside Jerusalem as Jesus of Nazareth draws his agonized last breaths. The Age to Come is invading the Old with a power that shakes the foundations of the world and raises the dead from their long-sealed graves. From henceforth the meaning of the universe is found, not in the old familiar movement past-present-future, but in the utterly unfamiliar, unlooked-for invasion of "the present evil age" (Galatians 1:4) by God's future. You understand that this is nothing like the futuristic thinking so beloved by the Speaker of the House.[61] That is only a dressed-up version of the Old Age, because all the predictions of the future come from projections out of the present. The Age to Come attested by the events of Good Friday are out of the mold altogether, coming as they do from the God who, as Paul writes in Romans, "gives life to the dead and calls into being the things that do not exist" (Romans 4:17). It is God's future that is decisive for the present. The earthquake and the splitting rocks signify to us the definitive entrance of God upon the scene, halting the entropic spiral of creation toward death and extinction. God has not abandoned his creation to its own fate. God in Jesus Christ places himself squarely in the path of this world's careening course toward self-destruction and reverses it. From now on, the Old Age movement from past to present to future is no longer determinative, so that at length T. S. Eliot can conclude his poem, "In my end is my beginning."[62] We orient ourselves not to what we have been, but to what by the grace of God we shall be.[63] And according to St. Matthew who tells us of the third great happening at the time of Jesus' death, the identifying mark of that Age to Come is the Resurrection of the Dead. "The tombs also were opened, and many bodies of the saints who had fallen asleep were raised. . . ."

You will notice that the dead who were raised were not just anybody. They were "the saints," the Old Testament believers who died, as the Epistle to the Hebrews says, in faith and the unflagging hope that the promises of God would come true. The resurrection life is not given indiscriminately; it is given through the death of Jesus Christ. How fortunate we are today to be here; many who come only on Easter Day will not fully grasp the dimensions of the reversal that God has wrought in the Cross of his Messiah.

Not every one wants to look at the Crucified One. The Corinthian Christians are the prototype. They loved Easter and hated Good Friday. To them Paul wrote, "I determined to know nothing among you except Jesus Christ and him crucified." Life is given to the dead through Jesus' *death.* Matthew also has a message for the "Corinthians" among us. The opening of the tombs takes place, not on the morning of the Resurrection, but at the moment of Jesus' last struggle for breath. Matthew is telling us that "the powers of death have done their worst" and they cannot contain him.

And so the sign of the open tombs and the risen saints is this: Jesus Christ did not enter death in order to give us an example of a good and brave death, not even in order to come back from the dead himself, but rather, to unlock our prison doors and lead us free. What is your prison door? Is it a fear of failure, of not making the cut, of not being good enough? Is it a loss of love, a sense of abandonment and disappointment, a feeling of being undervalued and uncherished? Is it the prison of jealousy, petty thoughts, and resentment? Is it estrangement from your children, your wife, your husband? Is it fear of growing older, losing physical potency, watching life and hopes slip away? These things are all signs of the Old Age of sin and death. This is the normal progression of our lives — a downward spiral through increasing weakness, loss, and deteriora-

Andrea Mantegna: Descent into Limbo,
also called The Harrowing of Hell

Mantegna painted this scene many times. Each of his versions shows a commanding risen Christ, seen from the rear, holding his banner of victory as he summons forth the faithful Old Testament dead. This wondrously moving painting is the only one of Mantegna's many versions to show the rapturous gesture of the patriarch as he sees his Savior standing at the door of Hades. Adam and Eve have emerged on the left and stand transfixed in awe (the identity of the middle figure is uncertain); Adam looks wonderingly up to the sky which he has not seen for millennia, whereas Eve gazes prayerfully back into the cave as a blast of air propels the resurrected man forward and upward, billowing his draperies as he reaches toward the Lord. The patriarch on the right is equally expressive in his movements of ecstatic welcome.

tion, through life towards death. Today, for all who are in Christ, the direction is reversed. The new direction is through death into life. Jesus' unconditional love of us all, poured out on the Cross to the last drop of his blood, has changed everything. His death has set us free — free from doubt and despair, free from sin and guilt, free from darkness and everlasting death, free for the praise and service and glory of our God who on this day makes you and me and the whole creation new. And that is why this terrible day is called Good.

AMEN.

MORE SERMONS FOR GOOD FRIDAY

The Hour of Glory

———⚚———

(preached for an evening service)
Texts: Various passages from the Gospel of John

You are the heart's core of the church tonight, the people who know that the only place to be on this day is with other Christians, watching at the foot of the Cross. It is the highest privilege of the year for me to be here with you.

We have just listened together to the reading of our Lord's Passion from the Gospel according to St. John. Before we begin to look deeply into it, there is something that needs to be said. Because John the evangelist repeatedly uses the term "the Jews" in speaking of the enemies of Jesus, and because the St. John Passion is traditionally read on Good Friday, this Gospel more than the others has been called into question in light of what happened to the Jews in the heart of Christian Europe during World War II. It is important that we be aware of this and understand that what happened to Jesus was not the work of "the Jews," but of all humanity. For one thing, John sometimes seems to use the term "the Jews" to mean, more or less, "the religious authorities," which makes Jews of a lot of us. Furthermore, Jews did not crucify people; crucifixion was a Roman punishment. More important still, however, and central to our worship here tonight, is the universal significance of his death. The very best way to put this across is to pay close attention to words of the hymn we will sing immediately after this sermon. Of all our Holy Week hymns, this one makes the point best. In this hymn we sing, "'Twas I, Lord Jesus, I it was denied thee: I crucified thee."[64]

"I crucified thee." This is the key insight. It was not "the Jews." It was us. As the choir sang last night, "For our sins this is thy pain. . . . For they are ours, O Lord, our deeds, our deeds." If there were any remaining doubt, it is dispelled by the dramatic reading of Palm Sunday, in which we ourselves shout, "Crucify him."

Let us now reflect tonight on a few crucial passages from John's Gospel. The first one is at the very beginning; John the Baptist sees Jesus for the first time, and says, "Behold, the Lamb of God, who takes away the sin of the world!" (John 1:29). This phrase, *Lamb of God,* is unique to the Fourth Gospel, but it has an echo in the words of St. Paul which we say at every Eucharist: "Christ our Passover is sacrificed for us" (1 Corinthians 5:7). Many good churchgoing people probably don't entirely understand that this really means that Christ our Passover *Lamb* has been sacrificed for us. The purpose of this sacrificial death, John the Baptist is telling us, is to take away the sin of the world. We cannot take away our own sin because we are slaves to it, as Jesus teaches in chapter 8: "Verily, verily I say unto you, every one who commits sin is a slave to sin. . . . So if the Son makes you free, you will be free indeed" (John 8:34-36).

Let's see if we can get the idea here. Human self-betterment is a major theme in our culture, but self-improvement can only bring us so far because it takes place inside the prison house of sin. What Jesus gives is deliverance from the prison altogether, and a completely new life to go with it. The primary meaning of freedom in the New Testament is not freedom to do whatever we choose. It is freedom from bondage to sin — freedom from everything that separates us from God. Think of all the things that you would like to do and be but have not been able to because of ingrained habits, personality flaws, harmful cravings, secret grudges and festering resentments within yourself. The Psalm that we just sang describes this condition:

Innumerable troubles have crowded in upon me;
my sins have overtaken me and I cannot see;
  they are more in number than the hairs of my head,
  and my heart fails me.

(Psalm 40:12)

There is a subtlety in the reading of this Psalm 40 on Good Friday that you might not catch if you haven't been tipped off. One of the characteristics of the Psalms is that the speaker is not always the same. Sometimes a human being is speaking and sometimes God is speaking, and we have to figure out for ourselves which it is. Throughout the history of the church, this shifting back and forth has proven to be a marvellous opportunity for interpreting the mission of Christ. Look at Psalm 40 again. It appears to be entirely in the voice of an ordinary human being: "I waited patiently upon the Lord; he stooped to me and heard my cry," and so forth. But when we read it on Good Friday, the speaker becomes Jesus himself:

Burnt-offering and sin-offering you have not required,
And so I said, "Behold, I come;
In the roll of the book it is written concerning me;
I love to do your will, O my God."

(Psalm 40:6-8)

If there were any question about who is saying this on Good Friday, it is answered by the reading from Hebrews that you just heard:

When Christ came into the world, he said, "Sacrifices and offerings thou hast not desired, but a body hast thou prepared for me. . . . I said, 'Lo, I have come to do thy will, O God,' as it is written of me in the roll of the book." (Hebrews 10:5-7)

So you see, when we read this Psalm on Good Friday we hear *Jesus himself* saying the words:

[199]

My sins have overtaken me and I cannot see;
  they are more in number than the hairs of my head,
  and my heart fails me.

(Psalm 40:12)

The same process will be going on when we read Psalm 38. The same thoughts are expressed in different words, and again, Jesus becomes the speaker: "My iniquities have gone over my head; they weigh like a burden too heavy for me" (Psalm 38:4).

The anthem that will be sung at the very end of this service is from Psalm 130: "If you were to note what is done amiss, Lord, who could stand?" (130:3). Ordinarily this is spoken by us human beings. The implied answer to the question is, no one. No one could stand if the Lord counted up what is done amiss. As we learned in the Maundy Thursday service, no one is worthy to stand before God without the washing of our Lord. Today he becomes the Lamb of God. It is not *his own* sin that overtakes him today, for he was free from sin; it is *our* sin that he carries to the Cross. Therefore, on Good Friday and Good Friday only, these words, this intolerable burden, are transferred to Jesus. There is a sense in which this burden begins to descend upon him at the Last Supper. He washes his disciples' feet, including those of Judas, saying to them all, "If I do not wash you," he said, "you have no part in me." Then, after he resumes his place at the table, John tells us that he began to be *troubled in spirit.* We wouldn't want to be too literal-minded about this, but nevertheless it does seem almost as though the sins he has washed off the disciples have begun to come upon him. He who has been without sin all his life is about to enter its prison-house. He and he alone has its key. He has explained this to his disciples already: "Truly, truly I say unto you, every one who commits sin is a slave to sin. . . . So if the Son makes you free, you will be free indeed" (John 8:34-36).

Continuing in the Fourth Gospel, Jesus speaks of his approaching death as the turning point in the history of the world. He is quite explicit about this. For this reason, chapter 12 is the turning point of this Gospel. Jesus proclaims: "Now is the judgment of this world." His *hour,* as he calls it, is the hour of judgment on the powers of Sin and Death, the domain ruled by the Prince of Darkness. He continues: "'Now shall the ruler of this world be cast out; and I, when I am lifted up from the earth, will draw all men to myself.' He said this to show by what death he was to die" (12:31-33). We learn from these words that the Lord's death will be not only a sacrifice for sin, but also a victory over the power of evil and death. The paradox at the heart of our faith is that the Son of God conquered this evil power, personified as "the ruler of this world," *precisely by submitting to him.* Jesus will cast out the ruler of this world by entering his domain of Death.

In John's Gospel, the Crucifixion is called, paradoxically, Jesus' hour of glory. In chapter 17, the Lord speaks directly to his Father in prayer: "When Jesus had spoken these words, he lifted up his eyes to heaven and said, 'Father, the hour has come; glorify thy Son that the Son may glorify thee, since thou hast given him power over all flesh, to give eternal life to all whom thou hast given him'" (17:1-2). The Father has given power to the Son to enter the domain of Death. As Christ says to Pilate, "You would have no power over me unless it had been given you from above" (John 19:11). The powers that confront one another in the Passion story are not equal powers. The power given to Christ as the Son of God is greater than the power of Sin and Death. It is helpful to understand this from the Biblical point of view as a real contest for lordship. The writer Flannery O'Connor never hesitated to put Satan into her stories. When she was asked about this, she wrote, "Our salvation is played out with the Devil, a Devil who is not simply generalized evil, but an evil intelligence determined on its own supremacy. . . . I want to be certain [she continues] that the Devil gets identified as the Devil and not simply taken for this or that psychological tendency."[65] The struggle for supremacy that we see going on during the Passion of Jesus Christ shows our salvation being "played out with the Devil," who on Golgotha is allowed for the first and only time to have a completely free rein. This is the moment of the glorification of the Son, in his victory over all evil. That's why Jesus said earlier, "Now is the judgment of this world, now shall the ruler of this world be cast out."

John, like Luke, shows Jesus reigning as King and Lord even on the Cross. In Luke, he remits the sins of his tormentors ("Father, forgive them; for they know not what they do") and grants the repentant thief entrance into the Kingdom of God ("Today thou shalt be with me in Paradise"). These are not the actions of a victim. They are the actions of a commanding figure who has power to direct the future of human beings. In John's Gospel, he creates a new human community, giving his mother and his disciple to each other ("Woman, behold thy son! Behold thy mother!"). Then, John tells us, Jesus says, "I thirst," not primarily because of the tormenting condition he is in but, rather, to place his suffering in the context of God's eternal purpose. These are the words of the evangelist:

> After this Jesus, knowing that all was now finished, said (to fulfil the scripture), "I thirst." A bowl full of vinegar stood there; so they put a sponge full of the vinegar on hyssop and held it to his mouth. When Jesus had received the vinegar, he said, "It is finished"; and he bowed his head and gave up his spirit. (John 19:28-30)

It is finished *(tetélestai).* In the Gospel of Mark, we read, "Jesus uttered a loud cry, and breathed his last" (Mark 15:37). It has been said by some of the older interpreters that John has given us the content of Mark's wordless loud cry. In John, "It is finished" is a cry of victory. When I was growing up in the church, I always thought that Jesus meant, "It's over." More of us now realize that that does not convey the full meaning. A better translation would be "It is accomplished." Other translations are "It is completed," or "It is perfected." The Latin version is best of all; even if you don't know any Latin, you will get it: *Consummatum est.* Even as death engulfs him, our Lord Jesus is his Father's victorious Son. The Father's purpose is consummated.

We will not conceal from you tonight that there are numerous Biblical scholars today who seem to enjoy announcing to the media that the "historical" Jesus did not say any of the things attributed to him in the Gospel of John. I attended a funeral recently in an Episcopal church where the rector announced to the congregation, "Jesus *is reported to have said,* 'I am the resurrection and the life.'" But if the Christian story is true, then Jesus is a living Lord who has shown to the church by the Holy Spirit what he says and does not say. A few years ago at Eastertime, Kenneth Woodward of *Newsweek* magazine wrote an article about the "Jesus scholarship" in which he said that reliance on the truth of the Bible "implies a bond of trust between those who live in the presence of Christ today and those who first carried the Easter message 2,000 years ago."[66] This is as close as a newsmagazine can come these days to a statement of faith.

That bond of trust is not forged in the pages of magazines or on the Internet, however, but in the context of the worshipping community "who live in the presence of Christ today." That is where we are, you and I, here and now. We have come together to reaffirm our trust in the Biblical witnesses. At the end of his Gospel, St. John writes these words:

> Now Jesus did many other signs in the presence of the disciples, which are not written in this book; but these are written that you may believe that Jesus is the Christ, the Son of God, and that believing you may have life in his name. (John 20:30-31)

Here again are the words of Jesus in his prayer at the end of the Last Supper:

> Father, the hour has come; glorify thy Son that the Son may glorify thee, since thou hast given him power over all flesh, to give eternal life to all whom thou hast given him. And this is eternal life, that they know thee the only true God, and Jesus Christ whom thou hast sent. (John 17:1-3)

Dearly beloved in Christ: Believe tonight. Take him into your heart and your life as he has taken you into his heart and into his eternal life.

Have innumerable troubles crowded in upon you? "If the Son makes you free, you will be free indeed."

Have your sins overtaken you? "Behold, the Lamb of God, who takes away the sin of the world."

Does your heart fail you? "God so loved the world that he gave his only Son, that whoever believes in him should not perish but have eternal life. . . . To all who receive him, who believe in his Name, he gives power to become children of God . . . we have beheld his glory, glory as of the only Son of the Father, full of grace and truth" (John 3:16; 1:12, 14, 17). As the Father has loved him, so has he loved us; dear friends, abide in his love tonight, tomorrow and for ever, for he alone is the Resurrection and the life (John 15:9; 11:25).

The Great Exchange

⸺⸺ ∞∞ ⸺⸺

(preached for a one-hour noonday service)

Here is the cover of *Newsweek,* March 27: "Visions of Jesus: How Jews, Muslims, [Hindus,] and Buddhists View Him."[67] This is an indication of how much our culture has changed. Twenty-five or thirty years ago, American Christians weren't much interested in what other religions thought about Jesus. The situation is very different now. Books by Deepak Chopra (a New-Age-*cum*-Hindu guru) and the Dalai Lama (the Buddhist leader) are bestsellers. These books and their authors vary in quality. The Dalai Lama, for instance, is admired worldwide for his leadership of a suffering culture, and he is a classical Tibetan Buddhist, not a hybrid like Chopra. Nevertheless, it has never been more crucial since New Testament times for Christians to understand the difference between Jesus as one generic religious figure among many others and the unique Christ whom we know as Savior and Lord. Your presence here at church on Good Friday therefore sends a signal. Not everyone understands about the singularity of Good Friday; if they did, they would be here. You are the avant-garde, the advance troops. As our culture drifts away from its Biblical moorings, we are going to need more people like you. It is becoming more and more difficult to help people understand that Christianity is not just one religion among many, that it can't be blended together with yoga and astrology and angel worship and self-help to make a bigger and better religious smorgasbord.

The *Newsweek* article was written by their longtime religion editor, Kenneth L. Woodward, a practicing Catholic who is usually able to balance fairness to other faiths with a staunch defense of his own. In this cover story, he discusses various ways of understanding Jesus from the standpoint of the various religions. Let me read you a few sentences.

> Nothing shows the difference between Jesus and the Buddha better than the way that each died. The Buddha's death was serene and controlled — a calm passing out of his final rebirth. . . . Jesus, on the other hand, suffers an agonizing death on the cross, abandoned by God but obedient to his will.
>
> Clearly, the cross is what separates the Christ of Christianity from every other [concept of] Jesus. In Judaism, there is no precedent for a Messiah who dies, much less as a criminal as Jesus did. In Islam, the story of Jesus' death is rejected as an affront to Allah himself. Hindus can accept only a Jesus who passes into peaceful *samadhi,* a yogi who escapes the degradation of death. The figure of the crucified Christ, says Buddhist Thich Nhat Hanh, "is a very painful image to me. It does not contain joy or peace, and this does not do justice to Jesus. . . ."
>
> That most of the world cannot accept the Jesus of the cross should not surprise [us]. . . . Jesus remains what he has always been, a sign of contradiction.

The Cross is a "sign of contradiction" for several reasons. For one thing, the Crucifixion was an actual event, not a religious idea. This is of central importance. The religion of the Hebrews — the faith of the Old Testament — was different from any of the religions around it because it alone was grounded in history. Our God has chosen to reveal himself, not through the individual "spiritual" journeys and searches so much spoken of today, but by breaking into world events. For example, Elijah, who heard the "still small voice" when he was alone in the wilderness, was not preserved for a contemplative life in a hermit's cave, but was sent back to the court of Ahab to confront the king with his sins. The stories of

Elisha in 2 Kings are so entwined with the interaction of nations and institutions that a commentary on that book is called *The Politics of God.*[68] The Old Testament is startlingly worldly compared to other faiths. In the Creed, we say that Jesus was "crucified under Pontius Pilate." Surely this is very strange. Why would a statement of religious faith go out of its way to enshrine the name of an obscure provincial Roman official? It has long been recognized that this peculiarity is of central importance for understanding Christianity. The birth, death, and resurrection of God's Son "for us and for our salvation" was not a cyclical happening that recurred every year with the seasons. It was the climactic occurrence of God's entrance into history at a specific time and place that we can reliably identify and date. Christianity did not arise out of the mystery religions of the ancient Near East.[69] Christianity emerged out of Judaism with its unique character: historical (not mythological), linear (not cyclical), materialistic (not world-denying). Without the Exodus from Egypt and the Incarnation of Jesus, the history of world religion would look totally different. The acting subject is not humanity with its longings, needs, wishes, and hopes. The acting subject is God. "The Word became flesh and dwelt among us" (John 1:14).

Besides this world-historical significance of Jesus, however, there are other contradictory features about his story and, especially, his death. We might be able to accept the martyrdom of a famous person; indeed, such martyrdoms usually enhance the stature of such a person — we need only think of the Kennedy brothers and Martin Luther King, Jr. Heroic figures, however, are not usually associated with disgrace, shame, and humiliation. Certainly this is true of religious personages. We want our objects of worship to be effulgent and serene, welcoming and uncomplicated. The most compelling argument for the truth of Christianity — as the *Newsweek* article suggests — is the undisputed historical fact of the crucified Messiah, a scandalous happening that runs counter to everything that the human religious imagination has ever produced. That's why St. Paul calls the Cross a stumbling block to Jews and foolishness to Greeks (1 Corinthians 1:23); we can paraphrase this by saying that the Crucifixion is "a very painful image," offensive to religious people and secular people alike.

How then are we to understand the centrality of the Passion narratives, the universal recognition of the Cross as the symbol of the faith, the strong emphasis of the historic creeds that he was "crucified, dead and buried"?

I don't mean to be suggesting that we can understand, in this life, the full dimensions of what happened on Good Friday. We have only hints and suggestions from the Bible.[70] But one thing we know. Over and over again, all of the New Testament writers in one way or another tell us that Jesus' death was *for sin*. That is why his death was uniquely terrible. The shameful nature of crucifixion as a method of execution stands in direct correlation to the shameful conduct of the human race. The Roman state was not concerned about "cruel and inhuman punishment." The method was supposed to be as cruel and inhuman as possible. That was its purpose. Americans don't grasp this easily; we do not have (thank God) a culture of deliberate, public, state-sponsored torture. The public nature of crucifixion is unimaginable to us; in America, there is controversy even if the families of victims are allowed to view death by lethal injection under strictly controlled conditions. Chaplains are provided for the prisoners doomed to die; they are not manhandled or cursed or mocked as they are escorted to the death chamber. We are protected in this way from confronting our own worst instincts.[71] In crucifixion, by contrast, the worst was not only permitted but, indeed, encouraged as passersby hurled insults and taunts. A man being crucified was not even allowed the dignity of a human executioner; he was forced to be his own executioner.[72] As a victim hung there gasping for breath, his own body turned against him, asphyxiating him.

Last year, Georgetown University commissioned contemporary artists and sculptors to design and make crucifixes for new classrooms. One of these artists, Charles McCullough, talked about his experience in making a crucifix, and this is what he said: "To draw, paint, or sculpt the Crucifixion is a terrifying experience. It is hard to overemphasize the extreme brutality of this death by torture. It is important, I believe, to represent the Crucifixion as state murder, not an abstract notion of death in general."[73] This arresting statement is helpful because it focuses our attention on the specific and gruesome nature of the method used by human beings to execute the Son of God. The Roman Empire, whatever else one may think of it, stood at the pinnacle of human achievement in its time. Likewise, the religion of those who collaborated with the Romans to crucify Jesus was the very highest and very best in the ancient world — the revealed religion of the God of Abraham, Isaac, and Jacob, our own parent religion. What we see going on here, therefore, is a conspiracy between the best government and the best religion to execute God's Messiah. This sort of collusion has happened over and over, ever since, in the history of the world. It is not in the least related to "the Jews" in particular, but to church and state in general, representative of human depravity at all levels. At this moment, evidence is being gathered that Catholic and Anglican priests, nuns, and even bishops collaborated with the Hutu to massacre huge numbers of Tutsi in Rwanda, even within the church buildings themselves. Perhaps you will think yourself incapable of such things. Who can say until he has been there? Today, the entire human race comes under the judgment of God — except that this entire race has all been gathered into the human body of one representative Person, which has made all the difference.

For what happened to Jesus was in a league by itself — not only because it was state-sponsored torture, but also for another supreme reason that we will now examine.

We will shortly sing a hymn with these words:

Lo, the Good Shepherd for the sheep is offered;
The slave hath sinned, and the Son hath suffered;
For our atonement, while we nothing heeded,
God interceded.[74]

"The slave" — you and me; "the Son" — Jesus. The shame was ours, but the effects fell upon him. It is what W. H. Auden called the Great Exchange, the greatest exchange the world has ever known.

Peter Paul Rubens: Descent from the Cross *(above);*
Max Beckmann: The Descent from the Cross *(right)*

The gorgeous picture by Rubens shows a massive, muscular Christ requiring all the exertion of several powerfully built men to take him down. The composition does not lead the eye down to the grave as Rembrandt's engraving

of the same subject (p. 136) does, but to the faces of two lovely women who do not look particularly distressed. A ruggedly beautiful St. John, bracing himself carefully on the ladder, handles the body with masculine tenderness. A richly human picture, full of compassion and warmth, it suggests that the seeds of resurrection lie within humanity itself. This, however, is contradicted by bleak twentieth-century portrayals of the dead Christ in the context of world war.

Like so many twentieth-century depictions of the Crucifixion, this modern one (painted during World War I) remorselessly depicts the ugliness and meaninglessness of death by torture. This dead body, already in the grip of rigor mortis, is past human hope or help.

As St. Paul wrote, "God made him to be sin who knew no sin, that in him we might become the righteousness of God" (2 Corinthians 5:21). His sinlessness is exchanged for our sin; his righteousness is exchanged for our unrighteousness. The First Epistle of Peter says much the same thing in a different way: "He himself bore our sins in his body on the tree, that we might die to sin and live to righteousness. By his wounds you have been healed" (1 Peter 2:24). His perfect health is exchanged for our sickness unto death.

In the Passion according to Matthew, the high priest says to the people: "You have heard his blasphemy. What is your judgment?" And the people — you and I — shout, "He is deserving of death" (Matthew 26:65-66). This is what we always say when the death penalty is handed down. We say, "He got what he deserved." But what does the Cross say? The Cross says that the one person who *did not deserve* to be crucified is the one who was. And the Cross says something else. It says, "It should have been us instead of him." That is what is meant by the Great Exchange. It should have been us there instead of him, because — as Paul wrote to the Romans — "the wages of sin is death." Death is the wage we rightfully deserve for our rebelliousness against God's good purposes for human life. Death is the wage paid to Adam in the Garden of Eden. In the Garden of Gethsemane, the Lord Jesus took that wage due to us and accepted it for himself.

Here is what Auden wrote:

Flesh grew weaker, stronger grew the Word,
Until on earth the Great Exchange occurred.[75]

Flesh grew weaker. Auden knew and understood the Scriptures as few do today. He knew what St. Paul meant by "flesh" (Greek *sarx*). When John wrote that "the Word became flesh and dwelt among us," he meant essentially that the Son of God, the second Person of the Trinity, took *human nature* upon himself. Paul, however, expands that idea of flesh as human nature with his use of the word "flesh" to mean, specifically, *corrupted* human nature — the human being in its total incapacity, not just bodily or sexual aspects. Paul described this predicament in words which thoughtful Christians have always recognized and claimed:

> I do not understand my own actions. For I do not do what I want, but I do the very thing I hate. . . . For I know that nothing good dwells within me, that is, in my flesh. I can will what is right, but I cannot do it. For I do not do the good I want, but the evil I do not want is what I do. Now if I do what I do not want, it is no longer I that do it, but sin which dwells within me. (Romans 7:15-20)

"Flesh grew weaker." Sin is too strong for us. Sin is not just a misdeed here and a mistake there. Sin is a Power that holds all human beings in its grip. Why don't we have peace instead of war? Because of Sin. Why don't we have racial harmony instead of racial animosity? Because of Sin. Why are children poor, abused, neglected, malnourished, sick from drinking bad water? Because of Sin. Because we go round and round in a cycle of selfishness, rapacity, indifference, greed, and vengefulness. If you don't believe that about yourself, believe it about the human race. If the twentieth century taught us anything, it taught us that the human being is capable of unspeakable atrocity on an unimaginable scale in the very midst of supposedly advanced civilization. We are profoundly, incurably, irrevocably unable to cure the human race from within. That is why the news that God has entered history from outside history must be preserved at the very heart of the Christian message. "Stronger grew the Word." He has entered our condition to substitute his capacity for our incapacity, his righteousness for our unrighteousness, his deserving for our undeserving.

We human beings like to say of another person, "He got what he deserved." The Cross says the opposite. It tells us, "While we were still helpless . . . Christ died for the ungodly." It says, "God shows his love for us in that while we were yet sinners Christ died for us" (Romans 5:6, 8). Not for the godly, the righteous, the religious, the moral; he died for the *ungodly,* the *unrighteous,* the *irreligious,* the *immoral.* There are all kinds of reasons that people give for opposing the death penalty, but for Christians, there is only one reason that really counts: according to our understanding of Christ's Cross, we were all deserving of death, yet he stepped into our place and took it away from us, undeserving though we were and are. Therefore Christians do not say, "He deserved it"; Christians say, "There but for the grace of God go I."

When we truly understand this, when it sinks into our hearts, we will never want to see another human being humiliated. We will never want to see another person get exactly what he or she deserves. We will want every person to receive mercy as you and I have received mercy. May we think deeply about these things as we sing the next hymn, and may we make these words our own.

> Therefore, kind Jesus, since I cannot pay thee,
> I do adore thee, and will ever pray thee,
> Think on thy pity, and thy love unswerving,
> Not my deserving.

AMEN.

The Crucifixion of Self-Help

———— ⚮ ————

(preached for a one-hour service)

God, who is rich in mercy, out of the great love with which he loved us, even when we were dead through our trespasses, made us alive together with Christ {so that} you who once were far off have been brought near in the blood of Christ.

(EPHESIANS 2:11-13)

O n Good Friday, the Christian gospel decisively defines itself. This is the day that differentiates the faith of the Church from religion in general. Some might interpret that declaration as a negative judgment on other faiths, but this is not our aim; rather, we desire with a single-minded intention to set before you this day the stark singularity of the Cross of Christ. We are so far removed from the gruesome reality of crucifixion as the ancient world knew it that we are scarcely able to imagine its offensiveness, its loathsomeness, its gross unsuitability as an object of religious reverence or worship. There is a sense in which this instrument of torture is the most irreligious thing that ever was. And yet, as theologian Jürgen Moltmann has written, the Cross is "the inner criterion of Christian theology."[76] He is telling us that we simply cannot have a sanitized Christianity. If you visit a typical Christian bookstore in America, you will see scenes of glorious nature everywhere: sunsets over pristine lakes, snow-crowned peaks without a sign of litter, forests untouched by acid rain, golden wheat waving over plains that never saw an interstate. The greeting cards we buy, the bulletin covers we hand out each week, the calendars that illustrate Bible verses all send a soothing message of tranquillity and beauty — you would never know that the central fact of the Christian narrative is a scene of unspeakable ugliness. Perhaps that is why the turnout is always smaller on Good Friday. A special welcome to those teenagers present today — this is a sign of your maturity, because this is the day that divides the men from the boys and the women from the girls. Pollsters tell us that a huge majority of Americans believe in God, but that can mean almost anything. The question that really matters is, "What do you think of Christ crucified?"

The reason we read the very, very long Passion narrative twice during Holy Week is that we seek to enter into the meaning of this death by state-sanctioned brutality. One thing is certain from the outset: this is not a day for contemplating the suffering of an innocent hero whom we might some day emulate or imitate. If we were to be drawn into that frame of reference, we might lose the argument to someone who might point out that others have suffered more horribly than Jesus, more stoically and for a longer period. The Biblical writers have forestalled any such discussion by their reticence concerning those very matters. Their entire attention is directed to something else. It is not physical suffering that dominates the Passion narratives. The evangelists are concerned with the inner meaning of the events. Mark pictures Christ derelict and rejected by God, yet precisely in that condition and at that moment publicly confessed for the first time as the only-begotten Son of the Father. Matthew also emphasizes the dereliction and the mockery, but he characteristically shows forth Christ as the Son of David and Messiah of Israel at the same time, bearing high titles, with mighty revelatory signs testifying to the true meaning of his rejected condition.[77] Luke depicts Jesus reigning as King even from the Cross, with power to determine the eternal destinies of men ("Today thou shalt be with me in Paradise"); and John interprets the Passion and death as the triumph of the Lamb, the "hour of glory" when he wins the victory over death and the Devil: "Now is the judgment of this world, now shall the ruler of this world be cast out; and I, when I am lifted up from the earth [on the Cross], will draw all humanity to myself" (John 12:31-32). These are the themes that the New Testament writers care about.

The Passion of Jesus is set in contrast to the behavior of the disciples and the other players in the drama. While the Master is on his way to his trial, torture, and death, everyone else in the story is protecting his own flanks. Judas, Peter, Pontius Pilate, and the disciples are thinking, not of Jesus, but of ways to vindicate themselves. That is precisely the point of difference between Jesus and us. Self-help is the American gospel, which translates into self-congratulation and self-protection. Much of our time is spent in protecting and securing what we have accumulated. Most of our energy goes into the maintenance of what we have earned or inherited — our businesses, our families, our clubs, our free enterprise system, our American superiority. Very often, even the Church becomes an idol that we seek to protect as a symbol of our patrimony, our way of life, our position at the top of the heap, so that the Cross becomes not a summons to self-sacrifice, but a symbol of hegemony — as has recently (and shockingly) been the case in Bosnia where the Serbian Orthodox have forced the sign of the Cross upon the Muslims as a sign of domination.[78] But we should not think of this as a characteristic of what is easily described as the notoriously volatile Balkan populations. Right here in the United States there are many immigrant groups who have been told to "go get your own church."

We Americans can excuse our attitudes on the grounds of the American creed: "God helps those who help themselves." This motif is eerily echoed, or parodied, in the taunts flung at Jesus on the Cross:

> Those who passed by derided him, wagging their heads and saying, "You who would destroy the temple and build it in three days, save yourself! If you are the Son of God, come down from the cross." So also the chief priests, with the scribes and elders, mocked him, saying, "He saved others; he cannot save himself.

He is the King of Israel; let him come down now from the cross, and we will believe in him." (Matthew 27:39-42)

It is easy for us, far removed from the scene, to distance ourselves from these hateful imprecations. Yet something about them is familiar to us; we expect people to reap what they sow, to get what they deserve, to make their own luck, to pull themselves up by their own bootstraps. "Is it nothing to you, all you who pass by?" This verse from Lamentations has traditionally been associated with Jesus on the Cross. The implied answer is, "Yes, it is nothing to us." This is the attitude of those who pass by on Good Friday. It is the attitude of city dwellers who become accustomed to walking past homeless people without a second glance. "They've chosen it," I have heard people say on many an occasion. The implication is, "Let them save themselves." Today, as we enter more deeply into the experience of Good Friday, we begin perhaps to see how the Son of God has entered into the condition of those who cannot save themselves, those who are defenseless, those who deserve to die. This was his free choice. In Gethsemane on Thursday night, he asked the Father if he might not be spared this final sentence, this death penalty; he rose from his knees knowing that he had chosen the path laid out for him since before the world began. In the garden that night, he shrank from the sentence of judgment that he did not deserve, but in the wrestling, in the struggle, in the agony that the disciples were too weak to share, he submitted to that sentence on our behalf — so that it would not fall on us. He went forth to arrest, trial, and execution; he became the Judge judged in our place.[79] He has written *our death sentence* in *his own blood,* and thereby has deflected it from us for ever.

Here is the way Ephesians describes what the Lord has done for us:

> You were dead through the trespasses and sins in which you once walked, following the course of this world, following the prince of the power of the air [Satan], the spirit that is now at work in the children of disobedience. Among these we all once lived in

the passions of our flesh, following the desires of body and mind, and so we were by nature children of wrath, like the rest of mankind. But God, who is rich in mercy, out of the great love with which he loved us, even when we were dead through our trespasses, made us alive together with Christ. . . .

Therefore remember that at one time you Gentiles [that's us] were . . . strangers to the covenants of promise, having no hope and without God in the world. But now in Christ Jesus you who once were far off have been brought near in the blood of Christ. (Ephesians 2:1-5, 11-13)

These are among the most wonderful words in all of Scripture, but they are difficult for many of us to hear. We do not like to be called "children of wrath" and "children of disobedience." Each epoch has its own way of describing the human predicament; the author of Ephesians has apparently thought of them all. Some generations have feared death: "we were dead." The Puritan era emphasized guilt: "the trespasses and sins in which you once walked." Estrangement was a major theme in the twentieth century; Ephesians has thought of that too: "You were strangers." The great novels are all concerned with these themes in one form or another, that is what makes them great. They all deal with the tragedy of human existence. Fear of loss, fear of decrepitude, fear of failure, fear of being exposed — all these things have been present to us to a greater or lesser degree throughout human history. Think of Conrad's Lord Jim, haunted all his life by one act of youthful cowardice, never able to rest assured that he is "good enough." All of these human anxieties are summed up in the Biblical expressions "children of wrath" and "children of disobedience."

Two words mark the turning point in the passage. "But God . . ."! Whenever you hear these words, *but God,* "lift up your heads, for your redemption is drawing near!" (Luke 21:28) The words "but God" and "but now," in the New Testament, always signal that we are about to hear the great good news of the gospel. We were children of wrath, we were children of disobedience, we were dead through sin, we were imprisoned by our own desires and passions, we were without hope in the world . . . *but God!* "But God, who is rich in mercy, out of the great love with which he loved us, even when we were dead through our trespasses, made us alive together with Christ. . . . You were strangers to the covenant of promise . . . *but now,* in Christ Jesus, you who once were far off have been brought near in the blood of Christ."

This glorious passage from Ephesians is acknowledged by almost everyone as a Class A summary of the gospel message. However, in spite of its clear reference to the blood of Christ, it is not usually associated with Good Friday. I'm assuming that you, being the inner core of this congregation, are up to the challenge of making the connections. The inner meaning of the hideousness of Jesus' death is revealed by the phrases "children of wrath" and "children of disobedience." The darkness of the day of his death corresponds to the darkness of the human heart.

The more we enter into the meaning of Christ's death, the closer we see into our own precariously balanced inner lives. A great many people go through life without ever facing their own potential for hurting others, for greed and rapacity, for selfishness and indifference to suffering, for cooperating with systems of evil. They are not here today. You are here in their place. You are not here for yourself only, but also for others. In a very important sense, therefore, you are doing something Christlike, aligning yourself with the vicarious action of our Savior, who is there on the Cross in our place while the world goes heedlessly by.

What is happening today as we gather is that we are recapitulating the story of Fall and Redemption. We are not just listening to it; we are placing ourselves within it; and by doing so we are also representing those who are not here, who think we can get ourselves out of the fix we are in. That is the great deception that we human beings practice on ourselves — but we here today know that we cannot follow through on it. We look at ourselves today with the Savior's eyes. Jesus looks at us and he knows that we cannot help ourselves. He looks at us this very day in the same way he looked at every human being that he encountered during his earthly life: with infinite sadness for our predicament, yet with unquenchable love

and with unflinching resolve to rescue us from certain condemnation and death, whatever it took, wherever it led, whatever the
price. "Self-help" is crucified with Christ — for as St. Paul writes,
"While we were *still helpless,* Christ died for the ungodly" (Romans
5:6).

Even on this day, therefore, we rejoice greatly. *Especially* on this
day we rejoice. We are not afraid to hear the phrase, "children of
wrath," for we know that we are such no longer. We are not afraid to
hear that we were walking in darkness, for we know that now we
walk in his light. We are not afraid to hear that we were "dead in
our sins," for we know that we are dead no longer:

> God, who is rich in mercy, out of the great love with which he
> loved us, even when we were dead through our trespasses, made
> us alive together with Christ [so that] you who once were far off
> have been brought near in the blood of Christ. (Ephesians 2:4,
> 13)

And, finally, let us gladly hear the rest of St. Paul's great words
in Romans 5:

> God shows his love for us in that while we were yet sinners
> Christ died for us.
> Since, therefore, we are now justified by his blood,
> much more shall we be saved by him from the wrath
> of God.
> For if while we were still enemies
> we were reconciled to God by the death of his Son,
> much more, now that we are reconciled,
> shall we be saved by his life.

Let us humbly thank God on this day of days for his infinite
mercy, and let us come to the foot of the Cross to praise him for his
help when we could not help ourselves. Lord Jesus Christ, my only
Savior and Lord, "help of the helpless, O abide with me."[80]

Good Friday Preaching 1976-2001

I owe a debt of profound gratitude to the following parishes, and to their rectors who issued the invitations. It is an incomparable privilege to bring the message of Christ crucified to those who make the extra effort to come to services on Good Friday. I will cherish the memory of these congregations all my life.

1976	Christ's Church, Rye, New York
1977	Christ's Church, Rye, New York
1978	Christ's Church, Rye, New York
1979	Christ's Church, Rye, New York
1980	St. John's, Larchmont, New York
1981	Bethesda-by-the-Sea, Palm Beach, Florida
1982	Grace Church, New York City
1983	Grace Church, New York City
1984	Trinity Cathedral, Columbia, South Carolina
1985	St. John's, Larchmont, New York
1986	Trinity Church, Portland, Maine
1987	Grace Church, New York City
1988	St. John's, Larchmont, New York
1989	St. Michael and St. George, St. Louis, Missouri
1990	Grace Church, New York City
1991	Christ Church, Greenwich, Connecticut
1992	St. Mark's Church, New Canaan, Connecticut
1993	Church of the Good Shepherd, Norfolk, Virginia
1994	St. Paul's Church, Augusta, Georgia
1995	Grace and St. Stephen's Church, Colorado Springs
1996	St. Francis' Church, Potomac, Maryland
1997	Christ Church, Grosse Pointe, Michigan
1998	St. Paul's Church, Shreveport, Louisiana
1999	Grace and St. Stephen's Church, Colorado Springs
2000	St. Bartholomew's Church, Hartsville, South Carolina
2001	Trinity Church, Hartford, Connecticut

SEPTEMBER 11, 2001:
A CROSS AT GROUND ZERO

Note to the reader

⸺⸺∞⸺⸺

This sermon was delivered in early October, 2001, at St. Paul's, Munster, Indiana, and in a slightly altered form at Christ Church, Sheffield, Massachusetts.

A Cross at Ground Zero

———⟨∞⟩———

*{Jesus said,} If it is by the Spirit of God that I cast out demons,
then the kingdom of God has come upon you. How can one enter
a strong man's house and plunder his goods, unless he first binds
the strong man? Then indeed he may plunder his house.*

MATTHEW 12:28-29; PARALLELS IN
MARK 3:27 AND LUKE 11:21

My fellow Americans:

On September 10th, in my wildest imagination I could not
have dreamed that there would ever come a time that I would address a Christian congregation as "my fellow Americans." But that
was last month, long ago, when we were young.[81] Two weeks after
the September 11 attack, *New York Times* columnist Frank Rich
wrote an article called "The End of the Beginning."

> Everything has changed. As we straddle this incredible moment,
> poised between Armageddon and a future only a fool would pre-
> dict, there is rampant hunger for certainty — a precious commod-
> ity.... In truth we don't know where we are.... We're in limbo.[82]

A *Wall Street Journal* writer commented that the famous "New
York swagger . . . is for the moment gone," replaced by "grief, inse-

curity and fear."[83] Everyone is rethinking everything. One woman who was interviewed said that her job in fashion no longer seemed important. Richard Johnson writes a gossip column called "Page Six" for *The New York Post.* Suddenly, he said, he could not seem to put it together; he wanted to be writing hard news.

Hard news. I realize that the word "hard" sounds, well, hard; but that is not what it means in this context. "Hard news" is the term used by journalists to distinguish articles about actual events from "soft" news about cultural trends, lifestyle issues, pop culture, and so forth. This distinction is useful for understanding the Christian gospel. The words for "hard news" in New Testament Greek are *evangel* and *kerygma,* meaning news, *good* news, proclamation, announcement. In this era of generic religiosity, Christianity stands out because it is based on actual events that happened in a specific, documented place at a specific, identifiable time. That's why we say "crucified under Pontius Pilate" in the Creed. The appearance of God's Messiah in human history is hard news; it is the real thing.

Here is a picture from Friday's *New York Times.* I am sure you have seen it in your local papers too. At the site of what used to be the World Trade Center, a piece of the destroyed steel structure has been raised over the wreckage. It is shaped like a perfectly symmetrical cross. The *Times* reporter wrote:

> The cross has become an inspiration to many workers and others at the site. Frank Silecchia [one of the ironworkers] found it the third day after the attack, as he was pulling bodies from the rubble and dust. He looked up at the light, saw the cross, and wept. "I was overwhelmed by it really," he said. Chris Ryan, of the Fire Department's Rescue 3, said, "It was pretty much miraculous. Without a doubt it is one of the few good things we have seen down here."[84]

Now we know that the sign of the cross can be used in demonic ways. Crosses have been burned in front of homes and churches by the Ku Klux Klan. Crosses have been forced upon Muslims in Bosnia as a sign of their defeat. The cross that was erected by a Catholic religious order near Auschwitz has deeply offended many Jews. We must take care, because the symbol of the Cross is not self-interpreting; it takes on meaning according to the meaning assigned to it in each concrete situation. But a cross raised above the desolation at Ground Zero speaks to us of the One who "suffered under Pontius Pilate, was crucified, dead, and buried." There is no other religious symbol so identified with an actual event, an event that has for two thousand years been proclaimed by Christians as the turning point of all the ages and the source of salvation for the whole world.

What does it mean to see the Cross rising out of the graveyard of four thousand unsuspecting, defenseless people? What does it mean to invoke the presence of a crucified man in the midst of so much pain? What does it mean to erect an instrument of torture and death over a scene of hatred and destruction?

Matthew, Mark, and Luke all report a parable that Jesus spoke to his disciples. It is not very well known, and sounds enigmatic; nevertheless it spoke to me as I was searching the Scriptures with "hunger for certainty, [that] precious commodity."

> [Jesus said,] If it is by the Spirit of God that I cast out demons, then the kingdom of God has come upon you. How can one enter a strong man's house and plunder his goods, unless he first binds the strong man? Then indeed he may plunder his house.

You and I have trouble understanding these words unless they are explained to us. In Jesus' time, though, his disciples would have known right away that the strong man is Satan, and the "house" of Satan is this world. Jesus calls Satan "the ruler of this world" (John 12:31). In Ephesians, he is called "the prince of the power of the air" who directs "the course of this world" and is at work in "the children of disobedience" (2:2). In the parable of the strong man, Jesus is saying that Satan is not going to give up his domain without a struggle. If he is not met with a force superior to his own, he will never yield. He is in possession of his kingdom until the one stronger than he renders him helpless and robs him of his goods.[85] That is exactly what Jesus is promising to do. He is already doing it as he goes about exorcising demons in his earthly ministry, but the decisive cosmic victory is not won until he is on the Cross. On the Cross, we read in Colossians, "God disarmed the principalities and powers, making a public spectacle of them, triumphing over them in [Christ]" (Colossians 2:14-15).

When we look at pictures of the planet Earth from space, it does not look like the house of Satan. It does not look like the domain of evil. It looks beautiful. When we see it in this way, we think of it as fragile and threatened only in an abstract sense because it seems small and vulnerable, a blue and white marble in deep space, looking as though it could at any moment be swallowed up by the surrounding blackness. What the Scripture teaches us, however, is that the world is fragile and threatened, not because of any threats from space but *because of the darkness of the human heart.* Ecclesiastes sums it up: "The hearts of men are full of evil, and madness is in their hearts while they live, and after that they go to the dead" (Ecclesiastes 9:3). The threat to our planet does not come from without, but from within.

I have a recording of a lovely Christmas carol by one of the great English boy choirs. It is called "See amid the winter's snow."[86] One of the verses has a phrase that came to mind on September 11. It says that Christ has laid aside his divine glory, that he "[has] come from highest bliss/ Down to such a world as this." That movement of our Lord from heaven to earth came to its earthly end in the Crucifixion. The Cross of Christ is the only symbol that matches the devastation at Ground Zero. Christ did not come for a holiday visit to a world of silver, blue, and white beauty. On the wings of a silver plane, out of the blue, came the black smoke and orange flames of hell. The photographs show it. Never was there a more crystalline blue day than September 11, but "the cloud-capp'd towers"[87] vanished into an inferno. *Such a world as this.*

September 29 was Michaelmas, the Feast of St. Michael the Archangel. He is the one, you know, who is commander of the Lord's army, the heavenly host. He is the one who serves under Christ's Lordship to bring an end to the rule of the great dragon

(Revelation 12:7-9). I have always loved this image of St. Michael defeating evil. I am too much the Protestant to pray to a saint, but on September 29 I found myself saying, "Michael, where were you? Where were you on September 11?"

And the answer seemed to come back, "I was there. I was there in the fire. I was there among the firefighters. I was there with those who laid down their lives."

Over and over, we have heard one particular story from the Trade towers. The versions vary slightly, but the basic theme is always the same. It is the story of those who were descending the stairs of the towers, leaving the buildings. As they were coming down, the firefighters were coming up. Over and over the same thing has been repeated: we were going down, escaping; they were going up, to their deaths. People cannot stop saying it. Garrison Keillor has written a song about it. This has been the single most powerful piece of testimony to come from the center of the cataclysm. Why is that? Because sacrifice for the sake of others is the most powerful thing there is.

Every day, *The New York Times* has a full page of pictures and profiles of the people who were killed. The page is called "Portraits of Grief." A lot of people are reading every word of this page every day. Let me read you just two of the notices. Here is a man named Zhe Zeng, a Chinese-American. When the first plane struck, he was safe on the street below. He could easily have stayed secure in his office at the nearby Bank of New York. But he did not. He was a certified emergency medical technician. He ran into his office for first aid supplies and then headed for the inferno. A video camera later that day caught sight of him, still wearing his business suit, ministering to someone on the street. He was not seen again.

Here is a second story. This man was named Giann Gamboa, a Hispanic American, the manager of the Top of the World Cafe in Tower Two. He was a devoted member of Iglesia Nueva Vida (the Church of the New Life) in Queens. "Friends are still talking about how he arranged for 70 children from the church to visit and pray atop the World Trade Center just a few months ago. 'He loved being a Christian and sharing his faith with people,' said Fernando

Montoya, his best friend. The last time anyone saw him, he was on the 78th floor about to squeeze into a crowded elevator . . . but he offered his spot to a young woman on his staff who was crying. . . . 'I'll just take the next one,' he told a friend, as the elevator doors shut."[88]

Our planes are preparing to bomb the Taliban. Our troops are going into Afghanistan. Even pacifistically inclined people like myself are solidly united behind our armed forces in this hour. But it is these little stories of people making the ultimate sacrifice, these hidden actions of individuals without glamour, without heroics, just ordinary people, that will be remembered in the Kingdom of God. Without doubt, there were many other stories that will not be told in this life because they were buried in the collapse of the towers; but the Lord knows each one, and speaks his word: "Well done, thou good and faithful servant" (Matthew 25:21). "Blessed are the dead which die in the Lord, saith the Spirit. . . . Their works do follow them" (Revelation 14:13).

I find myself thinking constantly, since 9/11, about Dietrich Bonhoeffer. In the spring of 1939, he was safe in America, but despite the entreaties of his American friends, he chose to return to Germany, to the belly of the Beast. What interests me these days is the way that this man of peace, this exceptionally gentle, non-violent Lutheran pastor with no military background, came to the decision not only to return to Germany but also to join a conspiracy to assassinate Hitler. He decided that he as a Christian should not expect someone else to do for him what he could not or would not do for himself. He did not want to be like the governors of states who sign off on the death penalty but expect someone else to do the executing for them. Dietrich Bonhoeffer was not going to do that. If the job had to be done, he was not going to stay clean by remaining apart from the consequences. You know the rest of the story: the assassination attempt failed, he and his co-conspirators were arrested, and he was hanged by the Nazis four days before the Liberation. Now he is in the gallery of twentieth-century Christian martyrs at Westminster Abbey, along with others who died for Christ's sake: Martin Luther King Jr., Bishop Romero of El Salvador, Anglican

Archbishop Janani Luwum of Uganda.[89] They took up the cross of Christ. Where was God when they died? God was present in their cross-shaped actions.

Bit by bit, the full story of United Airlines Flight 93 is being pieced together. I was fortunate to see the full-length interview that Jane Pauley did with Lisa Beamer. Only the complete interview can give the full picture of the valor and faith of the young Christian knight, Todd Beamer, and his amazing wife. His was the plane that crashed in western Pennsylvania, killing all on board. Lisa and Todd met when they were both students at one of the top Christian colleges, Wheaton in Illinois. This deeply committed young Christian couple married and produced two sons. Every morning, Todd delighted his little boys with the greeting, "Let's roll, guys!" Todd is the one who spoke to the telephone operator from Flight 93, because his credit card did not work when he tried to reach Lisa. He asked the operator to say the Lord's Prayer with him, and he spoke of his faith in Jesus. Then he let the telephone drop and the operator heard him issue the final order to the men on board Flight 93, "Are you ready, guys? Let's roll!" In this way, a target in Washington, most likely the White House or the Capitol, was delivered from destruction. Lisa, pregnant with their third child, is convinced that the Lord was acting through Todd and the other passengers that day. He was with them in the flame.

This heroic story has thrilled and inspired the whole nation. It will be told for many years to come.[90] But there are other stories as well. There are stories of tiny, anonymous actions: warm cookies brought to the workers, church pews offered for firemen to sleep, Christians escorting Muslims to the supermarket so they won't be harassed. Each of these works of mercy is a sign of the Cross raised over the ruins. Never think that there is nothing you can do. Right here in your own community you are enabled to act as a congregation that knows it is not living in limbo. We *do* know where we are. "All my hope on God is founded," you just sang. We do not look for a future only a fool can predict, because "Christ has died, Christ is risen, Christ will come again." Cross-shaped acts of Christian courage, no matter how small, testify to the coming Day of the Lord's ultimate triumph over evil. A moving story appeared in the paper the other day, telling of the death of a young mother from breast cancer. She had fought the disease for four years. Her husband testified: "To me, she was as much a hero as the police officers and firefighters that are heroes now to everyone else. I consider her one of the most courageous people I have ever known."[91] That was the unconquerable gift she gave to him and to their children.

I'm sure you noticed that the hymn we sang contains these lines: "tower and temple fall to dust. But God's power, hour by hour, is my temple and my tower."[92] Our "hunger for certainty, the precious commodity," is found not in the towers and temples of worldly power, not even in the great cathedrals that cannot last for ever, but in the place we would have least expected it, in a sign of pain and contradiction, a symbol of torture and death — which against all merely human possibility has become also our token of Christ's victory over the strong man. The Stronger Man (Mark 1:7) is here. He became subject to human sin, cosmic evil, and ghastly death — and in so doing wrested Satan's goods away from him. Our Savior has plundered the house of the ruler of this world, but he did not do it from a safe distance. He came "down to such a world as this." He did not run away from the fire. He entered into it. Remember the words of the firefighter about the steel-beam cross? "Without a doubt it is one of the few good things we have seen down here." Note the phrase "down here" — down here where the fires of hell have tried their best to extinguish the good. But they cannot. The Stronger Man has already gotten "down here," with us. In his Resurrection he has overcome evil. We do not know what the future will hold, but we know who holds the future: "I am the Alpha and the Omega, the beginning and the end, who is and who was and who is to come" (Revelation 1:8; 22:13). This is the hard news. This is the gospel.

And so I close by addressing you once again: Fellow sinners; fellow saints; fellow servants of our Lord Jesus Christ: we are not afraid of anything the devil can do. The future belongs to those who share in the victorious sacrifice of Jesus Christ.

AMEN.

PART FIVE

The Day of Resurrection: Easter Day

Brute beauty and valour and act, oh, air, pride, plume, here
  Buckle! AND *the fire that breaks from thee then, a billion*
Times told lovelier, more dangerous, O my chevalier!

GERARD MANLEY HOPKINS,
"THE WINDHOVER: TO CHRIST OUR LORD"

Midnight in the Kingdom of Death

———— ✗✗✗ ————

Text: John 20:1-10

Up in Stockbridge, Massachusetts, on top of beautiful Eden Hill, a Polish Catholic monastic order has its home. On the hilltop there is a small cemetery set within a grove of tall evergreen trees. Here the fathers and brothers are buried when they die. The tombstones are white crosses, all alike, with no indication of who was superior over whom — all equal in death. There is one very large cross, however, that towers over the others. It is not a grave marker; it is the centerpiece of the whole. On it there is carved a Biblical text, in Latin: *Qui credit in me, etiam si mortuus ferit, vivet.* This verse from John's Gospel (11:25) is from the story of the raising of Lazarus from the dead. In that story, Martha accosts Jesus on the way to the tomb and more or less accuses him of allowing Lazarus to die. The Lord challenges her with these words: "I am the Resurrection and the life; *whoever believes in me, though he die, yet shall he live,* and whoever lives and believes in me shall never die. Do you believe this?"

Do you believe this? Is any of this true? What were we doing out in the cemetery just now? What do you think people driving by might think we were doing in the graveyard in the dark? Was that

---

(Note to the reader: This sermon was preached in the dark of the Easter Vigil, before the sunrise of Easter morning. The service began in the church graveyard and then continued inside the church building.)

some kind of spooky clandestine ritual like the voodoo scene in *Midnight in the Garden of Good and Evil?* How is the Easter Vigil any different from that?

The symbolism of night and darkness pervades the Gospel of John. At the very beginning we hear the proclamation that the light of the Incarnate Word of God comes to shine in the darkness (1:5). Nicodemus came to Jesus by night so that no one would see him; Jesus issues a warning that "men loved darkness rather than light, because their deeds were evil" (3:19). Repeatedly in this Gospel, Jesus teaches that he brings light to the world; without him, it is night (3:20-21; 9:4-5; 11:9-10; 12:25-26, 46). We read that "Jesus spoke to them, saying, 'I am the light of the world; he who follows me will not walk in darkness, but will have the light of life'" (8:12). Most portentously, the master dramatist John tells us in his account of our Lord's last evening on earth that he was "troubled in spirit," saying, "One of you will betray me." He dips a morsel of bread into the wine and gives it to Judas. After the morsel, we are told, "Satan entered into Judas . . . he immediately went out; *and it was night*" (13:21-30).

It was night. This is the night in which Sin and Death reign. In the words of Jesus from Luke's Gospel, "This is your hour, and the power of darkness" (Luke 22:53). The service on Maundy Thursday dramatized it for us; the altar was stripped, the candles were extinguished, the lights were put out. The liturgy is designed to show that as Jesus dies, every human hope is obliterated. The realm of darkness appears to be victorious. There is nothing left of the Messiah but the grave. And so we read that Joseph of Arimathea came to Pilate to ask permission to take down the body from the Cross. Nicodemus also, we are told, "who had at first come to [Jesus] by night," brought spices for anointing, which were traditionally used in an admittedly vain effort to fend off corruption. They bound the body tightly with the spices wrapped in linen bands, "as is the burial custom of the Jews," and placed it in Joseph's own new tomb (19:38-42). This would have been late Friday afternoon. There the corpse lay all during the night and all day during the Sabbath, the day in which all work, including the visiting of tombs, was forbidden. This is an echo of Jesus' own words in the ninth chapter: "As long as I am in the world, I am the light of the world. Night comes, when no one can work" (9:4-5).

Jesus has entered the realm of Death. The mythology of the Greeks and Romans is by no means wrong here; the dead must cross over the black waters of the river Styx into the kingdom of darkness from which no one can ever return.[1] The Son of God, by his own permission, has been given over to the realm of night. This is where he has gone. We say in the Creed, "He descended into hell." Death rules there. Satan rules there.[2] The corpse lies there twenty-four hours, thirty hours, thirty-four hours. It is night.

Have you buried someone? If you haven't, you will. You will come to know the cold clasp of death. You will know it in the literal sense, when someone who means the world to you is gone, when you yourself must stare it in the face. You will come to know it in a hundred other ways, as the death of a friendship, the death of a career, the loss of youth, the loss of health, the death of happiness, the death of dreams. It will seem to you like the tomb of hope. This, in part, is what John's Gospel means by *night*.

The Gospel of John, chapter 20, verse 1: "On the first day of the week Mary Magdalene came to the tomb early, while it was still dark."

While it was still dark. In the middle of the night. This is the night of the end of human hope.

Why does Mary come? Why do any of us go to cemeteries? Regardless of the burial customs, the symbolism is the same. Whether you throw the ashes into the ocean or bury them in a garden, the reign of Death is stark, merciless, irrevocable. I have a dear friend whose daughter died tragically. The rest of the family were determined to scatter the ashes on the beach. He was heartbroken about this. He begged and begged until they finally agreed to let him have a small portion of the ashes to bury in the family plot. He told me that he was grateful to have something of her left where, as he put it, "I can go to be with her." These little comforts are the best that we can do to cope with our grief and loss — walking on a beach, sitting by a grave. These are the few shreds of solace that we are able to snatch from the jaws of Death before we, too, disappear. In the famous line from Samuel Beckett's play, *Waiting for Godot:* "[Human beings] give birth astride of a grave, the light gleams an instant, then it's night once more."

Mary Magdalene came to the tomb early, while it was still dark. Why do we go to graveyards? My friend, the bereaved father, goes to lay flowers, to remember, to seek some connection, some comfort. Some visit cemeteries to read the inscriptions and try to imagine the lives of those buried there. Thrill-seeking young people, who by definition think they are immortal, go to cemeteries at night for the shivers and chills of defying specters and ghosts. When I go to the cemetery in Stockbridge, as I often do, I go to read the words of Jesus on the tombstone. Absolutely no one goes to visit a grave because they expect some one to rise out of it. The very thought would make even the teenagers' hair stand on end.

Why did Mary go to the tomb in the middle of the night? We are not told, but one thing is for sure: she was not expecting the Resurrection. All over the Mediterranean there were dying and rising gods, but none of them were actual historical figures, let alone "crucified under Pontius Pilate." Dying and rising gods were a dime a dozen; they came and went every year with the cycle of plant life. No one, absolutely no one, expected to see such a thing happen to a real person. That is why, when the Magdalene came to the tomb in the dark and saw that the stone had been removed, she ran to Peter and the others with the news that Jesus' body had been stolen. What other explanation could there be for an empty tomb?

And so the men run to see for themselves. They are running to see if the body has been stolen.[3] Then what happens? Let John tell us:

> The other [younger] disciple outran Peter and reached the tomb first; and stooping to look in, he saw the linen cloths lying there, but he did not go in. Then Simon Peter came, following him, and went into the tomb; he saw the linen cloths lying, and the napkin, which had been on his head, not lying with the linen cloths but rolled up in a place by itself. Then the other disciple, who

**Matthias Grünewald: The Resurrection
(a panel from the Isenheim Altar)**

This spectacular painting presents the greatest possible contrast to the Cruci-fixion scene shown earlier. Christ explodes out of the tomb in the middle of the night, accompanied by blinding golden light that seems to emanate from his own radiant transfigured countenance. His drapery billows and soars around him with the force of his emergence. The soldiers are knocked back, rendered helpless. The skin of the risen Christ seems to glow from within; a more extraordinary contrast to the tortured, riven, putrid flesh of Grünewald's crucified Jesus could scarcely be imagined.

reached the tomb first, also went in, and he saw and believed; for as yet they did not know the scripture, that he must rise from the dead. (John 20:3-9)

Remember this: the evangelist wants us to know that the Resurrection was truly inconceivable. The two disciples did not know what had happened until they got there. It was the sight of the cloths that revealed to them what was otherwise unthinkable. No grave robber would stop to unwrap the winding sheet. Jesus' body had simply passed through them.[4]

The Resurrection happened *at night.* No one was there when it happened. When the women and the disciples arrived, he was gone. He arose from the kingdom of Death and carried away its spoils. The rising sun revealed the victory already accomplished.

And so the risen, living, reigning Christ says to us tonight as he said to Martha, "I am the Resurrection and the life; whoever believes in me, though he die, yet shall he live, and whoever lives and believes in me shall never die. Do you believe this?"[5]

Let our answer be hers: "Yes, Lord; I believe that you are the Christ, the Son of God" — and in believing, receive the gift of eternal light and life in his name (John 20:30-31).

Alleluia! Christ is risen!
The Lord is risen indeed! Alleluia! Alleluia!

Face to Face, Hand in Hand

⸎

*The first man {Adam} was from the earth, a man of dust; the
second man {Christ} is from heaven. . . . Just as we have borne
the image of the man of dust, we shall also bear the image of the
man of heaven.*

(1 CORINTHIANS 15:47, 49)

The Archbishop of Canterbury was quoted recently on the subject of e-mail and the Internet. He acknowledged the power
and usefulness of the Net, but observed that a lot of people thought
they were having real relationships by e-mail when in fact there can
be no real relationships without face-to-face contact. I know two
couples who met on the Internet, and they have given me permission to say that that is the absolute truth!

"I believe in the resurrection of the *body.*" That's what we say
when we recite the Apostles' Creed. The Apostles' Creed is what we
say at Morning and Evening Prayer. Many of us have been saying
"resurrection of the dead" in the Nicene Creed for so long that we
have forgotten the phrase "resurrection of the body." "Resurrection
of the dead" is itself a unique affirmation, but it doesn't make the
point as explicitly as "resurrection of the body." St. Paul's letter to
the church in Corinth addresses this issue head-on. In his famous
chapter on love, he speaks of the future day when we will know the

Lord and one another, not "through a glass, darkly" ("in a mirror dimly" — RSV) but "face to face." He goes on, "Now I know in part; but then I shall know even as also I am known" (1 Corinthians 13:12).

The Corinthian congregation that Paul had founded and nurtured was turning away from the revolutionary Christian proclamation of the resurrection of the body. They were returning to the much more familiar religious idea of the immortality of the soul. In fact, the Corinthians thought that they had already gained immortality. They had a "spiritualized" idea of the resurrection that bypasses the body. Paul writes to them, explaining that if they are going to go that way, they are going to be giving up the foundation of the Christian faith: "How can some of you say that there is no resurrection of the dead? . . . if there is no resurrection of the dead, then Christ has not been raised; [and] if Christ has not been raised, . . . your faith is futile and you are still in your sins" (1 Corinthians 15:13-17).

Immortality of the soul was such a commonplace belief in the Hellenistic world of Jesus and the apostles that, even though it was not a Jewish idea, no one would have been surprised to hear it. Similarly, we today hear people talk of rebirth, life after death, personal immortality, reincarnation, and all kinds of other generic religious beliefs almost as a matter of course. Only Christianity speaks of the resurrection of the body. Suppose for a moment that the angel in Mark's story had stood outside the still-closed tomb and said to the women, "The spirit of your Master lives on," or "The immortal soul of Jesus has gone into heaven." Maybe this would have comforted the women. Maybe it would have encouraged them to pick up their lives, warmed them with a religious glow and a sense of possibility. Maybe. In view of what they had witnessed at Golgotha, I doubt it. In any case, this is *not at all* what Mark describes. His Gospel ends like this:

> Entering the tomb [for the stone had been removed], they saw a young man sitting on the right side, dressed in a white robe; and they were amazed. And he said to them, "Do not be amazed; you

seek Jesus of Nazareth, who was crucified. He has risen, he is not here; see the place where they laid him." . . . And they went out and fled from the tomb; for trembling and astonishment had come upon them; and they said nothing to any one, for they were afraid. (Mark 16:5-8)

This is a very peculiar way to end a Gospel. Some additional verses were added later, but most interpreters now believe that Mark meant to conclude this way.[6] The news of the Resurrection caused the women to run headlong from the scene. Maybe this image would convey the message better than the usual one of the women kneeling reverently and peacefully, bathed in the rays of sunrise. Maybe the best Easter card would show the women hurtling pell-mell out of the empty tomb, terrified. Indeed, I found a card this year that conveyed something of this. The painting on the card was done by a Guatemalan artist in a primitive style. It showed the women reacting to the angel's message in vivid action. The hair of one is standing straight up as though she had received an electric shock. Another was throwing her pottery jar into the air as though it had suddenly become radioactive. Yet another was shown with her legs and arms splayed out as if she were leaping like a Cossack dancer. The Gospel of Matthew also conveys something of this sense that something truly staggering has taken place: "And behold, there was a great earthquake; for an angel of the Lord descended from heaven and came and rolled back the stone, and sat upon it. His appearance was like lightning, and his raiment white as snow. And for fear of him the guards trembled and became like dead men" (Matthew 28:2-4). This is not a story about the immortality of the soul.

The tomb was empty; the body was gone. All four Gospels report this.[7] Yet in a certain sense, the Easter Day sermon is the most difficult of the year because it is impossible to talk directly about the Resurrection. It is often noted that the various accounts in the Gospels do not agree. Most of us who are believers think that these discrepancies simply reflect the ineffable nature of the Resurrection, an event so transcendent as to belong to another order of meaning altogether. Yet in spite of the differences about the numbers and names of angels and witnesses, all evangelists agree that the tomb was empty. The body was nowhere to be found. Only the grave clothes were left behind. "And the disciple saw, and believed."[8]

All of the Gospel accounts of the Resurrection convey a sense of something completely unlooked-for that has happened, something altogether without precedent, something that stuns and astonishes with its inexplicable power. Yet this event is revealed — in various stages — as being the Resurrection of Jesus to a *bodily existence.* To be sure, it is a *different* body, which passes through doors, isn't always recognized, and appears only to a chosen few; yet it is a *real* body that eats fish (Luke 24:42-43), cooks breakfast (John 21:12), and bears the marks of the nail wounds (John 20:27). The risen Lord was not a disembodied spirit, but a real body with whom the disciples had a continuing face-to-face relationship, as in his dialogue with Peter: "Jesus said to him, 'Simon [Peter], son of John, do you love me?' [Peter] said to him, 'Yes, Lord; you know that I love you.' [Jesus] said to him, 'Tend my sheep'" (John 21:15-16). This exchange, repeated three times, corresponds to the three times that Peter denied the Lord before his Crucifixion. This kind of intimate human encounter, with all that it conveys of forgiveness, repentance, and restitution, cannot take place without bodily presence.[9]

Paul writes quite sharply to the Corinthian church: "If the dead are not raised, then Christ has not been raised." If immortality is what we are talking about, then everything we apostles have told you about what happened to Jesus Christ is a lie: "If Christ has not been raised, then our preaching is in vain," Paul says. Furthermore, if you want to just go back to some kind of general belief in a soul that lives on after death, all the benefits of Christ's Cross are lost to you: "If Christ has not been raised, your faith is futile and you are still in your sins." Not only that, Paul continues, you need to know that if Christ has not been raised, your eternal future is at stake also. If there is no Resurrection, then "those who have fallen asleep in Christ have perished." Thus in various ways Paul seeks to remind the Corinthians that the Resurrection is a completely new happening in the world: the single, definitive, and unique action of God to vindicate and enthrone the crucified Messiah.[10]

St. Paul is no fool. He always anticipates objections. He goes on (v. 35): "But some one will ask, 'How are the dead raised? With what kind of body do they come?'" And Paul's answer is, basically, "That's a stupid question." He's annoyed that the Corinthians are so literal-minded. He wants them to understand that the Resurrection body, though it is recognizably the same person, is of another order of reality altogether: "You foolish man! What you sow does not come to life unless it dies. And what you sow is not the body which is to be. . . . God gives it a body as he has chosen." At this point Paul finds himself in a difficulty, and he is not altogether successful in getting himself out of it. He is trying to explain how the Resurrection body is different from an earthly body, so he starts talking about seeds and plants, birds and fish, stars and suns. The preacher is sympathetic to Paul's predicament here. It is always tempting at Easter to talk about how the ugly brown bulb is transformed into a gorgeous, colorful tulip or daffodil. The analogy doesn't really work, however, because flowers come up every spring and we expect them to, whereas the Resurrection was totally unexpected and explosively new. Paul, as he dictates, seems to sense that these illustrations from the natural world are not working so he abandons them and goes on to a much more arresting set of Biblical images.

> The first man [Adam] was from the earth, a man of dust; the second man [Christ] is from heaven. . . . Just as we have borne the image of the man of dust, we shall also bear the image of the man of heaven.

Here Paul has more success as he begins to show how Christ is from another world order altogether. Together with us, Christ has borne the image of "the man of dust"; indeed he has borne it to its bitter and shameful end at Golgotha; but because he is "the man of heaven," his death and Resurrection are the evidence planted within human history that God has broken through from beyond human history, from beyond human imagining, from beyond human capacity. That is what Paul means when he says crisply, "I tell you this, brethren: flesh and blood cannot inherit the kingdom of God, nor does the perishable inherit the imperishable." The Gospel of John says the same thing in a different way: "To all who received him, who believed in his name, he gave power to become children of God . . . born, not of blood nor of the will of the flesh nor of the will of human beings, but of God" (John 1:12-13).

Just as the Crucifixion has always been problematic, so too has the doctrine of the Resurrection of the body. We don't seem to want to believe in resurrected bodies. We want to be "spiritual." But bodies are important. When Yitzhak Rabin was assassinated, the whole world was touched by the grief of his young granddaughter who wept that she would never feel his warm hands again.[11] I'm sure that you remember the famous photograph taken at the scene of the Oklahoma City bombing — the big husky fireman cradling the tiny dead toddler. The impact of the picture, reproduced around the globe, came from the sight of the bloodied little limp body cradled in the huge hands of the fireman with the compassionate face. Bodies matter.[12] Faces matter. We want to hold a warm hand, we want to see a beloved smile. I remember when I was young in Virginia and a wise older person said, "Virginians think they love Robert E. Lee. They don't love Robert E. Lee; they love their *image* of Robert E. Lee. In order to love someone, you have to have them right there."

Jesus is right here. He is right here in a way that no one else has ever been. Even now there is a real sense in which you can, as the song says, "put your hand in the hand of the man from Galilee." It is very difficult to describe how this can be, but just as the beloved disciple grasped by faith that Jesus' body had passed through the grave clothes, so also we today may grasp by faith that he is risen and alive. Let us return to Paul's words:

> If Christ has not been raised, your faith is futile and you are still in your sins. Then those also who have fallen asleep in Christ have perished. If for this life only we have hoped in Christ, we are of all men most to be pitied.

But in fact Christ has been raised from the dead, the first fruits of those who have fallen asleep. For as by a man came death, by a man has come also the resurrection of the dead. For as in Adam all die, so also in Christ shall all be made alive.

Can you imagine anything more wonderful than this? On the contrary, we can scarcely begin to imagine it, for it does not come from human imagination but from God. All our sins wiped away, all evil done to death forever, the devil and his hosts destroyed, our loved ones restored to us, all the injustices and wrongs of human history made right in a new heaven and a new earth.

These things are neither humanly possible nor religiously possible. *Flesh and blood cannot inherit the kingdom of God.* But as Jesus himself said, "All things are possible with God" (Mark 10:27). Paul continues his letter in a sort of rapture:

Behold! I tell you a mystery. We shall not all sleep, but we shall all be changed, in a moment, in the twinkling of an eye, at the last trumpet. For the trumpet will sound, and the dead will be raised imperishable, and we shall be changed.

Changed! our sinfulness exchanged for his righteousness, our mortality for his immortality, our sorrow for his joy, our bondage for his freedom, and our deteriorating human body for an altogether transformed one that will nevertheless be our very own and no one else's, a body with which to love others and be loved in return with all the love of Christ himself. "So when this corruptible shall have put on incorruption, and this mortal shall have put on immortality, then shall be brought to pass the saying that is written, 'Death is swallowed up in victory'" (1 Corinthians 15:54).

AMEN.

PART SIX

Easter Week

〜⊗⊗⊗〜

*Even the womb is a body of death if there be no deliverer . . . yet
he hath the keys of death {Revelation 1:18}, and he can let me
out at that door. . . . Though from the womb to the grave, and in
the grave itself, we pass from death to death, yet as Daniel
speaks, "The Lord our God is able to deliver us, and he will deliver us" {Daniel 3:17}.*

JOHN DONNE

Note *about the Easter Week sermons*

⸺⸙⸺

The week immediately following Easter Day is the most thrilling of the year, so it seems a pity for it to be neglected because of the emphasis given to Lent. The setting for two of these sermons (dated 1997) was a simple but festal service at 5:30 each weekday evening during Easter Week at St. John's Episcopal Church in Salisbury, Connecticut. These were not Eucharists, but preaching services with prayers; the dominant note was celebration and joy. The church remained richly decorated with Easter lilies and spring flowers. In addition, the organist, Natasha Ulyanovsky, treated us to some of the most brilliant festival pieces in the repertoire.

I have preserved this arrangement for this book as an offering. Such services as these during Easter Week are not customary, but no special effort was required from anyone except the organist and the preacher. The organist was happy to show off a number of exciting organ works, and I postponed my Easter vacation to the following week.

The sequence is not quite as originally delivered; one service had to be cancelled on account of a snowstorm (!) and two others were too site-specific to include here. Three other Easter Week sermons from different times and places have therefore been substituted to fill out the five days, Monday through Friday.

Like the sermons for Monday, Tuesday, and Wednesday of Holy Week, these were delivered to smaller congregations largely made up of the inner core of the faithful. When one knows one's congregation, one can probe more deeply into difficult subjects — like death, without which, after all, there can be no Resurrection.

Beyond Possibility

———— ✺ ————

With God, all things are possible.

(MARK 10:27)

There was a violent earthquake, for an angel of the Lord came down from heaven. Going to the tomb, he rolled back the stone and sat upon it. His appearance was like lightning, and his clothing was white as snow. The guards were so afraid of him that they shook and became like dead men. The angel said to the women, "Do not be afraid, for I know that you are looking for Jesus, who was crucified. He is not here; he is risen. . . ."

(MATTHEW 28:2-6)

The Easter greeting that we have just exchanged is very ancient. It goes back to the first centuries of the Christian church. As I'm sure you know, the Greek Orthodox people, to this day, say *Christos anesti! Alethos anesti!* ("Christ is risen! He is risen indeed!") to each other during Easter Week. What a wonderful custom.

Well, we have said it. Now let me ask you a question. Do you believe what you have said?

A great many churchgoers have gotten the idea that you can't believe in the Resurrection if you want to be a sophisticated person.

In the midst of all the articles about the mass suicide of cult members in Rancho Santa Fe, there have been many sneering comments about religion.[1] One writer said that religion led to bizarre cultic behavior because it thrived on "repression, exclusion, and control." These messages, heard over and over, have their effect. The cumulative result is to make Christians feel sheepish about their faith. St. Paul was not immune to this effect in his own time; that's why he wrote to the Roman Christians, "I am not ashamed of the gospel" (Romans 1:16).

It is a feature of our time that preachers in the mainline churches, if not ashamed exactly, are embarrassed to say anything straightforward about the Resurrection. I went to hear a sermon preached in an Ivy League chapel by a Ph.D. student whom I knew to be a believer. You wouldn't have known it from his sermon. I asked him afterward why he had been so timid, and he murmured something about the congregation being "very skeptical and urbane." Well, indeed: the "uneducated, common men" (Acts 4:13) who became apostles after the Resurrection might have been similarly intimidated. If they had, however, you and I would never have heard the name of Jesus Christ.[2]

I have heard and read many Easter sermons in my day and I have a lot of them in my files. Here are some actual quotes:

"On Easter Day, the world takes a turn for the better."

"The Resurrection is the divine inspiration for us, giving us the strength and courage to emulate Jesus."

"Peter is a symbol of human weakness; his discovery of acceptance and forgiveness is personified in the idea of the risen Jesus."

"In their table fellowship after the Crucifixion, the heartbroken disciples gradually came to sense that Jesus was still with them."

"The early Christians came to believe that love is stronger than death."

Piero della Francesca: The Resurrection

This surpassing masterpiece was called "the greatest painting in the world" by Aldous Huxley. The characteristically sculptural quality of Piero's human figures is displayed here to full effect. His signature skill in rendering volume and mass is shown in the single figure of Christ as he issues forth from the tomb, a massive physical reality occupying real space. In contrast, however, the face of the risen Lord conveys something transcendent, as though, having passed through unspeakable ordeals, he now belongs to another order of existence — as indeed he does. (On the left, nature is barren and wintry; on the right, trees burst into leaf. The sleeping soldiers suggest uncomprehending humanity, unaware of the gift of eternal life.)

"The disciples came to believe that Jesus lives forever in the faith of those who trust his message."

Over and over in these sermons, the same words appear: the disciples "came to believe" something about Jesus. In other words, the impulse for belief arose out of themselves. The New Testament says something quite different. The words of the angel announce something completely foreign to human possibility: "He is not here. He is risen." On the road to Emmaus, the two disciples did not recognize Jesus until "their eyes *were opened.*" The syntax clearly indicates that their recognition of the risen Christ was initiated by God. Think about this: in the quotations from the sermons I just read, God is not the acting subject of any of the sentences. A large number of Easter sermons today seem timid because the speakers do not seem confident that God can, or that God did, do anything outside of human capacity.

In one sermon that I heard myself, the preacher said that Easter is about "the enduring symbols of ultimate truth." But you could hear that message anywhere; it is no different from any number of sayings having only the most tenuous connection, or no connection, to the Christian faith. It does not seem likely to me that anything so abstract as an enduring symbol of ultimate truth could have galvanized, virtually overnight, a tiny band of scruffy fishermen and other assorted nonentities, all of them completely discredited in the eyes of the world because they were disciples of a man who had been gruesomely and publicly executed by the highest authorities of church and state. Do you think that commonly held but nature-bound ideas about life after death could have been the motivating force that took hold of those men and women and transformed them into an unstoppable force that within a few years was setting the whole Mediterranean world ablaze?[3]

A world-famous figure of our own day, a woman nurtured in the church, was widely quoted at the time of her husband's death; she said, "All the world's religions teach that there is some sort of life after death. I cling to that hope."[4]

Many people are comforted by thoughts such as this. Apparently it was enough for her. Maybe it is enough for you. I confess that it is not enough for me. More important, such reflections fall far short of the New Testament message. In my ministry I have learned to recognize the look, the feel, and the smell of death. I have been present with people at the time of death many times and I have never become immune to the change that comes over the body. The New Testament refers to death as an enemy (1 Corinthians 15:26). Even in the case of what we call a merciful death, there is still a horrible indignity, a fearsome intrusiveness about death that causes us to feel its presence as a hostile, invading Power that robs the human being of everything it was ever meant to be. I keep thinking about an inconsolably bereaved husband I knew, a prominent and vigorous man in his early sixties who was looking forward to a happy twenty-year retirement in a new house he and his wife had just built. A hit-and-run driver has robbed him of his companion. Death has destroyed their hopes. He is one who can testify that nothing can ever replace a uniquely loved person. Nebulous messages about some sort of religious hope for an afterlife simply do not have the power to stare down the stark ugliness of death. Such messages sound too much like wishful thinking to me. We cannot seriously imagine that, after watching their Master pinned up to die like an insect, an object of utmost contempt and public disgust, the disciples would suddenly be transformed by being reminded that there was always a hope for some sort of life after death.

We owe it to those first Christian disciples to do our very best to understand the utter hopelessness of their situation after the Crucifixion. They had invested their whole lives in what appeared to be a diabolical joke. They had seen their beloved Master scourged almost to death, dragged through the streets, nailed to a cross and abandoned to suffer public agony in the face of the obscene mockery of everybody in Jerusalem. Once they had basked in the reflected status of a celebrity who had been mobbed by large crowds; now he had been judged a nonperson, fit only for the most degrading and sadistic death that the human mind was capable of devising. If there had been any solidarity among his followers, it had vanished; not one person had dared to come forward in the Master's defense, and their supposed leader, Peter, had cravenly denied Jesus three times. There was nothing left. It is preposterous to think of them pulling themselves together with the sorts of thoughts available to them from the mystery religions surrounding them. Frankly, their Jewish faith, based in the utterly realistic and unromantic Hebrew scriptures, would not have allowed any such vague and generic hopes. The Messiah was supposed to usher in the kingdom of God; for those disciples who had staked their lives on Jesus being that Messiah, it cannot be stated too strongly: *there was no hope.*

Everyone who has studied the New Testament agrees that something happened to change the situation. Even the skeptics who seem determined to demystify the Resurrection into something bland and predictable will agree that *something happened.*

But what was it? If it wasn't an experience of personal forgiveness or renewed hopefulness or positive thinking, *what was it?*

Imagine that you are one of the women going to the tomb in the early hours of the morning. We do have a way of going to visit graves, don't we? But why do we go? Isn't it because we want to try to hold on to some kind of shred of closeness to the dead person? There were flowers here in our local cemetery on Easter Day; this is a way we have of saying we haven't forgotten, we miss you, we love you, we wish you had not gone away. We most definitely do *not* visit a grave because we expect to see somebody rise out of it.

The women were not going to Jesus' grave with any sort of expectation whatsoever. The New Testament is quite clear about that. They set out for the tomb because they felt a longing to have some sort of contact with what was left of their dead Master. They were hoping for no miracle. Dead people don't come back. In fact, so little did they expect a miracle that the sole subject of discussion was who was going to roll away the stone. If they didn't think that the power of God could roll away the stone, they most assuredly did not think the power of God would raise Jesus from the grave.

St. Matthew explains that the tomb of Jesus had been sealed by an express order of Pontius Pilate, and that a guard of Roman soldiers had been posted. At dawn on the first day of the week, the women came to the tomb. As they approached, St. Matthew tells us,

There was a violent earthquake, for an angel of the Lord came down from heaven. Going to the tomb, he rolled back the stone and sat upon it. His appearance was like lightning, and his clothing was white as snow. The guards were so afraid of him that they shook and became like dead men. The angel said to the women, "Do not be afraid, for I know that you are looking for Jesus, who was crucified. He is not here; he is risen. . . ."

If that doesn't make your hair stand on end, I have not read it right. Matthew means for it to strike us with utter, dumbfounded, stupefied awe. Perhaps this retelling gives you at least some sense of the unprecedented, unlooked-for, unimaginable nature of the event. Note the action of the angel. Why does he roll away the stone? To let Jesus out? No indeed; Jesus is already gone. Why does the angel roll away the stone then? He does it to let the women look in, to see that the tomb is empty. Jesus was raised out of death into life during the night, before the women got there.

I can feel the goosebumps on the back of my neck as I say this. Yes, I know all the objections: I know that the Gospel accounts seem to contradict each other; I know that the Roman soldiers never wrote up a report; I know that medical science scoffs at this; I know that none of it can be proved; I know it isn't possible as we understand possibility. But I also know that this is a message that would explain everything that happened afterward. *He is not here; he is risen.* That, truly, is a piece of news to shake the foundations of the Roman Empire and the stronghold of death itself.

"Go quickly," said the angel to the women in Matthew's account, "Go quickly and tell his disciples, 'He has risen from the dead and is going ahead of you into Galilee. There you will see him.'" What other message on earth or in heaven could reverse the effect of a crucifixion? I do not believe that there is any news ever uttered by human tongue equal to the announcement that the citadel of Death had been stormed by the only Power capable of bearing away its standard.

The battle imagery is right. The New Testament is pervaded by battle imagery. In the words of the well-loved Easter hymn: "The strife is o'er, the battle done; the victory of life is won. . . . The powers of death have done their worst; but Christ their legions hath dispersed." Can there be anyone who has not thrilled to a victory parade? Well, this is the greatest triumphal parade of all time; Jesus has beaten down death, routed the hosts of Satan, and driven the enemy into full flight. As we read in Colossians: "He [God the Father] disarmed the principalities and powers and made a public spectacle of them, triumphing over them in him [Jesus]" (Colossians 2:15). This is no time for wishy-washy sentiments about springtime in the heart; this is a time for fanfares and drum rolls and choruses from the book of Revelation:[5]

> Hallelujah! For the Lord our God the Almighty reigns. (19:6)

> The kingdom of this world has become the kingdom of our Lord and of his Christ, and he shall reign for ever and ever. (11:15)

> We give thanks to thee, Lord God Almighty, who art and who wast, that thou hast taken thy great power and begun to reign. (11:17)

> The salvation and the power and the kingdom of our God and the authority of his Christ have come, for the accuser of our brethren has been thrown down. . . . Rejoice then, O heaven and you that dwell therein! (12:10, 12)

> I saw heaven opened, and behold, a white horse! He who sat upon it is called Faithful and True, and in righteousness he judges and makes war. His eyes are like a flame of fire, and on his head are many diadems; and he has a name inscribed which no one knows but himself . . . and the name by which he is called is The Word of God. And the armies of heaven, arrayed in fine linen, white and pure, followed him on white horses. . . . On his robe and on his thigh he has a name inscribed, King of kings and Lord of lords. (19:11-16)

Now *that* is dynamite; dynamite enough to strengthen these apostles that you see around you in stained glass to defy the Roman

Empire and go to exile, prison, or death so that you and I might say to one another two thousand years later, "The Lord is risen! He is risen indeed!"

May we all rejoice together on this snowy New England day, knowing that his Resurrection is not dependent on the weather. "O ye ice and snow, O ye frost and cold, bless ye the Lord; praise him and magnify him forever." Spring will come. Spring will come, not because it is in nature, but because God has raised his Son from the dead. May God confirm this miracle in our lives, now and in the hour of our death, so that we may remember the angel who descends like lightning from heaven, who rolls the stone of doubt and fear from our hearts, who invites us into the very bastion of Death to show us that the tomb is empty, that the Enemy has been routed, that the unthinkable and the impossible has happened: *He is risen; he goes before us; we will see him.* May this incredible message give you joy today and always, and may the God of Jesus Christ our Lord be praised for ever and ever.

Recognizing Jesus

―――― ∞∞∞ ――――

When he was at table with them, he took the bread and blessed, and broke it, and gave it to them. And their eyes were opened and they recognized him; and he vanished out of their sight. They said to each other, "Did not our hearts burn within us while he talked to us on the road, while he opened to us the scriptures?" And they rose that same hour. . . .

(LUKE 24:30-32)

During the past month, a number of articles about our Lord Jesus Christ appeared in major magazines and newspapers. Here is *TV Guide;* here is *U.S. News and World Report;* here is the *Wall Street Journal;* here is *Newsweek;* and here is a review from *The New York Times.* There isn't anything really unusual about this; it seems to happen every year at Eastertime. What *is* new, however, is the note of debunking that dominates some of these articles.[6] Until recent years, no one would have published anything radically skeptical about Jesus in the mass market media. To be sure, there were "God is dead" articles back in the sixties; but attacking Jesus himself? Definitely not. Now, however, it has become commonplace to do so. The *U.S. News and World Report* article draws the reader into what *seems* to be a straightforward retelling of the story of Jesus, adding some genuine insights about his political importance along the way; only at the end do you realize that you have just read a subtle and adroit diminishment of Jesus' stature and of Christian faith in him. He has become "an enigmatic Jewish rabbi," nothing more.[7]

This trend did not seem particularly alarming at first. The media has its secular angle on things, but the church knew what the real story was. Or so we thought. Now, however, skepticism about Jesus has deeply penetrated the church as well. It is downright unfashionable in some circles to confess Christ as Son of God and unique Redeemer of the world. One is accused of being fundamentalist, reactionary, unmodern, irrational, intolerant of other faiths, and all sorts of other crimes against enlightened thinking.

Such perspectives are shaped by articles like that in *U.S. News and World Report.* This article presents the Crucifixion as a fact; it states that Jesus "was crucified." It does not say he "was raised," however; it says that the disciples *believed* he had been raised. It says that the disciples *became convinced that* Jesus was alive. It says that the small core of disciples who had been his followers were "energized *by that belief.*" I wonder what you would think if the preacher got up in the pulpit this evening and announced, "Jesus' disciples *came to believe* that he had risen from the dead." That would be an interesting statement about a historical development, but it certainly wouldn't hold out any transforming or world-shaking hope.

The *New York Times* article lays the challenge right out: Telling the story of Jesus straight, in the traditional fashion, can be "a foolhardy venture" because "there is not a shred of historical evidence outside the Bible itself to support the existence of Jesus."[8] This sounds shocking to those who have not heard it, but it is absolutely correct. It cannot be shown through historical research that Jesus of Nazareth ever even lived, let alone rose from the dead. It can be, and often is, argued that he is a purely literary presence, like Sherlock Holmes. Hundreds of people still write letters to 221-B Baker Street, London, as though Holmes were a real person, still alive. Is it like that with Jesus? We need to ask ourselves what we mean when, during the Great Fifty Days, we say "The Lord is risen! He is risen indeed!" Some are suggesting something like this: "Some of

Rembrandt: The Disciples at Emmaus

Both of Rembrandt's versions emphasize the humble setting and intimacy of
this Resurrection appearance. Both take place in stillness and in silence as the
Lord breaks the loaf of bread. Nevertheless, the earlier version (above) is one
of the most dramatic scenes that Rembrandt ever painted. It shows his famous use of light to special advantage. As the Biblical passage from Luke indicates, it is evening, so darkness has fallen. In the background, a servant
works by candlelight, oblivious to what is happening. In the foreground, the
profile of Christ is silhouetted against an invisible candle flame. The eye is
drawn first to the silhouette, then to the brightly lit face of the disciple in the
center, then back again in an interplay between the One whose identity is revealed as he breaks the bread and the dawning realization of the disciple,
whose facial expression and raised hands tell the whole story. Another disciple, almost invisible in the shadow, has already recognized the Lord and,
knocking over his chair, falls at Christ's knees.

 The other, later Emmaus picture (right) is better known. Here, too, is

the moment of recognition, but this time the drama is understated, so that the attention is drawn exclusively at first to the ineffable expression of Jesus, who seems to bear the story of his Passion in his eyes, and only then to the disciples, whose gestures are very subtly conceived; the one on the left raises his hand, while the more prominent one on the right is just beginning to push himself away from the table as the revelation comes upon him. As in the first picture, the servant, who did not know Jesus in life, is unaware of what is happening.

Jesus' disciples *believed that* he was not dead, and started talking about him *as if he were* still alive." People talk like that about Elvis Presley. If that's all that happened, why do we bother with church at all?

A few minutes ago we heard the reading of a passage from the Gospel according to Luke. It tells us how the women who went to the tomb at dawn on Easter morning came back and told the disciples that the body of Jesus was gone and that they had seen an angel who said that he was risen. The disciples, Luke reports, did not believe a word of it. It seemed to them to be *an idle tale.* I think we can really understand the disbelief of the disciples here. Disbelief forms a significant part of the Resurrection narratives. This Sunday we will hear the story of how Thomas flatly refused to believe the Lord was risen, even when all the other disciples swore they had seen him. Skepticism about the Resurrection is not something that was invented by our own age. The evangelists are not fools. They know about disbelief and they have incorporated it into their stories.

Luke goes on to tell us that on Easter Sunday afternoon, the day that the women first told their "idle tale," two disciples of Jesus "were going to a village named Emmaus, about seven miles from Jerusalem." These two people, one named Cleopas and the other not identified, are on foot.⁹ Jesus' disciples are always walking; they were too poor to keep an animal. We don't know anything about these disciples; they weren't famous, they weren't members of the Twelve, they weren't leaders — they were just common, garden-variety disciples like you and me. As they walked along they were "talking with one other about all the things that had happened." This little scene is remarkably ordinary and lacking in distinction; it is not a dramatic setting for a great event. There is no angel, no empty tomb. It is just two friends, clinging together in common misery, trying to comfort each other, going over and over the events as if the mere repetition of them would bring relief, seeking desperately to understand and accept, but dazed and numb with shock and grief. Their humdrum, obscure lives had been lifted out of the ordinary by the Master; they had been so proud, so hopeful, as they followed him. Now he was not only dead; he was disgraced and discredited in the eyes of the whole world. It is important to understand that the Crucifixion was not only a horrible and obscene way to die, but more important, it was a state-sponsored method of declaring a person to be contemptible, subhuman, not even fit to be executed in a decent way. Crucified victims were victims of extreme shame, and after their deaths their names were blotted out of human history. We do not know the identity of any other pre-Christian victim of crucifixion. *If the story of Jesus had ended with his death we would never have heard of him.* It is important to keep this in mind as we continue with the story of the road to Emmaus.

Because of the nature of Jesus' death, we must assume that his disciples were experiencing complex and turbulent emotions. Pain and sorrow is not all they felt. Feelings of anger and betrayal must have been there too. Perhaps they felt that they had been duped and victimized. In any case, we may be sure that the natural world around them offered no consolation for the public degradation and execution of their Master. They did not derive any hope or comfort from the birds that caroled along the roadside, the sprouting wheat, the flowers that bloomed. The miracle of the Resurrection did not arise out of nature or human perception. As St. Paul wrote, "Flesh and blood cannot inherit the kingdom of God, nor does the perishable inherit the imperishable" (1 Corinthians 15:50). Human eyes and ears can see and hear, but unless there is divine intervention, there is no comprehension. Thus they did not jump for joy when, as "they were talking and discussing together [on the road], Jesus himself drew near and went with them."

The One who was crucified comes close, walks alongside his grief-stricken disciples, steps matching steps. They do not come to him; he comes to them. Yet they do not know him; he alone has the power to make himself known. In a very important verse, we read, "Their eyes *were kept* from recognizing him." Not, "they did not recognize him," but "their eyes *were kept* from recognizing him." Whenever you see that passive form of a verb in the Bible, it means that God is at work. The initiative in revealing Jesus is God's, not man's.

Or did they imagine all this?

Jesus said to them, "What is this conversation which you are holding with each other as you walk?" And in sheer misery and despair they stop in the middle of the road, looking at this interloper with eyes of pain. "Are you the only visitor to Jerusalem who does not know the things that have happened there?" And the stranger in the road says "What things?"

"What things?" What a question. It must have been extremely painful for them to answer. The disciples' reply is, we may imagine, recited almost by rote — mechanically, dully, lacking now in conviction: "Jesus of Nazareth," they explain, "was a prophet mighty in deed and word before God and all the people, and our chief priests and rulers delivered him up to be condemned to death, and crucified him." These facts that they recite will soon become the kernel of the apostles' preaching, but at this point none of that has registered. The two disciples *know* the facts, but they do not *understand* the facts. "We had hoped," they say with infinite disillusionment, "that he was the one to redeem Israel" . . . and now, they continue, some of the women in their group are telling a crazy story. "They were at the tomb early in the morning and did not find his body; and they came back saying that they had even seen a vision of angels, who said that he was alive. Some of those who were with us went to the tomb, and found it just as the women had said; *but him they did not see.*" Wouldn't you think that they would be putting two and one together by now? If flesh and blood could inherit the kingdom of God, these two would have been able to figure out who this third person was. According to Luke, however, God is in control of their understanding. Recognition was withheld from them until the moment that God chose.[10]

Now those of us who are in church tonight are in the same position as those two disciples. We have heard the testimony of the women, we have heard about the empty tomb and the angels, *"but him we did not see."* These words are of great importance for us. Luke was writing for Christians who were *not there* and *had not seen.* They were surrounded, as you and I are, with those who do not know the risen Lord and think it is only an idle tale. Disbelief is always going to be with us. Sophisticated people turn up their noses at the Resurrection of Jesus. And you know what? Religious people are leery of it too. If you don't believe me, just look at what has happened to Easter cards. The empty tomb and the risen Lord are quickly absorbed into generalized religious messages about renewal and rebirth that have nothing to do with a crucified and risen Messiah.

Luke's story continues: Jesus said to the two disciples, "'O foolish men, and slow of heart to believe all that the prophets have spoken!' . . . And beginning with Moses and all the prophets, he interpreted to them in all the scriptures the things concerning himself." That was the Bible study to end all Bible studies. Think of it! The risen Lord, walking along, began to teach them the real meaning of the Old Testament. It is all about himself! — how he would suffer and die for the sin of mankind, how he would complete his work on our behalf and then enter into his glory. The true expositor of Scripture is Jesus himself; he is its content, he is its message, he is its interpreter. During the next two hours, the three continue walking the seven miles to Emmaus, as the divine and resurrected One patiently leads the disciples into the living Word of God of which he himself is Author and subject. What a scene for the ages!

Or did they imagine all this?

The evangelist continues, "They drew near to the village to which they were going. He appeared to be going further, but they constrained him, saying, "Stay with us, for it is toward evening and the day is now far spent." So he went in to stay with them. Yet, though clearly by now they are powerfully drawn to him, still they do not know him. They go in together to the inn and they take a table and are served a meal. The disciples are the hosts and Jesus, of course, is the guest. It is the role of the host at the Jewish table to bless and break the bread, but in this case it is the guest who takes over as the host. "When he was at table with them, he took the bread and blessed, and broke it, and gave it to them. And their eyes were opened and they recognized him; and he vanished out of their sight."

They recognized him. Or did they imagine it all? Was it just a projection of their wishes and dreams?

No one outside the circle of faith can answer those questions. Jesus did not show himself to everyone. He only drew near to those who were his disciples already, and then, later, to that other person whom he chose, the Pharisee named Saul. No one ever stated the truth of the Resurrection more definitively than that man who became Paul the Apostle. The earliest account of the Resurrection in the Bible was written by Paul, in 1 Corinthians 15. Did Paul make it up? Were Paul and the four evangelists deceived? Was the whole early church deceived? Is the story of the road to Emmaus a literary depiction of what the disciples "came to believe," as some would say? I read an article of literary criticism last week that mentioned Richard the Third. The point being made was that the "historical" Richard was less interesting than Shakespeare's Richard. Is Jesus like that? Have the evangelists created a Jesus who is more interesting than the real one? Does he live only on the page, or stage, or TV screen? That is what some would say. But what would *you* say? Where is he alive right now?

Think for a minute about why you came tonight. Some of you, I'm sure, are here with your childhood faith intact. Others of you have serious questions about it all. There is nothing that the evangelist or preacher can say that will convince a stubborn unbeliever. The Resurrection cannot be proved by normal means, and the writers of the New Testament seem to understand that. Faith is a mysterious thing. It is not a human work. It is a gift of the Lord himself.

Listen to what the Emmaus disciples say to one another after Jesus disappears: They say, "Did not our hearts burn within us while he talked to us on the road, while he opened to us the scriptures?" Remember how we said that was the Bible study to end all Bible studies? But that is just a manner of speaking. It is, rather, the Bible study to *begin* all Bible studies, because the Lord is the Author and the Holy Spirit is the interpreter of the Scriptures. A Bible study undertaken today, twenty-one centuries later, has the very same power as the first one. "Beginning with Moses and all the prophets," the living Lord continues to interpret to us "in all the scriptures the things concerning himself." Jesus has drawn near to us in his living Word tonight.

Or is this just the preacher's imagination? Have all the Resurrection messages over the centuries been based on nothing more than preacherly flourishes?

"Him we did not see." But *"when he was at table with them, he took the bread and blessed, and broke it, and gave it to them. And their eyes were opened and they recognized him."* The impact of those simple words, if we can only meditate upon them for a moment, is simply indescribable. Jesus was crucified, dead, and buried before their eyes; now he is alive, and he is with them, breaking a loaf of bread. Some of you will remember Rembrandt's small painting of the moment. Nothing seems to be happening; it is just a little picture of three men sitting at a table in a plain, humble room. A serving maid stands by with a water jug. Then you look more closely and you see that one of the figures is pushing himself back from the table. It is the simplest gesture in the world, and the most eloquent. Light is dawning upon him. He is recognizing the Lord. O glorious and unutterable joy! O most mighty wonder! It is He himself!

Here is a modern story about two ordinary disciples of Jesus. They are my father, who was about eighty-six at the time, and his older sister, Mary Virginia, about ninety-two. She had been totally bedridden in a nursing home for seven years, following a stroke. My father visited her often, but the visits were very difficult for him and usually depressed him deeply. Mary V., as we called her, spoke very little during these years, almost not at all. One day, however, she said something. My father came straight home and wrote it down. I still have the paper that he wrote on. This is what it says:

> Mary V. said today "Am I going to die soon?" I told her I could see no sign of it, and that such things were, for her and me "in the hands of the Lord and I trusted him." She thought a minute and said "Yes, I love the Lord." And after a minute [she] said, "Do you love the Lord?" I said yes, I certainly did, and she closed, with a suspicion of a tremble in her voice, "I thought you did."

Imagine yourself passing by the door at the nursing home at that moment and looking in. Nothing seems to be happening; it is just a little scene of two extremely old people in a plain, humble room. My father wrote at the bottom of the paper, "End of episode."

But it was not the end. That moment gave life to my father and it has given life to my husband and our children and to me. For those who love the Lord, the end is the beginning.

In the retelling of this story this evening, Jesus himself draws near to you. He is present in his Word in this hour as surely as he was alive and interpreting the Scriptures on the road to Emmaus. Does your heart burn within you? Do you recognize him? If you do, it is the work of God. It is the Lord Jesus Christ, present with us to-night — drawing near to us, opening the meaning of the Scripture to us, gathering us at his table as he will on Sunday, breaking the simple loaf of bread to show us that the final word is not death but life, not judgment but mercy, not loneliness but the fellowship of his unconquerable love forever and ever.

Alleluia! The Lord is risen! He is risen indeed!

The evening service concluded with the Collect for the Presence of Christ, based on the Emmaus story (Episcopal Book of Common Prayer, *70).*

Lord Jesus, stay with us, for evening is at hand and the day is past; be our companion in the way, kindle our hearts, and awaken hope, that we may know thee as thou art revealed in Scripture and the breaking of bread. Grant this for the sake of thy love.

AMEN.

The Undoing of Death

—— ∞∞ ——

*Jesus cried with a loud voice, "Lazarus, come forth!" And he
that was dead came forth, bound hand and foot with graveclothes . . . and Jesus said to them, "Loose him, and let him go."*

(JOHN 11:43-44)

You probably noticed that there is a very unspiritual detail in
the story of the raising of Lazarus. When Jesus came to the
grave of his friend, he ordered the bystanders to roll away the stone
from the entrance to the tomb. Martha, the sister of the dead man,
said to him, "Lord, by this time there will be an odor, for he has
been dead four days." The King James Version, in its robust Jaco-
bean style, puts it more pungently: "He stinketh."

I don't know how many of you have had an experience of actual
death in front of your very eyes. One does not forget one's first time.
I had never seen a dead body until I was a priest in my mid-thirties
and was called to come to the bedside of a dying man. He was lying
on the sofa in the living room with his family around him. While I
was saying the prayers for the dying, he drew his last breath. I will
never forget the shock of seeing the change that came over his body.
Something enormous and alien had entered the room. The under-
takers arrived. The family left the room. I stayed because I felt that
someone should be present. The way they handled the body gave

me a second shock. They were not rough, exactly, but they were certainly businesslike. They spread out a rubber sheet on the floor, hoisted the body off the sofa and down onto it, wrapped it up and carried it off as if it were nothing more than a sack of garden mulch. Twenty minutes before, there was a live human being who would have been moved only with the greatest care and delicacy; now there was nothing but an object to be disposed of as quickly as possible.

Death has a horrible color; I have seen it many times since. Death has a terrible icy feel, too. Not long after this episode I was asked by a parishioner to slip a ring onto the finger of the corpse of his dead wife. I had never done anything like that before. I had heard of rigor mortis but I had never touched it. I was not prepared; it was all I could do to perform my task. The hand did not feel like anything human. For any person who values warm human contact, the difference between a living hand and a dead hand is frightful.

> Try — can you stir the awful rivet —
> Try — can you lift the hasps of steel!
> Stroke the cool forehead — hot so often —
> Lift — if you care — the listless hair —
> Handle the adamantine fingers
> Never a thimble — more — shall wear — [11]

It is a compliment to this Easter evening congregation that we are talking about such things. You are not the average Sunday crowd. You, I know, are ready for stronger challenges. The reason I am talking about death in such stark terms is that the Bible talks about it. Death is one of the main characters in the Biblical drama. Death stalks around everywhere, threatening to destroy everything.[12] The Bible is blunt about death. "He stinketh, for he has been dead four days." Earlier generations were not as squeamish about depicting death as we are; look closely the next time you see a Greek or Russian icon of the raising of Lazarus. The bystanders are holding handkerchiefs to their noses. Death was a visible, smellable fact of life for Biblical people and, indeed, for all people everywhere

Giotto: The Resurrection of Lazarus (detail)

This early Renaissance painter, whose ground-breaking greatness still remains unchallenged after 600 years, is able to show Jesus' majesty with the simplest of means: powerful composition, riveting facial expression, and forceful gesture. The strong modeling of the Lord's face, standing out against its solid blue background, is designed to strike even the viewer standing at a distance (the fresco is high on the chapel wall), as the command is given to Lazarus to come forth from the stronghold of death. The two figures of the disciples on the left do not gasp or exclaim as though Jesus had just done a trick, but register solemn astonishment, even fear, as though they know they are in the presence of a power far beyond anything they have ever imagined before.

until about a hundred years ago when we started calling in the morticians to hustle the bodies out of sight. I have a Bible that belonged to my great-grandmother, my namesake; she died in childbirth when she was only in her twenties. She has underlined verses that few young people would underline today. For instance, Psalm 90:10: "Though men be so strong that they come to fourscore years, yet is their strength then but labor and sorrow, so soon it passes away and we are gone." In the nineteenth century, people lived with these thoughts as a matter of course. Not so in these tender-minded times. Our culture is infamous for its unceasing attempts to manage death, to get it out of sight, to perfume it and embalm it and cover it with flowers, but the truth remains. A modern writer who has battled cancer three times observes that

> There is a peculiarly modern predilection for psychological explanations of disease, as of everything else. Psychologizing seems to provide control . . . [but] death is the obscene mystery, the ultimate affront, the thing that cannot be controlled. . . .[13]

St. Paul wrote to the Corinthians, "Flesh and blood cannot inherit the kingdom of God" (1 Corinthians 15:50). Contrary to popular belief, Scripture does not teach that there is any natural carryover of life past death into the beyond. The Old Testament makes this very clear; over a thousand years the children of Israel were patiently taught by God to love, fear, and serve him without even a hint of any promise of life beyond death.[14] It would be a good thing, perhaps, if all Christians went through this process. Paul was frustrated with the Corinthian church because they apparently believed in some sort of immortality. That's why he says to them, "The perishable cannot inherit the imperishable." There is an "infinite qualitative distinction"[15] between human life and the divine life. The entire human person lives under the sway of Death. It is the reigning phenomenon of our existence. Lay theologian William Stringfellow writes,

> Death survives all other powers, apart from God, in this world. . . . Death is the obvious meaning of existence, if God is

ignored, surviving as death does every other personal or social reality to which is attributed existence in this world. Death is so great, so aggressive, so pervasive and so militant a power that the only fitting way to speak of death is similar to the way one speaks of God. Death is the living power and presence in this world which feigns to be God. . . .

It is the presumption of sovereignty over *all* of life that marks the power of death, [and] that makes the employment of the name of the Devil, as unusual or archaic as it may nowadays seem, wholly apt and, so to speak, respectful of such an exceeding great power.[16]

So I think we do God great honor to speak with awe and reverence of Death tonight. Death is "the last enemy" of man and God (1 Corinthians 15:26). Flannery O'Connor was wise about many things; at the time of John F. Kennedy's funeral, she wrote in a letter to a friend, "Mrs. Kennedy has a sense of history and of what is owing to death."[17] The Corinthian congregation's problem was that they did not understand what was owing to death. They would have loved "The American Way of Death."[18] Just like us, they wanted to hustle death offstage; they preferred to think of death as a mere blip on the screen of immortality. The entrance of Christ into the world, they believed, meant that death had been made irrelevant. Paul wrote to correct them. Death, he said, was the last and greatest antagonist of all. Death is the one great, overwhelming, final reality of human existence: "In Adam, all die" (1 Corinthians 15:22).[19]

It is unfortunate that we seem to be moving away from the traditional Anglican funeral service. This is a great loss. Until recent years, the liturgy from the Prayer Book was regularly used. It was designed to show what was owing to the solemn reality and power of Death. The presence of the body in the church (in a closed coffin covered by a draped pall) reminds us that something irrevocable — humanly speaking — has happened; "the powers of death have done their worst."[20] The classical Anglican order for burial is Biblical and noble in its unflinching view of what has taken place.[21] Memorial services tend to be more Corinthian and less Biblical, because they celebrate the person's life independently of the power of Death. There can be no true proclamation of the Resurrection until there has been an acknowledgement of the power and the finality of Death. It is indeed "the obscene mystery, the ultimate affront, the thing that cannot be controlled."

Everything I know about grief and mourning tells me that when someone we love dies, we cannot go on with our lives in a healthy way unless we come to terms with the fact of that person's death. We often need to prolong or postpone the process, so that we will not be overwhelmed all at once, but sooner or later we must face it. Death is ugly, a rotten deal; it is a cheat, a thief, a grinning mockery — like a skull. In the story of Lazarus, we see Jesus face to face with that reality. "He stinketh." Martha, the sister of Lazarus, seems to have a clue that Jesus might be able to do something about her brother ("even now I know that whatever you ask from God, God will give you" — John 11:22), but it is evident that she thinks he might do it on a "spiritual" level, certainly not in the presence of actual, corrupted flesh. Jesus, however, approaches closely to the tomb and, we are told, he "was deeply moved in spirit and troubled" (11:33). John repeats three times that Jesus "wept" and was "deeply troubled." Interpreters have long seen that this is more than grief for Lazarus; this perturbation of spirit is caused by the presence of the Great Antagonist. God is revealing, through the Son, that he hates Death and pities us because we must bow our necks under its terrible stroke. Jesus is deeply moved in spirit because he is gathering his forces for this mighty confrontation with the "exceeding great power," the Supreme Enemy of all that God has purposed.[22] This is a truly cosmic duel.

But in the end it is no contest.

Jesus cried with a loud voice, "Lazarus, come forth!" And he that was dead came forth, bound hand and foot with graveclothes . . . and Jesus said to them, "Loose him, and let him go."

Nicholas Froment: Resurrection of Lazarus

This painting, the center panel of a triptych, shows the raising of Lazarus, who begins to sit up while Jesus says "Unbind him, and let him go." Martha, on the left, is in the process of removing her handkerchief from her nose as she realizes that Lazarus, having been resurrected to life, does not stink after all. (The donor, on the right, has been painted into the action as well.)

Here is a question for us this evening. When Jesus said, "Lazarus, come forth," did Lazarus have a choice?

The story of Lazarus is mysterious. Why is it not told in any other Gospel? Why weren't his enemies silenced by this drop-dead proof of Jesus' power? Why don't Paul or any of the other writers in the Epistles refer to this amazing episode? We don't know. But here is something that St. Paul did say: "God . . . gives life to the dead and calls into existence the things that do not exist" (Romans 4:17). For whatever reason, Paul may not have known the story of Lazarus; but the resurrection of the dead is at the heart and center of his proclamation. Flesh and blood cannot inherit the kingdom of God, nor can the perishable inherit the imperishable; *but God can bring into existence the things that do not exist.* Could Lazarus have said "No!" to Jesus' command? Think about it from the opposite angle. Could Lazarus have said "No!" to the summons of Death? A lot of people have tried it! — but as the stricken Hamlet says to his friend Laertes, "this fell sergeant, Death, is strict in his arrest."[23] In the midst of life we are in death: dust we are, and to dust we shall return.[24] There we remain unless there is an intervention from beyond this world order. Only a Power greater than that of Death can countermand that strict arrest.

When Jesus Christ the Son of God steps forward to the door of Lazarus' tomb and speaks, it is the same voice that was heard at Creation: "Let there be light!" *and there was light.* Did the light have any choice about the matter? Could the light have said "No"? In the words that open John's Gospel, we see with perfect plainness how the Incarnate Son is One with the Creator and the Spirit invoked in the beginning of the book of Genesis: "In the beginning was the Word, and the Word was with God, and the Word was God. He was in the beginning with God; all things were made through him, and without him was not anything made that was made" (John 1:1-3). This is the Word that *raises the dead and calls into existence the things that do not exist.* This is Jesus Christ, the Word Incarnate who "dwelt among us, full of grace and truth" (1:14).

We pathetic human creatures preen and pose, defying Death with our illusions of immortality, but we are helpless:

. . . all our yesterdays have lighted fools
The way to dusty death. Out, out, brief candle!
Life's but a walking shadow, a poor player
That struts and frets his hour upon the stage
And then is heard no more.[25]

But now, dearly beloved of God and of his Son Jesus Christ, hear this news:

Descending from the realm of light and life, invading the impenetrable darkness of the kingdom of Death and plundering it of all its treasure, comes One "who is and who was and who is to come, the Almighty" (Revelation 1:8). To his infinitely precious children by baptism and the Holy Spirit he says, "I am the resurrection and the life; he who believes in me, though he were dead, yet shall he live; and he who lives and believes in me shall never die" (John 11:25-26). He is the Alpha and the Omega, the root and the offspring of David, the bright morning star, risen with healing in his wings: Wonderful Counselor, the Mighty God, the Everlasting Father, the Prince of Peace.[26]

"Believest thou this?"

Out of Our Control

⸺⸎⸺

Why do you seek the living among the dead?

(LUKE 24:5)

No one saw the Resurrection of Jesus of Nazareth. In two thousand years of Christian art, there have been many great paintings, mosaics, and frescoes of the event, depicting the Roman soldiers lying unconscious, the tombstone pushed aside, the glorified body of the Lord emerging with the banner of victory and a blaze of light. Some of these paintings are great masterpieces, yet in a sense they are misleading. We search the New Testament in vain for a description of the Resurrection itself. No one saw it — not Peter, not John, not Mary Magdalene, not the Roman soldiers, not anyone. Jesus was already gone from the tomb when the stone was rolled away. The manner in which the Resurrection occurred remains a mystery. God intended it that way. He never meant for it to be within our comprehension. It is out of our range of understanding because it comes from another sphere of reality.

St. Luke gives us a clue about this mystery in the declaration of the angel at the door of the tomb: "Why do you look for the living among the dead? He is risen: he is not here." The angel's rebuke reverberates across the centuries. To this day we continue to seek for new life in all the wrong places, hoping to gain mastery over the pitiless advance of dissolution.

I remember not so very many years ago reading an article about Brazil. It said that almost all well-to-do Brazilian women of a certain age had face-lifts. I distinctly remember thinking to myself, "Thank God I don't live in Brazil." Well, my thanksgiving was short-lived. Since that article was written, cosmetic surgery in America has become a growth industry, to the point where not only women but also men are looking in the mirror and pushing at their faces. (I do it about ten times a day.) What is this if it is not *looking for the living among the dead?* As a side comment, however, I will mention that I did read an article a few months ago that said the rage for cosmetic surgery was affecting the entire country, "except perhaps for rural New England." So I said to myself, "Thank God for rural New England."[27] All kidding aside, I also remember being struck by an eloquent letter to the editor of a glossy magazine a few years back. I no longer have the clipping, but I can remember it almost verbatim. It was in response to an article about the mania for fad diets, aerobics, exercise machines, and spas. The letter-writer, in protest, summoned up an image of her grandmother's generation who, she wrote admiringly, "accepted their imperfect bodies" and concentrated on "grandchildren, community service, religious pursuits, and spiritual beauty." Remembering that one letter has been tremendously helpful to me as I get older and struggle with this question of where to find real life.[28]

The tendency of the human race to *set our minds on things that are on earth,* to *seek the living among the dead,* pervades every aspect of our lives, though we rarely stop long enough to realize it. Any newspaper these days gives ample evidence. Fury and frustration all around the globe are producing a bloodthirsty spirit everywhere. We are seeing an exponential escalation in the demand for capital punishment. The NRA continues to hold America hostage to its worst instincts. Our prison system is growing larger and larger as it becomes ever more mindlessly brutal. I watched an interview with former judge and convicted felon Sol Wachtler on television this morning. Just out of prison himself, he has made good use of his incarceration; he has written an insider's book about the system, detailing its many irrational cruelties and its failure to distinguish between violent criminals and others who can be reclaimed for useful lives.[29] An article on the front page of today's *New York Times* tells an appalling story about the abominable treatment of a Nigerian political refugee, seeking freedom in America from the regime that tortured his father to death, only to be brutally abused by the American immigration authorities for two years. This should cause the whole Christian community to rise up in outrage. I believe we are becoming desensitized as a people. I have never heard anyone dispute the fact that violence breeds more violence, and yet the fear of losing what we have in life seems always to produce in the human race a movement in the direction of death — more prisons, more executions, more weapons, more torture, more police brutality.[30] What does this suggest about the condition of our souls? We are looking for life, but we are investing in death.

What about the death industry in America? It was been powerfully lampooned by Evelyn Waugh and Jessica Mitford, but the machinery grinds on. I have a good relationship with our local undertaker, but it has taken a lot of work and a lot of teaching about what the church believes and expects. If we are not vigilant, they will not only undertake, they will take over. Ms. Mitford stated in an interview recently that her famous book about the industry, *The American Way of Death,* had had a significant impact for a while, but in recent years the situation had gotten even worse. I have in my files a favorite article from *The Wall Street Journal:*

> Personalized caskets, complete with one's monogram and the symbol of a favored club or religious order, are offered by Major Casket Company of Memphis. The company says a psychological study it made showed that such personal symbols tend to give a bereaved family "the feeling of having control over a situation that might otherwise be uncontrollable."

Might otherwise be uncontrollable, indeed. One of my favorite *New Yorker* cartoons depicts the doorway of a New York City apartment. The door is open, and its occupant stands just inside. He is a fiftyish, professional type. Standing just outside the door is his visitor — a figure wearing a long, black, hooded garment. This figure is holding in its hand — a scythe. The man in the apartment is saying, "Oh darn — just as I was beginning to take charge of my life!"[31]

Taking charge of life, taking charge of death; all over America this is a preoccupation. Christians should be concerned about the current enthusiasm for assisted suicide. I overheard a conversation in the Detroit airport the other day. A tall, fashionably dressed young man was saying to a group of friends, "So all those people killed themselves in California? What's the big deal? If they want to kill themselves, that's their right." He is not alone in this opinion. In recent months the well-known, long-established suicide-prevention hot-line called Samaritans (a good Biblical name) has begun to have trouble getting volunteers. Leaders in the organization believe this is because we are seeing a change in society's attitude toward suicide; people are starting to think it is not such a bad thing. The Dr. Kevorkians and the Derek Humphreys have done their work. For what it's worth, I will just note in passing that a Christian response to the very real problem of prolonged pain and decline lies in the direction of palliative care, pain management, the consoling presence of loved ones, and in some cases a decision on the part of an elderly patient simply to stop eating. These means seem to me to be appropriate for Christians, whereas death by fatal dosage, injection, or plastic bag is not the way of the believer who puts his or her trust in the Lord and Giver of life. I'm telling my children that when I am an old lady they had better not come at me with any plastic bag. "The Lord giveth, and the Lord taketh away; blessed be the name of the Lord" (Job 1:21 KJV).

In my big fat file on death, I have numerous clippings about Elizabeth Kübler-Ross. She has in many ways revolutionized the way we think about dying, and some of her work has been of great value.[32] However, her approach often fails to acknowledge what is owing to the solemnity of death. When speaking at the Washington Cathedral, no less, she was asked if she thought it was advisable to take a child to a funeral. Her reply was, "It's all right if he is accompanied by an adult who is feeling OK about death."[33]

Is that a good idea, to "feel OK" about death? Flannery O'Connor didn't think so; she wrote that the grim grandeur of the John F. Kennedy funeral was "a salutary tonic for this back-slapping gum-chewing hiya-kid nation."[34] Jesus certainly did not "feel OK" about death when he approached the tomb of Lazarus "deeply troubled in spirit" (John 11:33). I have another clipping in my file, an interview with a woman who has terminal cancer. She said:

> There are some people I want to scream at. I can accept the fact that I am terminal and facing death, [but] I want to say to them, "Stop giving me your saccharine words." I get so angry at the euphemisms about death with dignity. Death is ugly, bald, miserable. . . .[35]

I have never forgotten something that a friend told me a few months before she died. I was visiting her in the hospital. We were discussing the theft of some of her beautiful antiques. "Oh, well," she said, "we can get the insurance, we can fix it." And then she said (these were her exact words): "Everything can be fixed — except death."

When the women went to the tomb on the morning of the third day, they knew that death could not be fixed. They knew it was out of their control. They were carrying perfumes and spices — cosmetic surgery for the corpse, so to speak — but that was because it was all they knew how to do. It was analogous to lining the coffin with satin. They were looking for the living among the dead, as we all do. They did not and could not see the Resurrection itself *because the Resurrection did not occur in the realm of the dead, but was an event from beyond this world order altogether.* They did not see the Resurrection itself, but what they saw later that day, later that week with the other disciples, transformed them forever. What they saw caused them to look for the first time in the right direction. For the first time they were enabled to look away from the old world of decay, despair, and death. Now they knew they could turn away from death toward the source of the only true and eternal life.

What they saw was the risen Lord Jesus himself; and then they knew.

The gathering of the Christian church on the day of Resurrection and on every Lord's day of the year celebrates that knowledge, celebrates that certainty. Only the scriptural witness, made present in the Word and the Sacraments, can tell us the truth about the Lord's disappearance from the tomb. The creation cannot do it. No one is suggesting that we do away with flowers; I am a passionate lover of flowers myself. I would have been bitterly disappointed if the Altar Guild had not produced these magnificent lilies for us this week. But here is the thing about the flowers and the other phenomena of nature: they can only *praise* the risen Lord; they cannot *teach* us of him. Only he can do that, and he only does it for those who serve and follow him. As you know, the risen Lord appeared only to those who believed in him (with one great and mighty exception, that of Saul of Tarsus, as though the Lord had said, See, I will do this thing out of time and out of sequence, just to display my freedom). Faith in the Resurrection simply is not available on general principles. It cannot be found in courses on death and dying. It cannot be inferred from the new so-called "openness and honesty" about death. It is not available to those who are "feeling OK about death." In fact, it is not "available" at all, in the sense that one can go to a store and buy what is available. Faith in the Resurrection comes to us as a pure gift.

I was making fun, earlier, of the idea that we could gain control over the uncontrollable with various human strategies like cosmetic surgery and embalming. There is another, better way of looking at this matter of control. I asked one of my psychoanalyst colleagues about a news article I had read; it said religious people were better at coping with death than nonreligious people, because religious faith gave a sense of control. I asked him what he thought about that. He reflected for a few moments, and then he said this: "I would put it differently. I wouldn't talk about control. I would talk about it in terms of power and powerlessness. Powerlessness creates anger and depression. Faith, however, is re-empowering. To have faith, like Christian faith in the Resurrection, is re-empowering precisely in the midst of powerlessness."[36] I wonder if you find that as arresting as I do. I think of the classic Anglican Burial Office which, it has always seemed to me, is the most re-empowering part of our Prayer Book.

A dear friend of ours, as most of you know, has been told that she has pancreatic cancer. I went to see her this afternoon. She said, in her cheerful, matter-of-fact way, "You know there's nothing they can do for me. In a matter of months I'm going to meet my Maker." She is preparing to move into the dreaded third stage at her retirement community. I asked her what she wanted to focus on in the time she had left. She said that she would be glad when the move was accomplished, so that she wouldn't have to dwell on possessions or the details of moving. "Someone said," she continued with a twinkle, "that you don't own your possessions; they own you." She knows better than to look for the living among the dead. I was reminded of the great Eastertide text from the Epistle to the Colossians: "If then you have been raised with Christ, seek the things that are above, where Christ is, seated at the right hand of God. Set your minds on things that are above, not on things that are on earth" (Colossians 3:1-2).

"Everything can be fixed except death." How true! Death cannot be "fixed." Life cannot be found by looking among the dead. Death is "ugly, bald, miserable," the last Enemy (1 Corinthians 15:26). It cannot be controlled. It is not OK. It can only be overcome by the One who comes from beyond this world order altogether. No wonder the Resurrection was hidden from our eyes; I suspect that our eyes could not have borne it. We still walk by faith and not by sight. But the news from the witnesses is that Christ has entered death and returned triumphant. He has won the battle. The tomb could not hold him. Our hymns celebrate it: "O sons and daughters, let us sing! The King of heaven, the glorious King, o'er death and hell rose triumphing: Alleluia!"[37] Scripture proclaims it: "Death is swallowed up in victory! Thanks be to God, who giveth us the victory through Jesus Christ our Lord" (1 Corinthians 15:54,

El Greco: Resurrection

El Greco's luminous, elongated forms are shown here to best advantage. A clearly transfigured, heavenly Christ soars above the tumult around him, his drapery and banner ballooning about him as though filled with the wind of the Spirit. The Roman soldiers react in varying postures of impotence; some are thrown to the ground while others vainly attempt with sword and shield to prevent him from escaping. He is untouchable; nothing on earth can harm him now. His gaze and gesture seem to say that his divine life is now definitively his, to be given freely to all who love him.

57). And the humblest Christian believer may claim it, for it was not the rich and famous who saw him on that first Easter Day, but those whose relationship to him is the same as yours and mine — those whose only claim to him is that of trust in his indestructible love and his transcendent power to bring us out of Death into life.

> Look there! the Christ, our Brother, comes resplendent
>   from the gallows tree —
> And what he brings in his hurt hands is life on life
>   for you and me.

> Good Jesus Christ, our Brother, died in darkest hurt
>   upon the tree —
> To offer us the worlds of light that live inside the Trinity.

> Joy! Joy! Joy to the heart and all in this good
>   day's dawning![38]

Refreshment Time

————⚬⚬⚬————

*Repent and return, that your sins may be blotted out, that times
of refreshing may come from the presence of the Lord.*

(ACTS 3:19)

When I came to the office on Tuesday, I passed the window of
a gift shop. There was a sign in the window — "All Easter
items ½ price." I made a mental note to come back later and stock
up. When I returned to the shop yesterday, I asked to see the items
on sale. The saleswoman shrugged apologetically and said, "They're
gone; we've put them all away." How quickly Easter comes and goes
in the secular mind! In the world of commerce, Easter is over. However, I look forward to going into my favorite Greek coffee shop
next week; I will be able to call out *Christos anesti!* (Christ is risen!)
with the certainty of receiving a joyful response: *Alethos anesti!* (He
is risen indeed!).

Easter is not over, either for the Eastern or for the Western
church. In fact, it has barely begun. Day after tomorrow will be
only the second Sunday of the Easter season. If you can find any
Easter cards for half price, this is a good time to send them, because
today is only the sixth day of the Great Fifty Days.

That has a rather grand sound to it, doesn't it? And why
shouldn't it? This noble designation refers to the season between

the Resurrection and the day of Pentecost. The word *pentekostos* in Greek means "fiftieth." So the Great Fifty Days is the time between the day when our Lord was raised from the tomb and the day that the Holy Spirit descended upon the church. The Paschal candle burns for these fifty days. If you have put out Easter eggs and other decorations in your house and don't quite know when to put them away, fifty days would be just right.

The Great Fifty Days includes the forty days that Jesus spent on earth after his Resurrection, appearing to his disciples; as St. Luke puts it in the first chapter of Acts, "He presented himself to his apostles and gave many proofs that he was alive" (Acts 1:3). At the end of the forty days, Luke says, "he was lifted up before their eyes, and a cloud took him from their sight" (1:9) as he ascended into heaven. Then there were ten more days of confident expectation, awaiting the promised gift of Jesus' own Holy Spirit, "proceeding from the Father and the Son,"[39] guaranteeing that Jesus will be with us "always, even to the end of the world" (Matthew 28:20). On the fiftieth day, the Holy Spirit descended with the roaring sound of a mighty wind and with tongues of flame (Acts 2:1-4).[40] On that day, the friends of Jesus became new people. They became apostles, not just disciples who learn from a master, but fully commissioned ambassadors of that Master, now "seated at the right hand of Power" (Matthew 26:64). They rushed out into the streets of Jerusalem and they never turned back. As the Lord had promised them, they had received "power from on high" (Luke 24:49). Then they remembered that he had said, "When the Holy Spirit comes upon you, you will be my witnesses" (Acts 1:8). Led by the restored and recreated Peter, they began to tell the people the incomparable good news of the Messiah Jesus, crucified, risen, and coming again. No one was able to stop this news from spreading, leaping from town to town and city to city, "from Jerusalem throughout all Judea and Samaria" and ultimately "to the farthest corners of the earth" (Acts 1:8). Many tried to stop the gospel from expanding, but it could not be contained; the power of it was greater than any obstacle, just as the power of God in Jesus had proven greater than the power of death.

And so, during the Great Fifty Days of Eastertide, we read the book of the Acts of the Apostles, because it unfolds before us the story of the explosion that took place in the world following the Resurrection of the Lord from the dead. Easter Day is only the beginning. You have a special opportunity this evening to understand that. On the night of Jesus' Last Supper, he told his disciples that they were to abide in him and in his love (John 15:4-10). You are here on a weeknight because you know that a quick fix on Easter Day isn't enough; you want *to abide in Jesus' love.* That wish is what brings us all together here, and we are all close and related to one another because we are part of the family that his love has created.

Part of *abiding in Jesus* is hearing his Word. As Acts begins, we see how the Spirit begins to give speech to the apostles that is not just human speech.[41] Behind and in and through the human words is the power of God which inhabits them and makes them living, creating agents just as he is himself. If we preachers did not believe that, we would have no business in the pulpit. The book of Acts is full of examples of the sermons that began to convince the Mediterranean world that a man who had been crucified as a common criminal was risen in power from the grave and had begun his reign as Lord of all life.[42] One of these sermons, preached by Peter, is aimed at the conversion of the hearers (as indeed all of the sermons are), and it contains these words:

> Repent and return, that your sins may be blotted out, that times of refreshing may come from the presence of the Lord. (Acts 3:19)

The word "refreshments" has a slightly quaint, retro sound to me. It doesn't sound quite like the way we talk today. We talk about "snacks," or we say we're going to grab a latte and a bagel. I started thinking about "refreshments" and what I thought of was Oreo cookies and juice at my Girl Scout meetings in Franklin, Virginia, in the 1940s. I thought of a jingle they used to play in between the newsreel and the feature at the movie theater: "Let's all go to the lobby." (Now that's *really* retro!) I thought of the dreary hour spent once a week in the headmistress's parlor by the girls at my boarding school, enduring ghastly conversation and — you guessed it — "refreshments." So the more memories I dredged up, the more it seemed to me that there must be more to "times of refreshing" than that.

So I puzzled a bit more over that word in Acts — "refreshing" — and I spent some time investigating it. I found some lovely things. The word in Greek means something like *relaxation, relief, respite, alleviation,* and *rest.* Most suggestive of all, perhaps, it means *breathing space.* It made me feel refreshed just to read that in the Greek dictionary.

A couple of days ago I came out of the front door and saw an elderly woman, very stooped and frail-looking, making her way arduously along the sidewalk. As she came closer, she caught sight of the tulip magnolia tree in full bloom. She stopped and gazed. As I passed, I heard her saying to no one in particular, just to herself, "Beautiful! Beautiful!" The sight of the tree was a respite for her, a breathing space.

Now those of you who are young and healthy may not think of yourselves as needing this sort of thing. Refreshment for you might be more likely to take the form of some sort of extreme sport. Some of the more driven among you might not want to admit that you even need a respite, except perhaps as one who takes a high-end break from the pressure of your intensely demanding career. It's a form of one-upmanship. If we are busy projecting ourselves onto the world as people in control, with no needs except to get ahead, we may not stop to look at flowering trees as we rush from one appointment to another. It's notable, really; the favorite saying among the young today seems to be "I'm stressed out." I don't remember saying anything like that in my day; it seems to have become fashionable to be continually under stress and continually pointing it out. It's almost like saying, "Don't bother me; you can't possibly understand my life; I've got so much more to worry about than you do, whoever you are." Those of us who find ourselves talking like this are, of course, more in need of a breathing space than we can admit even to ourselves. After all, when one has had a time of respite, one is able to turn more readily to the needs of others. Those of you who are caring for sick or elderly relatives know that after you have had a break you are able to be more patient and sympathetic.

As your clergy know very well, even in this prosperous and self-possessed-looking crowd of people there is tension, depression, strife, and unspoken pain. If you are in touch with the reality of your life, you will know how precious it is to have a moment of refreshment. During the Battle of Britain, everything in the British Isles was rationed; privation was severe. The earthenware factories even ceased to make teapots. However, the tea itself kept coming, for as Lord Woolton, the Minister of Food, said in 1940, "In Britain, tea is more than a beverage." The cup of tea was a means of survival, not because it was a drink but because, with its associations of comfort and home, it was soul-strengthening; it was "a time of refreshing." Those of us who are from the American South feel this way about iced tea. *The Theological Dictionary of the New Testament* describes "refreshing" this way: "to cool by a breath, or by water."[43] That beautiful definition strikes a chord in each one of us, I believe. Even the frenetic among us can recognize this.

Sooner or later, however, there are times in our lives when our pain is so great from loss and grief that tea, whether hot or iced, just won't do it. Not even the sight of a magnolia tree in full bloom will alleviate the deepest of our anxieties. That's why T. S. Eliot — who knew something about anxiety — wrote, "April is the cruellest month."[44] Just this week there was a piece in *The New York Times* that began, "Spring scares me. Everything pulsating. All the longer daylight hours mean to me is that I have to lower the window shades earlier to watch TV."[45] That, I suspect, is a person suffering from depression. Looking at a tree might not help. An authentic, lasting time of refreshing must be based on something more than the evanescence of springtime. Spring turns to autumn and then winter — and then comes melancholy. Robert Frost, contemplating the brilliance of the spring leaves in New Hampshire, wrote a poem, "Nothing Gold Can Stay."[46] Life teaches us that lasting refreshment must be grounded in something that is not ephemeral, but permanent.

The liturgical rhythm of the church during Lent, Holy Week,

and Easter has this purpose and this purpose only: to draw us into the one permanent thing, the one gold thing that will stay. The drama of Holy Week and the Great Fifty Days lays it out before us. Those of you who came to church on Good Friday will remember how it looked. Every single pretty article had been taken away, to remind us of how Jesus was taken away. There were no flowers, no vestments, no candles, no silver, no brass, no brocade, no lace — nothing. It looked dreadful — stripped, bare, stark. I'm sorry to tell you, but if you weren't here on Good Friday you can't fully appreciate the way it looks today. Make no mistake, however; the lavish profusion of Easter lilies and all the other gorgeous trappings in the church this week are not the source of our joy. The lilies will turn brown and drop off and we will have to throw them out. Even if we plant them in our gardens and they manage to come back for a couple of years they will eventually wear out just as you and I will. Let's be sure we get this straight: we do not feel refreshed because the church is in its Easter finery. The Easter finery is refreshing *because Christ is risen.* Even if there had been a tornado and there were no Easter finery, *Christ would still be risen.*

And so the "times of refreshing" that the Lord is pleased to give us are not ends in themselves. They point beyond themselves to the golden gates of the kingdom of Heaven that will never be destroyed. One of our beloved members, recently widowed, told us this week how much the Holy Week and Easter services had meant to her. Even in the midst of her grief and loneliness, God had given her a breathing space; he had refreshed her along the weary way. He had refreshed her not with the water that cools thirst only for an hour, but with his own "living water" that had "become in [her] a spring of water welling up to eternal life" (John 4:14).

At the very end of *Pilgrim's Progress,* that great masterpiece not only of Christian faith but also of the English language, we read of the pilgrims on the last stretch of their journey. They have suffered many hardships and they are struggling with weariness, discouragement, and fear. John Bunyan writes:

> . . . a great Mist and Darkness fell upon them all . . . nor was there on all this Ground so much as one Inn or Victualling-House,

therein to refresh the feebler sort . . . and the Children began to be sorely weary, and they cried out unto Him that loveth Pilgrims, to make their way more Comfortable. So [when they] had gone a little further, a Wind arose that drove away the Fog, so the Air became more clear.

Dear brothers and sisters in Christ, the promise today is that the Lord will give us "times of refreshing." He will cool us with springs of living water and will make our way more clear with the breeze of his Holy Spirit. He will send us unexpected signs of his mercy and sudden surprises of his grace. But don't forget; God intends also to use you, yourself, as a sign of refreshment for someone else. When you walk out of here, you can take some of this Easter joy with you. The smallest thing done for someone else can be a cooling breeze of the Spirit. You don't have to do it with a heavy hand; after all, the Spirit is doing it, not you — so let him. And do it with a light heart; as the bumper sticker says, practice random acts of kindness. Let somebody go ahead of you in line. Show friendship to someone different from you. Help the handicapped person on the bus. Give away some of your money. Any little thing done by one of Christ's servants can become a time of refreshing for someone else.

Because, you see, Easter is not over. Easter will never be over. Refreshment time is only the beginning of God's eternal and never-ending party when we will eat and drink in the kingdom of God.[47] This is our future. It is not just pretty words. When St. Paul wrote about God's promises, he was grounding them not in human hope, but in the hope that is beyond human hope because it is grounded in the Resurrection of our Lord. Therefore, in the midst of sorrow, struggle, and pain, he could say, "I am *confident* that neither death, nor life, nor angels, nor principalities, nor things present, nor things to come, nor powers, nor height, nor depth, nor anything else in all creation, will be able to separate us from the love of God in Christ Jesus our Lord" (Romans 8:38-39).

AMEN.

PART SEVEN

Eastertide, Also Called the Great Fifty Days

———✸———

There we leave you in that blessed dependency, to hang upon him that hangs upon the cross, there bathe in his tears, there suck at his wounds, and lie down in peace in his grave, till he vouchsafe you a Resurrection, and an ascension into that kingdom which he hath purchased for you with the inestimable price of his incorruptible blood. Amen.

JOHN DONNE

Low Sunday or High Sunday?

———— ⤫ ————

*God raised him on the third day and made him manifest; not to
all the people but to us who were chosen by God as witnesses, who
ate and drank with him after he rose from the dead.*

(ACTS 10:40-41)

The congregation that gathers for worship today is very special.
Did you know that? There is something intentional about
coming to church on the second Sunday of Easter. It isn't automatic
or obvious. Like the people who are present on Maundy Thursday
and Good Friday, those who come today tend to be clued in. You're
here because you know the Christian life isn't just a couple of big
splashy occasions twice a year. Many of you are here because you are,
in one sense or another, members of the family, and you know
what's important to the life and health of the family. It is a special
joy to see each and every one of you this glad morning, the second
Sunday of Eastertide.

We are aware, though, of the hundreds who did not come
back. It's always hard, I think — at least it is for me — to see the
falling-off after the tremendous upsurge of attendance on Easter
Day without a twinge of disappointment. Of course we love to see
that big Easter attendance and would be very sorry indeed if we
didn't get it; still, it is perplexing to note, year after year, that this

discrepancy in attendance always continues to occur. That's why we ruefully nickname this day "Low Sunday." Every year one hopes that *this* will be the year that so many people will be convicted by the truth of Jesus' Resurrection that they can hardly wait to return the following Sunday; but it never seems to happen.

Why is it that so many people flock to the churches on Easter Day, listen to the message that Jesus has been raised from the dead, receive their Easter Communion, and then don't return? If you were invited to dinner with someone who had risen from the dead and they asked you to come again the following week, wouldn't you want to go? Especially if you were assured of participation in that new and risen life, wouldn't you want to come back more than anything else you might be invited to do? Who would lie in bed and watch *Meet the Press* if they could receive eternal life? As I thought about this, it occurred to me that the reason people don't come back on the Sunday after Easter is that they don't really believe that anything unusual has taken place. Something nice, maybe; something cheerful and up-lifting; but not an honest-to-God resurrection from the dead.

The Biblical text for today is actually lifted from last week's reading. I was forcibly struck by it when I heard it read on Easter Day. It seemed to me to be addressed exactly to this problem of Low Sunday. During the Great Fifty Days of Easter, we read selections from the book of the Acts of the Apostles. Here is a portion of one of St. Peter's sermons delivered soon after the Resurrection:

> Good news of peace by Jesus Christ: . . . how God anointed Jesus of Nazareth with the Holy Spirit and with power; how he went about doing good and healing all that were oppressed by the devil, for God was with him. . . . They put him to death by hang-ing him on a tree; but God raised him on the third day and made him manifest; not to all the people but to us who were chosen by God as witnesses, who ate and drank with him after he rose from the dead. (Acts 10:36-41)

Not to all the people, but to those who were chosen by God as witnesses. I never particularly thought about those words before, but when the lay reader read them on Easter Day, they jumped out at me. God did not make the risen Lord manifest to all the people, just to those he had chosen to be witnesses. I wondered if this might not be relevant to the discrepancy between the numbers of people who have the opportunity to hear the message of Jesus raised from the dead and those who actually believe it and stake their lives on it.

According to the New Testament witnesses, the risen Lord did not make himself known to anyone and everyone. After his Resurrection, he appeared only to those who had been his disciples and believed in him before he was put to death.[1] The Roman cohort never saw him risen from the dead; Caiaphas the high priest never saw him; Pontius Pilate never saw him. Those who saw him were Peter and James and John and Mary Magdalene and several hundred other disciples whose names, for the most part, we do not know.[2] This fact is one of several indications in the New Testament that Jesus' risen body, though it was palpably real, was of a different order from his earthly body. He revealed it to those whom he chose and to no one else. The initiative in that matter was his alone.

So, it follows that there will be many people who will come to church on Easter morning and see the flowers and hear the music and even receive Communion and still never see the risen Lord.[3] The Resurrection of Jesus was not a proof given by God to stun unbelievers into faith. Rather, it was the vindication of the trust of those who were reeling from the shock of having put their faith in a Messiah who ended up getting himself crucified. The Resurrection did not create new faith so much as it validated the faith that had already been placed in the One who was hanged on a tree. That's why Jesus displayed his *wounds* to "doubting Thomas" after the Resurrection. Those who participate in his Resurrection are those who identify with him in his suffering. Those who will inherit the promise of the Resurrection are those who bear the wounds of Christ. Thus St. Paul described the life of a Christian apostle:

> We are afflicted in every way, but not crushed; perplexed, but not driven to despair; persecuted, but not forsaken; struck down, but

not destroyed; always carrying in the body the death of Jesus, so that the life of Jesus may also be manifested in our bodies. For while we live we are always being given up to death for Jesus' sake. . . . (2 Corinthians 4:8-11)

On second thought, reading a passage like that may be the best answer to why a lot of people don't come back for more on the second Sunday of Easter. Maybe they sense that more will be asked of them. Maybe they're right.

Are you perhaps getting worried about where this is going? Maybe you're beginning to wonder why you came today after all. Maybe you are thinking that you might not want to be one of God's chosen minority. It doesn't sound like an unmixed blessing, does it? Here's another of Paul's comments: "I think that God has exhibited us apostles as last of all, like men sentenced to death, because we have become a spectacle to the world" (1 Corinthians 4:9). He is thinking of the entering procession at the Roman gladiatorial circus, where the last people to enter the arena are the ones sentenced to die.[4] He is speaking especially of the apostles, but by extension this means all of us in the apostolic faith. Christ has called all of us to "take up the cross and follow me" (Matthew 16:24). The Resurrection can't be detached from the self-sacrificing way of the Cross.

This was the problem of the Corinthian congregation. Much to Paul's distress, they wanted to leap over the Cross altogether; they felt that they had already attained eternity. That's why Paul used strong words to emphasize the Cross. One of his main themes is that "there is no distinction" among human beings because we are all in bondage to sin (Romans 3:22-23), but here he does not hesitate to divide humanity into two groups: "The word of the Cross is foolishness to those who are perishing, but to us who are being saved it is the power of God" (1 Corinthians 1:18). Again, here is the idea that the message about Jesus may indeed be *heard* by those who have not entered into his saving life, but it is not *received*. To those who have looked on Christ as a mere religious phenomenon, both the word of the Cross and the raising of the Lord from the dead will be similar to the eggs and lilies that we use for decorations

— lovely to have for special occasions, but packed away like the winter coats for most of the year. After all, the real business of the season is the filing of the income tax and the renting of the beach house, isn't it? The resurrection of the dead seems like an irrelevant distraction from the actual preoccupations of daily life. Thus it is that Jesus was raised from the dead and most people never even noticed.

That is, they never noticed until the disciples of Christ, who had been made apostles in the meantime,[5] began making a stir with their insistent message: Jesus had been put to death by all the best people, "but God raised him on the third day and made him manifest; *not to all the people but to us who were chosen by God as witnesses,* who ate and drank with him after he rose from the dead. And he commanded us to preach to the people, and to testify that he is the one ordained by God to be judge of the living and the dead" (Acts 10:40-42). Those chosen men and women, under orders from God to proclaim the crucified Messiah as the Lord of the universe, burned so brightly with the flame of the gospel that the entire Mediterranean world was soon alight with the Name of Jesus Christ. The transformation of that ragtag bunch of disciples into a fearless force for the conversion of the world is one of the strongest arguments for the truth of the Resurrection.

Yet as we know, not all were converted. Not all believed. Many went through the motions, but as we know, that is not the same thing as showing forth in our lives what we say with our lips. Even after we have marshaled all the evidence and made the case as strongly as we can, many — perhaps the majority — will remain untouched. Easter remains for most people a vaguely reassuring festival of spring. Is it possible that the truth is too threatening for most people? "The Lord is risen indeed!" is not a cheerful message about longer hours of sunshine. It is a world-overturning announcement about the reorientation of our entire existence.

Uneasy though it may make you feel to be singled out in this way, there is a strong possibility that you who are here this morning are among those whom God has chosen to be his witnesses. You may doubt this, or even be frightened by it, but I invite you to take it seriously. God has chosen you for something more than azaleas and hyacinths and a new spring outfit. You are those who "ate and drank with him after he rose from the dead," and you have come to eat and drink with him once more. God has made him manifest to you. You have come back to be with him again on this second Sunday after the Resurrection. Something — some One — has brought you back. I suggest to you that you think of this as good news, because for those who are being saved, the gospel of Christ is the power of God.

The power of God! That is what descends upon the early disciples: "power from on high" (Luke 24:49). The Great Fifty Days of Easter comes to its mighty conclusion on Pentecost, the day when the Holy Spirit came down upon the disciples in tongues of flame. This has always seemed to many of us to be even more remote and baffling than the Resurrection. Most of us haven't a clue about tongues of flame, let alone speaking in tongues. But think about it this way. The Holy Spirit is the engine of Christian faith and Christian life. The Spirit is the fuel, the horsepower, the explosive force that made world-transforming agents out of a group of provincial nonentities.

The book of Acts, you might say, has two heroes, Peter and Paul (Paul, to be sure, would have been something more than a nonentity with or without the Holy Spirit). That's speaking about the human actors, though. The two driving forces behind Peter and Paul and all of the other Christians, male and female,[6] who move through the book of Acts are the Holy Spirit and the Name of Jesus.[7] One of the most memorable scenes in Acts is the one where Peter and John come upon a lame man begging at the city gate. Peter fixed his eyes upon the man, we are told, and said,

> "Silver and gold have I none; but such as I have give I thee: In the name of Jesus Christ of Nazareth, rise up and walk." And he took him by the right hand, and lifted him up: and immediately his feet and ankle bones received strength. And he leaping up stood, and walked, and entered with them into the temple, walking, and leaping, and praising God. (Acts 3:6-7 KJV)

Now you may think this is too farfetched to believe, and I think so too, except that once when I was a very young and inexperienced priest I was summoned to visit a young woman, just graduated from an Ivy League college, who had been diagnosed with some sort of crippling arthritis. Never having met her or her family before, I hadn't a clue what to expect. When I arrived, I found her sitting alone in a wheelchair in the back yard. This was one of my very first pastoral calls; you can't imagine how inadequate I felt and how little I knew about what to do as she and I talked. In the back of my mind, though, was the experience my husband and I had when our younger daughter was born with multiple life-threatening problems. All three of the clergy of our church came repeatedly to the hospital, sometimes as often as twice a day, yet not once did they ever pray with us. Remembering this, I put my hand on the young woman's knee and stumblingly asked Jesus to heal her.

He did. She was out of the wheelchair in a matter of weeks and now, twenty-some years later, she has had no recurrence. I have never told this story before and may never tell it again; it scares me still.[8] Nothing like that has happened in my ministry since. But you never know. You see, it is not up to me. It is not up to you. It is the Three-in-One God in his sovereign freedom who acts as he pleases. The power of the Holy Spirit and the Name of Jesus can work in you and through you in ways that you never imagined. I don't understand why we Episcopalians got this idea that using the Name of Jesus is tacky — something that only provincial nonentities do — but in the ineffable parlance of today, "Get over it!" Because as we read in the book of Acts,

> Peter, filled with the Holy Spirit, said to them, "Rulers of the people and elders, if we are being examined today concerning a good deed done to a cripple, by what means this man has been healed, be it known to you all, and to all the people of Israel, that by the name of Jesus Christ of Nazareth, whom you crucified, whom God raised from the dead, by him this man is standing before you well. . . . And there is salvation in no one else, for *there is*

no other name under heaven given among men by which we must be saved." (Acts 4:8-12)

Dear people of God: when you made the decision to come to worship today, the Holy Spirit of Jesus Christ was drawing you, whether you knew it or not. Do not go out from here with a furrowed brow, worrying about what you are supposed to do for him in return. That would not be good news at all. He will show you what he has for you. He has already prepared good works for you to walk in.⁹ He has chosen you. You are his witnesses. That's the way the news is spread. The beloved pastor of Madison Avenue Presbyterian Church in New York, David H. C. Read, told his congregation: "One of the reasons I believe in the Resurrection is that my mother told me. And to this day a strong element in my belief is the number and quality of the people who told me." You today, are a person of that quality, not because you are some paragon of virtue, but because you "ate and drank with the Lord Jesus after he was raised from the dead." Tell your children. Tell your grandchildren. Tell your friends. Bring the news especially to those who are suffering, because thereby you will carry his Cross. I know it isn't easy, but tell them even if you stumble over the words, because the Holy Spirit will be in your words. God raised Jesus on the third day. He is alive. He is here with us at this moment. This is the power from on high. May God the Father, God the Son, and God the Holy Spirit be praised for ever.

AMEN.

My Taste Was Me

———— ❧❧❧ ————

*(preached at St. Joseph's Roman Catholic Church
in Greenwich Village, New York City)*

*Peter was grieved because {Jesus} said to him the third time,
"Do you love me?" And he said to him, "Lord, you know everything; you know that I love you." Jesus said to him, "Feed my
sheep."*

(JOHN 21:17)

Eight years ago I was invited to preach here, and I still regard
that occasion as one of the greatest privileges I have had in my
entire ministry. I am thrilled to be with you again. I have the greatest regard for this congregation and all that it stands for. Furthermore, although to be sure there are some serious theological issues
dividing Protestants and Catholics, I nevertheless repeat what I said
in this pulpit in 1993 — we have many reasons to be deeply grateful to you. Your visibility, numbers, and centralized leadership give
you a voice and presence in the global village that we Protestants
can only envy.[10] You have used that voice fearlessly on behalf of the
poor, the oppressed, the powerless and dispossessed. Since I was last
here, Bishop Belo of East Timor won the Nobel Peace Prize. Since I
was last here, the Bishop of San Cristóbal, Mexico, was pictured in
The New York Times wearing a helmet to protect himself from government snipers who hate him for his "passionately egalitarian mes-

sage" to poor Indians who "are routinely abused or ignored."[11] Since I was last here, Bud Welch, the father of one of the Oklahoma City bombing victims, a devout Catholic, has been travelling the country in opposition to the death penalty, and calls Timothy McVeigh's father on the phone every couple of weeks.

And since I was last here, Pope John Paul II visited Jerusalem and the world watched as this frail, elderly man made his painful way across the open plaza to the Western Wall, where he inserted a prayer of confession and petition into a crack between the stones. His pontificate will long be remembered as the one which made the most significant overtures toward reconciliation between Christians and Jews. This subject has been very much before us these last two weeks. In case you've been out of town or temporarily deafened, here's the story: a Jewish reporter assigned to do an article on the New York Knicks attended a team Bible study led by player Charlie Ward.[12] The players had been friendly to the reporter and interested in his Judaism, so it was quite a surprise to him when Ward asked him why the Jews killed Jesus. This has caused an uproar. Last Tuesday morning, the entire Don Imus radio program was devoted to the subject. Charlie Ward has apologized handsomely, generously, and at some length, but the intensity of the reaction indicates that this issue is going to be front and center for a long time to come.

Because of the Holocaust, or the Shoah as many prefer, we do not read the Bible in the same way that we once did.[13] Take for example the portion of the book of Acts that is appointed for today. The Apostle Peter is standing before the Jewish council, the Sanhedrin, and he says, "The God of our ancestors raised Jesus, though you had him killed by hanging him on a tree" (Acts 5:30). You will agree, I think, that those words certainly seem to say that the Jewish council killed Jesus. The book of Acts and the Gospel of John, both of which we are reading today, are particularly given to negative statements about "the Jews," which have led over the years to the idea that the Jews were uniquely guilty of Christ's death. We might indeed wish that Luke and John hadn't done that. There really may not be any satisfactory way of dealing with these negative references. Nevertheless, the church is tackling the error on many fronts, for instance by reminding us that Jesus himself was Jewish, that all the disciples were Jewish, that crucifixion was a strictly Roman form of execution, and that the spitting, flogging, and mocking were all carried out by Roman soldiers.

More important still are the broader theological assertions that can be made. Many commentators over the centuries have stressed the point that Jesus was condemned by church *and* state, the religious *and* the secular authorities, the point being that he was intolerable to everybody. This should have removed any stigma attached to Jews in particular. Most crucial of all, however, is the deep theological truth that Jesus died for the sins of *us all,* every one of us. In my Anglican tradition as well as yours, we read the Passion narrative dramatically on Palm Sunday, with the congregation taking the part of the crowd. We *all* shout, "Crucify him!" All of us good churchgoing Christians call out, "His blood be on us and on our children!" Who killed Jesus? All of us sinners killed him. We will just have to keep on saying that and remembering that, so that these terrible misunderstandings will no longer occur.

Now on this glorious morning of Eastertide, let us turn our attention to today's story from the Gospel of John. It takes place a few days after the Resurrection. The disciples must have been in a state of shock; it was unnerving for them during those forty days before the Ascension when the risen Lord was turning up here and turning up there, materializing out of nowhere, now in the upper room, now on the beach. There was no telling where he might reveal himself next. In those days just after the Resurrection it must have been like breathing pure oxygen. No wonder Peter said, I gotta get outta here! "I'm going fishing" (John 21:3). Remember, it was Peter who said, on that very same shore at an earlier time, "Depart from me, for I am a sinful man, O Lord" (Luke 5:8). If any proof of that were needed, Peter has certainly given it. Peter was guilty of one of the worst things a human being can do to another, let alone to the Son of God.

We need to stop and think about this. As it happens, a great deal has been written lately about snitching. Betraying a friend is thought to be one of the greatest offenses of all. Two situations in particular have called forth recent thoughts about this, one being the so-called "blue wall of silence" that surrounds the police departments, and the other being the Columbine High School phenomenon. As of course you know, it has been very difficult to prosecute any police for anything, because of the informal but near-absolute prohibition against snitching on a fellow officer. Similarly, betraying a fellow student has been considered so heinous that high school officials have had difficulty persuading kids to report suspicious conversations.

Multiply these attitudes toward betrayal by an infinite number to get an idea of Peter's guilt. You remember Peter, the most outspoken of all the disciples. His personality emerges from the pages of Scripture with remarkable clarity. He must have been an adored child in his family, the type whose every utterance is thought to be too cute for words. He never seems to think before he speaks, blurting out whatever comes into mind, for better and for worse. For example, at the Last Supper, the Master predicted that all his disciples would abandon him. "Peter declared to him, 'Though they all fall away because of you, I will never fall away.' Jesus said to him, 'Truly, I say to you, this very night, before the cock crows, you will deny me three times.' Peter said to him, 'Even if I must die with you, I will not deny you'" (Matthew 26:33-35). It is really quite shocking to remember that Peter said these things in view of what happened later that very night. We are told that after Jesus was arrested, Peter followed at a distance into the courtyard of the high priest. All four Gospels tell us that three times he was asked if he wasn't a friend of Jesus, and three times he solemnly denied it. Matthew reports that the third time Peter swore and cursed and denied Christ vehemently. Only a few hours after his passionate protestations of exceptional loyalty, Peter became a traitor, just as Jesus had predicted.

So we can imagine, can't we, the feelings of Peter when the Lord was raised from the tomb? The Gospel accounts suggest strongly that joy was uppermost in his mind, but it must have been mingled with considerable dread as well. How could he ever survive the guilt and the shame? Shame is the right word here, surely. Peter must have understood that Jesus forgave him, being the kind of Savior that Peter knew him to be, but how was Peter ever to hold his head up again? We may imagine that Peter had a hard time eating his breakfast of fish and bread there on the beach with the man whose love and trust he had basely and dishonorably denied. Peter must have choked on the food; the words of Gerard Manley Hopkins in one of his sonnets describe it perfectly.

> . . . God's most deep decree
> Bitter would have me taste: my taste was me.[14]

When they had finished breakfast, Jesus turned to Peter and, using the form of his name that he used at the very beginning (John 1:42) when he called the big fisherman from his nets, he said to him "Simon, son of John, do you love me more than these?"[15] Those words, "more than these," can be interpreted two or three different ways, but many commentators have found the meaning in the earlier protest of Peter when he said, "Even though all these others leave you, I never will."[16] When Jesus says, "Do you love me more than these?" it recapitulates Peter's boast that he loves more than the others. Peter then responds simply, "Yes, Lord; you know that I love you." There can be no doubt of Peter's sincerity here. The human being may be cowardly, may be devious, may be desperately corrupt as Jeremiah says (Jeremiah 17:9), but if the heart is turned toward Jesus, that is the sign that the Lord's redemption is at work. When Peter says this, Jesus replies to him, "Feed my lambs." Then after a little while Jesus said to him again, "Simon, son of John, do you love me?" and Peter said, "Yes, Lord; you know that I love you." Jesus said, "Tend my sheep." Then Jesus said to Peter the third time, "Simon, son of John, do you love me?" This time, we are told, Peter was terribly hurt. Rarely are we told anything in the Bible about a person's inner feelings, so this is a striking statement. What more can Peter say? The distress with which he replies must have registered with the Lord, for he does not ask him a fourth time.[17] The third and final exchange goes like this: "Peter was distressed that Jesus had asked him a third time, and he said, 'Lord, you know everything; you know that I love you.' And Jesus said to him, 'Feed my lambs.'" Peter is not only forgiven, you see; he is completely made new; to use the word of the Apostle Paul, he is *justified.* He, too, is raised from the dead. He comes forth to us a man recreated. He is now to carry the divine life of Jesus to others. He is given his commission. Jesus entrusts him with the pastoral future of the Christian community in the same terms that Jesus uses of himself in John 10:11: "I am the good shepherd. The good shepherd lays down his life for the sheep." Peter's apostolate will be that of Jesus himself.[18]

And so we see that there is no crime so atrocious, no shame so abysmal, no failure so profound as to put us beyond the transforming power of the risen Lord Jesus Christ. The secular world ridicules us for believing this. Catholics in particular come in for constant scorn, as I don't need to tell you. Peter Steinfels writes about this in *The New York Times* frequently; thank God he is there. "The rhetoric of disbelief and ultimate Godlessness reigns as generally uncontested in important sectors of American culture," he commented last week. This is especially true in artistic, literary, and intellectual circles in New York City. Yet I came across a very surprising statement in a review last week by a respected cultural critic, Daniel Mendelsohn. He was reviewing the new book called *Walking the Bible,* written by Bruce Feiler, a Jewish man who set out on foot to visit all the scenes described in the Torah (Pentateuch).[19] Mendelsohn writes that he had been eager to read the book because "like many nonreligious people I harbor a secret, lingering desire to be persuaded."[19] That amazed me. Doesn't that feel like a breath of fresh air? But what would persuade him? What would persuade any Jew since the Shoah to take Christianity seriously? What would persuade journalists and artists and professors?

In the final analysis there is nothing that will persuade anyone except the example of transformed, Christlike lives that illustrate the preaching of the gospel. That was the power of St. Peter and St. Paul. That is the power of Bud Welch, who says that at first he wanted to see Timothy McVeigh "fry." "Then I came to myself," he said, using the same words that Jesus used of the Prodigal Son; "Revenge does the opposite of healing you."[21] All over the country, good reporters are covering the McVeigh situation. Who will lead them to consider the truth of Christ? The people calling for blood vengeance? Or the nuns of the Sisters of Providence in Terre Haute who will keep a vigil on the day of the execution? "You have to stay clear and consistent," Sister Joan Slobig says in a recent *Times* article. "If life is holy, we don't have a right to take a life under any circumstances."[22] Are these not the examples that point beyond themselves to Christ "the Lamb of God, who takes away the sin of the world" (John 1:29)?

Here is the issue. Do you see yourself, do I see myself as the final arbiter of "God's most deep decree"? Or have you tasted yourself? Do you know, along with Peter and Father Hopkins and your preacher this morning, that the taste of yourself is bitter? Listen, dear people of St. Joseph's, if you know that bitter taste it is because you are already safe in the hands of the One who died for you. You would not see yourself so clearly if you did not already know the love of the Savior. You are already incorporate in his risen, divine life. That is what gives us the strength and courage to arise from our pain and sorrow, our shame and disgrace, our sin and perversity, to go forth as new creatures in Christ Jesus.

"Simon, son of John, do you love me?" Through the power of the living Word at this very moment, our Lord asks you this question. He does not ask you if you have been good. He does not ask you if you have obeyed the rules. He does not ask you how many credits you have piled up. He just asks you, *Do you love me?* There is not one person here today who cannot answer that question with a full heart: *Lord, you know that I love you.* Come now to receive the Sacrament of his supper in complete confidence that his sacrifice for you is complete and perfect, now and for ever.

AMEN.

The Peace from Somewhere Else

———— ∞ ————

Out of Zion shall go forth the law, and the word of the LORD
*from Jerusalem. . . . they shall beat their swords into plow-
shares, and their spears into pruning hooks; nation shall not lift
up sword against nation, neither shall they learn war any more.*

(MICAH 4:2-3)

One of the texts appointed for today is from the book of the
prophet Micah. "Out of Zion shall go forth the law, and the
word of the LORD from Jerusalem." These words were written several centuries before Christ. It should be obvious by now, some
twenty-five centuries later, that whatever hopes Christians, Jews, or
Muslims may have had for Jerusalem as an actual source of peace for
the world at large have long since been revealed as religious day-
dreaming. No place on earth has caused more contention or been
more disputed. Attitudes seem hardened beyond hope of retrieval.[23]
But it is not necessary to look far away into the Middle East to
see the fault lines in the human community. I have been in South
Carolina for several weeks. Just a few days ago, *The State* newspaper
ran a big story and color picture on the top of the front page.[24] In a
classic confrontation between traditional community values and new
development, Richland County voted to approve a major development project in three old working-class villages.[25] The century-old

cotton mills will be turned into upscale condos, offices, shops, and art galleries. The plan was delayed for a year by the fierce and emotional opposition of many local residents who fear the destruction of the social fabric that they cherish. One person said, "The whole neighborhood is in an uproar over this. I'm truly sad about what this project has done to the community. We've always been together, and now we're forming groups against each other." Spokesmen for the development, on the other hand, said that there were always going to be people opposed to "progress" and it was time to "move forward" in spite of the opposition.

At this point in the story, a group of Tibetan Buddhist monks became players in the drama. At the time of the vote, they were finishing a four-day sand painting project sponsored by one of the art galleries which eventually hopes to move into the complex. On the climactic fourth day, according to time-honored Tibetan custom, the intricate sand painting was destroyed to indicate the impermanence of all life, and the remaining sand, with high ritual and ceremony, was poured into the Congaree River. A large color photograph on the front page of the paper showed this happening; the caption was, "Monks offer healing in time of change: the sand is poured into the river to disperse the healing energies of the mandala (oval-shaped sand painting) throughout the world." Gallery owner and project sponsor Jack Gerstner said to a reporter that the monks' visit was not a coincidence, but might have played a role in the county's vote. Thus do healing energies serve commercial interests.

The romanticizing of Tibetan Buddhism is one of the more interesting things going on in America today. As I travel around the country, Tibetan monks and sand paintings are everywhere, often in churches. There is much talk of healing energies. But what exactly is this Tibetan ceremony going to do to heal the community where the proposed development will displace so many? And where is this healing to come from?

Here is another story about Buddhist monks that I read only two weeks ago in *The New York Times*. The setting is Cambodia. The devastation left behind by the Khmer Rouge has produced a moral wasteland where there is virtually no system of justice at all. "Lynch law" prevails. Suspects are beaten to death in the streets with large crowds watching. A French historian and resident of Phnom Penh named Olivier de Bernon was walking to an appointment and came across one of these lynchings in progress. He was seized by both fear and anger, so that he began trembling uncontrollably, but his instincts overmastered his fear and he rushed in to stop the savage beating. A journalist who was watching said that "the crowd fell back at the sight of the determined foreigner." For two hours M. de Bernon stood over the unconscious victim until finally an ambulance arrived. As he talked about the episode to a reporter later, he said that the thing that unnerved him most was not the beating itself, not even the sight of the dozen police officers who watched the whole thing passively and made no move to help him. What bothered him most was the behavior of a group of Buddhist monks in their orange robes. The monks did not actively participate in the attack, but as the Frenchman stood guard over the body, they not only did not help, they laughed and "giggled" and pointed their fingers at M. de Bernon as though he were some sort of freak. This, at any rate, was his testimony according to the news report.[26]

I do not tell these stories in order to make any particular point about Buddhists or Tibetan monks.[27] We all know about the numerous atrocities committed over the centuries in the name of Christ. We all know about Christians who have stood by as other people attacked Jews or blacks or homosexuals. The point is not about Buddhists. It is about human sin, which pervades all cultures and all religions. Another recent *Times* article reported that some of the leaders of the Tibetan community in exile in Dharamsala, India, were growing weary of all the Americans who come there seeking for a smiling, idealized, "spiritual" Tibet.[28] Americans have a sentimental streak that allows us to think that there is such a thing as innocence, but as all great writers know and have shown us, there isn't. I think of Flannery O'Connor, who defined sentimentality as a premature rush to believe in innocence without grasping the reality of the Fall.[29] The Adam and Eve story doesn't have anything to do with the theory of evolution; it has to do with the original and primordial rebellion against the Creator in which all of humanity without exception is involved. Unaided humankind cannot lift it-self up out of its incessant warfare.

Now I am going to read to you the eucharistic Proper Preface for the Easter season, which you will hear in a few minutes as the celebrant begins the Great Thanksgiving. Listen to its concreteness, its references to something that has actually happened in human history. First we say that "it is right and a good and joyful thing to give thanks to you, Father almighty, Creator of heaven and earth." Then we continue,

> But chiefly are we bound to praise you for the glorious Resurrec-tion of your Son Jesus Christ our Lord; for he is the true Paschal Lamb, who was sacrificed for us, and has taken away the sin of the world. By his death he has destroyed death, and by his rising to life again he has won for us everlasting life.

Here, embedded in our Prayer Book, are these tremendous claims. The Son of God is the true Passover lamb whose sacrificial death has taken away the sin of Adam. By undergoing death, Christ has destroyed death, and in his Resurrection, he has won the victory for us also. We say these mighty things so often that perhaps we for-get to notice how staggering they are. The promise of the gospel is that the course of the world has been definitively changed by the in-tervention of God to save us from self-destruction. This is very dif-ferent from "healing energies."

The risen Lord says to his disciples repeatedly, *Peace be with you.* The Hebrew prophets spoke of God's *shalom,* or peace. St. Paul speaks of the peace that passes human understanding (Philippians 4:7). This theme of peace permeates much of the Old and New Tes-taments, but we may well ask ourselves if it isn't just sentimental. Micah's images of the swords bent into ploughshares and the spears bent into pruning hooks are well-known, but they sometimes seem like a mockery. "Nation shall not lift up sword against nation, nei-ther shall they learn war any more." Given human nature, isn't that a pipe dream? Much has been written about men's love of war. Of course men hate war, too, but if we are honest we must admit that they also love it. Many military men report that there is a type of male bonding in wartime that, we are told, is more intense than any other kind.[30] Watching an infantry charge at the height of the battle of Fredericksburg, Robert E. Lee turned to General James Longstreet and said, "It is well that war is so terrible — we should grow too fond of it!"[31]

I often think about firemen sitting around in their firehouses waiting for an alarm. It is probably pretty boring. When the signal goes off, I would imagine that the rush of adrenaline would be quite exciting.[32] Many people go out looking for that jolt, that rush; they sky dive, bungee-jump, rock-climb, go canyoneering, ride white water. Maybe peace is really not what we want. Maybe peace would be boring. Maybe "the peace of Christ" is not such a compelling thing.

But think of it another way. Think of how war cuts off creative activity, destroys family life, and kills promising young people. Think of how bombing consumes not only lives and buildings but also irreplaceable books, art, photographs, letters, scientific work. What we need to be truly human, it would seem, is two seemingly contradictory things; we want the rush of adrenaline, the almost aesthetic (and certainly almost erotic) thrill of rescue, success, and victory — but without the violence and destruction. We need the male bonding — without the killing. These thoughts suggest to me that Biblical peace is something quite different from the absence of conflict. After all, conflict and struggle are necessary for real productivity. Most great art and literature, most scientific breakthroughs, most human achievements of any kind arise out of tremendous effort, and everyone who has worked very hard for a goal knows the sense of euphoria that comes when work begins to pay off. There is nothing more thrilling in the world. Biblical peace is linked to that. Micah writes that "every man shall sit under his vine and under his fig tree" (Micah 4:4). The image here is one of hard work rewarded, as each person enjoys the fruits of his labor. In the kingdom of God, creative activity will flow unhindered, and the euphoria will never end.

The book of Ecclesiastes gives much insight here. We read

that "there is nothing better for a man than that he should . . . find enjoyment in his toil" (Ecclesiastes 2:24). But because of fallen human nature, things do not work out that way. The writer says, "I came to hate all my toil in which I had toiled under the sun, seeing that I must leave it to the man who will come after me" (2:18). He takes no pleasure in all the mighty works he has done. "I saw that all toil and all skill in work come from a man's envy of his neighbor. . . . What is done under the sun was grievous to me; for all is vanity and a striving after wind" (4:4; 2:17).

Don't let the literary beauty of Ecclesiastes fool you into mistaking its significance. It is a remarkable book of the Bible because it gives us a brutally unsentimental picture of the disappointments of life. Round and round we go in a ceaseless cycle of vanity and meaninglessness. Same old, same old, as we say. Same old wars, same old greed, same old folly. It is important that we take this picture seriously. It is a foil for the promises of Micah. Those words about bending the swords into ploughshares are engraved on a wall at the United Nations, but as of this morning, more than three hundred U.N. troops — "peacekeeping" troops — are held hostage by the rebels in Sierra Leone. Same old, same old.

What then do we mean when we speak of God's peace? What does Jesus mean when he says, "Peace be with you?" You can make retreats to as many monasteries as you like, Christian or Buddhist, but as honest monks will tell you, backstage behind the curtain of tranquillity there is just as much pettiness and rivalry as any other place. How then can God's peace be anything more lasting than sand poured into the river?

It all depends. It depends on who God is, who Jesus is, and whether the Biblical testimony is true. Today's Gospel reading from Luke 24 ends with verse 48, but if we read on to verse 49 we find the promise of Pentecost, which reads, "Behold, I send the promise of my Father upon you; but stay in the city, until you are clothed with power from on high."

Power from on high. Now let's not take this literally, the way some of the Bible-debunkers do. The apostles and evangelists knew what a figure of speech was. They never meant that "power from on high" was power from the top level of a two-tiered universe. It's a metaphor; it means power from another sphere, another realm, another order of existence. There is no hope of peace from within this world order. Something has to break the cycle. For centuries, the prophets of Israel promised just such a breakthrough. There would come a time when God would decisively intervene and reverse the downward spiral. In spite of all appearances, the prophets taught, history does have a plan and purpose; it moves toward the final revelation of the kingdom of God where they will study war no more. The message of the New Testament is that this final intervention, so long promised by the prophets, began with the Crucifixion and Resurrection of Jesus Christ. In a famous analogy made by a New Testament scholar (Oscar Cullmann) some years ago, the Cross and Resurrection was like D-Day. The beachhead has been established, the enemy is on the run, the war is going to be won. As the little animals of Narnia say in *The Lion, the Witch and the Wardrobe,* "Aslan has landed." There are terrible battles yet to be fought, but the end is not in doubt.

Our weapons in this warfare are Biblical. Sentimentality is not one of them. Neither is a belief in any sort of religious innocence. Pilgrimages to find holy people and holy places lead to preachers with clay feet and churches where gunmen enter and massacre the worshippers. There is no escape from the world into Shangri-La. The promise of the new Jerusalem does not mean a life free of disappointment in this world. The Pope's recent trip to the Old City of Jerusalem was a case in point. During the week of his visit, according to news reports, a sort of peace did seem to descend. Within hours of his departure, the old animosities were back in place as though he had never been there. And yet, and yet . . . his presence, old, frail, and stooped as he was, conveyed a message. He has held onto his beachhead for the Lord. He has not yielded it to the enemy. He was an embodiment, however feeble, of Christ's ultimate victory over our ancient hatreds.

What is your beachhead for the Lord? Each of you has one, and your congregation has more than one. It might be prison ministry, or bringing up your children as Christians, or being honest and fair in business. It might be far away in Belize, or nearby at Emmaus House. It might be helping a sick neighbor, or mounting a campaign for better protection of the environment, or enduring cancer with grace. Whatever it is, large or small, when you trust in the Lord, it is not sand poured in the river. Unaided human activity is "vanity and striving after wind," but we are *not unaided.* The peace of God is not peace as the world gives; it is peace that comes from another source. In God, our toil is meaningful, purposeful, and lasting, because he gives us *power from on high.*

Believing that makes all the difference in the world. Martin Luther King Jr. believed it in prison. Dietrich Bonhoeffer, hanged by the Nazis, knew his death was not in vain. Our fellow Southerner Will Campbell has trusted in Christ's victory through all these decades of civil rights work while continuing to be a gospel presence to the Ku Klux Klan. One of the most impressive Christians of this or any other age is Bishop Tutu of South Africa. He has trusted *the power from on high* for more than forty years of suffering and struggle. He has remained stalwart and faithful through temptations and pressures that you and I cannot even imagine. Through it all he has never lost his unquenchable high spirits. He trusts God's future, "the Jerusalem which is above, which is free" (Galatians 4:26). This is what Bishop Tutu says about the meaning of the Christian struggle. He says, "I've read the end of the book! We win!"

> Out of Zion shall go forth the law, and the word of the LORD from Jerusalem. . . . they shall beat their swords into plowshares, and their spears into pruning hooks; nation shall not lift up sword against nation, neither shall they learn war any more . . . *for the mouth of the LORD hath spoken it.*

AMEN.

It Ain't Necessarily So

———∞∞∞———

If Christ has not been raised, your faith is futile and you are
still in your sins. . . . But in fact Christ has been raised from
the dead, the first fruits of those who have fallen asleep. For as
by a man came death, by a man has come also the resurrection of
the dead. For as in Adam all die, so also in Christ shall all be
made alive.

(1 CORINTHIANS 15:17, 20-22)

Here is a review of a book called *The Bible Unearthed.*[31] Written
by two leading archaeologists, it is about the latest discoveries being dug up in the Biblical lands and what these finds might
mean for the interpretation of the Scriptures. This book review was
written by a highly respected Old Testament scholar who taught for
many years at my seminary. Reading her review has been a good reminder for me that things have changed since I was in theological
school. In the 1950s and 60s when I first started studying the Bible,
we were constantly being cheered on by the latest news from the
digs. The more the archaeologists uncovered, we were told, the
more their finds corroborated the stories of the Biblical ancestors —
Abraham, Moses, Joshua, David. Now, forty years later, the whole
thing has been reversed. To the great delight of the Bible-
debunkers, the stories in the first part of the Old Testament cannot

be shown to be historically dependable. The Exodus did not happen as described; the swift conquest of Canaan never took place; the great King Solomon was probably just a local tribal chieftain.[34] The authors of *The Bible Unearthed,* according to this review, show great reverence for the Hebrew Bible, but (they believe) it is "not a miraculous revelation, but a brilliant product of the human imagination." It all reminds me of the words of the Gershwin song, "The things that you're liable to read in the Bible/ It ain't necessarily so."

Now let's fast-forward to the New Testament. The text for today's sermon is the fifteenth chapter of the first letter of the Apostle Paul to the Christians in the city of Corinth. Paul makes some very big claims in this letter — staggering and unbelievable claims, as a matter of fact. In order to give you the full picture, I will be referring to the whole of chapter 15.

Paul was very worried about the Corinthian Christians. They were drifting away from the path of truth and life. Paul writes to call them back. He begins chapter 15 with these words: "Now I would remind you, brothers and sisters, in what terms I preached to you the gospel, which you received, in which you stand, by which you are saved, if you hold it fast — unless you believed in vain." In this climactic chapter — one of the most powerful passages that he ever wrote — Paul is saying, This is it, Corinthians. It's this or nothing. What I proclaimed to you as good news is nothing less than the salvation of the world, unless you want to throw it away. Everything — *everything* — depends on whether I told you the truth or not.

In the next two or three sentences, Paul sums up the Christian message that he preached everywhere he went. What is that message? Could you sum it up in three sentences? How would you do it? Here is how Paul does it: "I delivered to you as of first importance what I also received, that Christ died for our sins in accordance with the scriptures, that he was buried, that he was raised on the third day in accordance with the scriptures, and that he appeared to Cephas [Peter], then to the twelve [disciples, later apostles]."

We need to notice several things about this summary of the gospel message. First, you will see that Paul does not offer religious ideas, inspirational sayings, or "spiritual" lessons. He simply declares that *something happened.* He describes it in four sentences:

Jesus Christ died.[35]
He was dead and buried.
On the third day he was raised from the dead.
He appeared to his disciples.

This is the message that converted the Mediterranean world and that is still creating new Christians around the globe. It is not a collection of generic religious principles. It is an announcement about *events that happened* and that can be described: Christ died; Christ was buried; Christ was raised from the dead; Christ appeared, living, to his disciples.

A second thing to notice is that Paul says twice, "in accordance with the scriptures." Twice in one sentence he says it. Apparently this is very important to him. He wants the connection between Jesus Christ and the God of the Old Testament nailed into place. He wants us to know that the God of Abraham, Isaac, and Jacob is the same God who is the father of Jesus Christ and that the whole thing was planned from the beginning. And, clearly, he thinks that the Scripture can be trusted. If David and Solomon were not exactly the mighty rulers that live in song and story, that is not the point. The point is that God was at work in them, and in the entire history of Israel, "with a mighty hand and an outstretched arm."[36]

Now we come to the section of the chapter that you heard a few moments ago. This passage is well known, but I don't know if you've noticed the uncompromising do-or-die, either-or quality of it. Again, we can break down the argument to its simplest components:

If there is no resurrection of the dead, then Christ has not been raised.
If Christ has not been raised, then the apostles' preaching is in vain.
If Christ has not been raised, your faith is futile and you are still in your sins.

Paul the apostle has not always been understood in the church. He was controversial and difficult in his own time and he is controversial and difficult today. For those who have really come to know him, however, there can be no question of his importance. We should always remember that Paul's letters were written much earlier than the four Gospels. Without Paul, the news about Jesus Christ would never have spread appreciably beyond what was then called Judea. Christianity would have remained a sect within Judaism and might eventually have been reabsorbed.[37] Without Paul, there never would have been a gospel for the Gentiles, meaning that you and I would never have heard it. More important still, without Paul the events of the life of Jesus would not have been given their definitive theological shaping. It is not an accident that Paul's letters take up more space in the New Testament than those of any other writer.

So when Paul says, "if Christ has not been raised, then our preaching is in vain," it is right that we should sit up and pay attention. Paul was writing these words only about twenty years after the Resurrection. There were plenty of people still around who could have challenged his version of events, and sometimes they did, but *not about this.* All early Christians agreed on the central testimony: God had raised Jesus from the dead.

There is an exceptionally interesting passage in Paul's Galatian letter in which he defends his apostolic credentials explicitly: I hope you can feel his energy and passion in this as I read:

> I would have you know, brothers and sisters, that the gospel which was preached by me is not a human gospel. For I did not receive it from human beings, nor was I taught it [by human beings]; it came through a revelation of Jesus Christ. For you have heard of my former life in Judaism, how I persecuted the church of God violently and tried to destroy it. . . . But when he who had set me apart before I was born, and had called me through his grace, was pleased to reveal his Son to me, in order that I might preach him among the Gentiles, I did not confer with flesh and blood, nor did I go up to Jerusalem to those who were apostles before me, but I went away into Arabia. . . . (Galatians 1:11-17)

And then Paul adds this exclamation: "In what I am writing to you, before God, I do not lie!" (1:20).

In this exceptional passage, Paul is fighting to defend his apostolic identity, which is being challenged in the Galatian congregation. He defends himself not for his own sake, but for the sake of the truth of the gospel. He states explicitly and vehemently that the good news from God which he proclaims is absolutely *not* "a brilliant product of the human imagination" but "a miraculous revelation." He did not learn it from Peter, James, John, Mary Magdalene, or any other human being; he learned it from the crucified and risen Jesus Christ himself. Returning to the 1 Corinthians text, here is the way he puts it in that letter:

> [After appearing to all the disciples,] last of all, as to one untimely born, [Christ] appeared also to me. For I am the least of the apostles, unfit to be called an apostle, because I persecuted the church of God. But by the grace of God I am what I am, and his grace toward me was not in vain. (1 Corinthians 15:8-10)

So you see, the story of Paul is really the story of God. That's why one of the best books about Paul is subtitled *The Triumph of God*.[38] The apostle reports in the Galatian letter that when he first burst upon the scene following his amazing conversion, those who met him "*glorified* God *because of me*" (Galatians 1:24) — in other words, they praised God for his miraculous revelation, not Paul for his brilliant imagination.

But now let us be realistic. The point of view expressed in the book review is now so widely held *within the church* that it is a full-time job to plug even one hole in the dike. There has been a drastic falling-off of Scripture-reading among members of our mainline denominations. Parents who want their children to know the Bible stories have to work overtime; most children today can name forty Pokémon characters whereas they typically don't know anyone from the Bible at all except maybe Noah with his ark full of animals. It's definitely a challenge. The visiting preacher can only do so much. You in this congregation — parents, grandparents, teachers, clergy

— must shoulder most of the responsibility. Yet every sermon, every exposition of a Biblical text is a precious opportunity to strike a blow against the prevailing fashion of regarding the Holy Scriptures as the product of human imagination. Let Paul speak again: "I delivered to you as of first importance what I also received, that Christ died for our sins in accordance with the scriptures, that he was buried, that he was raised on the third day in accordance with the scriptures." Does that sound to you like a man who is in love with his own imagination? Or is it not rather a man who is reporting, not amorphous religious ideas, but the most important thing that has ever happened?

I recently attended the funeral in New York of a 58-year-old man named Cook Kimball. Cook was one of the most stalwart Christian believers that I have ever met. Not only was he a believer; he was a true disciple, living as Christ's follower every day of the week. He had been in poor health for some years and had been waiting for a kidney transplant. He died before he could receive the kidney; his death is a tremendous blow to the church because he was such an indefatigable defender of its mission in so many ways. Naturally there was a great outpouring for the service. When I arrived, everyone was talking about an odd thing that had happened, almost as if Cook had had a premonition. On Sunday two weeks ago, a portion of St. Paul's Resurrection chapter was appointed to be read. Cook was due to be an usher that day. It seems that he came to the church early; he spent a good deal of time at the church anyway. He took the list of people appointed to do various things in the Sunday service, and crossed off his name from the usher list. Then he crossed off the name of the man who had been appointed to read the second lesson and inserted his own name, moving the other man to the usher position. Thus it came about that Cook Kimball read the Resurrection lesson in church six days before his own death. But that's not all. He read the lesson at his own funeral. As it happened, the service was being taped that Sunday morning. The recording of Cook reading was retrieved — he was a superb reader of Scripture, always deeply engaged by what he was reading — and when the time came for the second lesson at the funeral, we all heard his voice, clear and strong, reading these words:

> Now if Christ is preached as raised from the dead, how can some of you say that there is no resurrection of the dead? But if there is no resurrection of the dead, then Christ has not been raised; if Christ has not been raised, then our preaching is in vain and your faith is in vain. . . .
>
> For if the dead are not raised, then Christ has not been raised. If Christ has not been raised, your faith is futile and you are still in your sins. . . . If for this life only we have hoped in Christ, we are of all men most to be pitied.
>
> But in fact Christ has been raised from the dead, the first fruits of those who have fallen asleep. For as by a man came death, by a man has come also the resurrection of the dead. For as in Adam all die, so also in Christ shall all be made alive.

Dear Christian friends: Cook Kimball declared the Word of God that morning, as Paul declared it two thousand years ago, as we now declare it to you today. The inexorability of Death has been reversed; its remorselessness has been overcome; its effects have been undone. We see this now by faith; in the Resurrection day we shall see it face to face. But be assured: it is not "necessarily" so. It is not so because we want it to be so, because we imagine it to be so, because we need it to be so. It is so *against* all human possibility, *against* all human expectation, *against* all human imagining. It is so by the miraculous intervention of our God who has not abandoned us to the grave.

"I know that my Redeemer liveth. . . . For now is Christ risen from the dead, the first fruits of them that sleep. . . . Thanks be to God who giveth us the victory through Jesus Christ our Lord."[39]

AMEN.

The Hidden Pathway to Joy

———— ✼ ————

Thou dost show me the path of life; in thy presence there is fulness of joy, in thy right hand are pleasures for evermore.

(PSALM 16:11)

I am come that they might have life, and that they might have it abundantly.

(JOHN 10:10)

My home town of Franklin, Virginia, has a cemetery that means a lot to me. Many of the gravestones have Bible verses on them, and I find that they bring much hope and comfort. My grandparents' stone has these words: *In thy presence is fulness of joy.* I wonder if you recognize those words; we just read them a few moments ago — Psalm 16, verse 11: "Thou dost show me the path of life; in thy presence there is fulness of joy, in thy right hand are pleasures for evermore." These words from the Old

---

(Note to the reader: The very specific references in this sermon are easily traceable to their subjects, but out of concern for a family's privacy and in order to make the sermon more universal and less directly personal I have eliminated the most recognizable local details.)

Testament have deep meaning for all those who have put their trust in Jesus Christ.

Everyone from this parish who saw the front page of the newspaper last Monday must have noticed the striking symbolism of the color photograph. The family in the picture has given me permission to talk about this. Here they are, father, mother, and daughter, singing a hymn, and over them is the angel of the Resurrection. The beautiful Tiffany window depicts the crucial moment in the story of the Christian faith. Without this moment there is no church, there is no baptism, there is no victory over death, and indeed without this moment there is no story of Jesus, for without this unimaginable and unprecedented moment, Jesus of Nazareth would have been like every other person who died a death by crucifixion in the days of the Roman Empire — that is to say, he would have been completely forgotten and we would never have heard of him. This window depicts the moment when the angel, standing by the empty tomb, says to the women, *He is not here; he is risen.*

This Easter message falls upon the ears of those condemned to die. Garrison Keillor reminded us of that last night at Tanglewood when he sang, "Gather ye rosebuds while ye may, for soon you will be dying." Everybody in this church today is living in the valley of the shadow of death, for as the Prayer Book says, "In the midst of life we are in death."[40] I had cause to quote that to my young granddaughter last week when her beloved cat died suddenly without any warning. But as all of you know, this family in the picture has been going through a series of ordeals such as most of us can scarcely imagine — first a fire, then the fatal accident that killed their older daughter, and now a cruel disease. The writer of the newspaper article quotes your rector, saying that this piling up of affliction upon one family has tested her faith. It is good that she said that. The Bible is full of prayers of complaint and lament, prayers in which the believers accuse God of abandoning them. For example, here is Psalm 102: "I lie awake and groan. . . . I have eaten ashes for bread and mingled my drink with weeping. Because of your indignation and wrath you have lifted me up and thrown me away." And here is Psalm 42: "My tears have been my food day and night, while all day long they say to me, 'Where now is your God?'" And here is Psalm 44: "Awake, O Lord! Do not reject us forever; why have you hidden your face and forgotten our affliction and oppression? We sink down into the dust." These are only a few examples; we could go on in this vein for an hour. Indeed, a whole book of the Bible is entitled Lamentations. Here in the very Word of God we are given permission to be full of doubts and accusations, to question God, to challenge him, to fling our unhappiness into his face as the ancient Israelites did. We may be very thankful that these passages are in our Scripture. We do not have a sentimental, fragile, wispy faith that shrinks away when the first sign of contradiction comes. This faith is for real life, real struggle, real suffering.

Notice something very important, however. The Psalms give voice to individual laments and doubts, but they were written to be prayed aloud in the midst of the congregation. The speakers, or singers, do not withdraw from the fellowship into private anger and bitterness. Among God's covenant people, tribulation is communal. As St. Paul wrote to one of his congregations, "If one member is honored, all rejoice together; if one member suffers, all suffer together" (1 Corinthians 12:26).[41] When the Psalmist protests to God about his troubles, the congregation does not say, "Count your blessings!" or "You should have more faith!" or "Look on the bright side!" The congregation and the clergy are protesting and questioning right along with the sufferer. The congregation is joining in with words like these: "I am full of trouble; my life is at the brink of the grave. . . . Lord, why have you rejected me? Why have you hidden your face from me?" (Psalm 88).

The more we know of life, the more we experience its disappointments and sorrows, the more we learn that things don't work out the way we wanted, the more the Bible has to offer us. The people of the Bible are not stained glass figures; they are like us. They are flesh and blood. They turn away from God, make deals with crooks, stab people in the back. They complain, argue, cheat, commit adultery, tell lies. They suffer; they are struck down in war, felled by disease, exploited by oppressors. Their children die, their homes are destroyed, plagues of locusts eat their crops. But here is the central fact. All of this happens in the sight of God and in the context of his faithfulness. That's why we often find two seemingly contradictory things in the same Psalm, for instance in Psalm 40: "Though I am poor and afflicted, the LORD will have regard for me." Or Psalm 38: "My loins are filled with searing pain, there is no health in my body; I am utterly numb and crushed . . . [but] in you, Lord, have I fixed my hope; you will answer me, O LORD my God." How can the Psalms be so filled with despair and hope at the same time? Is this what is frequently called "the triumph of the human spirit"?

No, it isn't. One of the central truths of Biblical faith is that the human spirit left to itself is doomed to self-destruct. The Biblical man, or woman, does not say "I am the master of my soul, I am the captain of my fate." We do not say, "I did it my way." We do not lift our heads pridefully in our own strength. Instead, we say with the Psalmist, "You, O LORD, are a shield about me; you are my glory, the one who lifts up my head." I went to my forty-fifth public high school reunion last month. Out of two hundred and fifty people from ten classes, one particular person, more than any other, was the center of attention. Her name is Nancy, and here is her story. Ten years ago she had breast cancer and was divorced. The next thing that happened was that she had two strokes, leaving her legally blind and her right arm paralyzed. Then she developed another severe type of cancer that reddens her skin. Finally, just four months ago, she fell and broke her neck. At the age of sixty-three she is now living in a nursing home. However, with the help of her son and daughter-in-law, she made it to the reunion, wearing beautiful clothes and looking a lot better than some of the rest of us. Everyone was in total awe of her. A bunch of us were sitting around a table, mesmerized, listening to her talk. Naturally, people began praising her for her courage. She would have none of it. I will never forget the fire with which Nancy answered (these were her exact words): "*I* don't have courage! *I* don't have spunk! *I* don't have bravery! Everything I have is a gift from God!" All of us at the table knew that we were in the presence of something extraordinary. Here was a person at the extreme limit of affliction, yet praising God. I thought of Psalm 75: "Do not toss your horns so high, nor speak with a proud neck . . . it is God who judges; he puts down one and lifts up another . . . but I will rejoice forever; I will sing praises to the God of Jacob."

"Thou dost show me the path of life; in thy presence there is fulness of joy, in thy right hand are pleasures for evermore." Is it true? Or is it just wishful thinking, like so much else that goes on in life? How can we believe this when all the evidence is against it?

Let us turn now to the New Testament, the tenth chapter of the Gospel of John, where we find the words of our Lord, speaking as the Good Shepherd: "The thief comes only to steal and kill and destroy [the sheep]; I have come that they might have life, and that they might have it abundantly." This phrase, *abundant life,* has captured the imagination of Christians for two thousand years. "In thy presence there is *fulness of joy!*" Can this be trusted?

The story of what God has done for us in Jesus Christ is so huge that words such as *fulness* and *abundance* can never be any more than hints. Another hint that Paul uses a lot in Ephesians is *"riches"* (Greek *ploutos*).[42] He writes ecstatically about "the riches of his glorious inheritance" (Ephesians 1:18), "the immeasurable riches of God's grace" (2:7), "the unsearchable riches of Christ" (3:8). These are his best attempts to say the unsayable. God has promised us the abundance of his own inexhaustible riches, not because we deserved them — Scripture teaches us we most decidedly did not deserve them — but because it was his purpose to give them to us out of his unbounded, indeed immeasurable love.

But what a strange story it is that the church tells! God did not come in the form of riches, or wealth, or worldly power. St. Paul puts it another way: "You know the grace of our Lord Jesus Christ, who though he was rich, yet for your sake he became poor, so that by his poverty you might become rich" (2 Corinthians 8:9). So it is a paradox, isn't it? God's riches are made known to us in a hidden way. In order to make us rich he became poor. In order to lift up our heads he lowered his own. In order to give us abundant life he "became subject to evil and death."[43] In doing all of this he enacted for us the way to be human before God — obedient and submissive to

[333]

the Father, yet defiant and unbowed before the Enemy, which is Sin and Death.

"In thy presence is fulness of joy. . . . I have come that they may have life, and may have it abundantly. . . . I am the Resurrection and the life [says the Lord]; he who believes in me, even though he die, yet shall he live; and he who lives and believes in me shall never die." There is much here that we do not yet understand. Are these promises about the future, or are they supposed to be true already? The answer is, both. When the Psalmist sang, *"In thy presence is fulness of joy,"* he meant right then and there, in the worship of God. When the ancient Israelite entered the temple to worship, that in itself was *fulness of joy.* We reserved Episcopalians don't entirely understand this. We want our Sunday service to be over promptly so that we can, as we say, "get on with our day." But we are a little bit deprived in that respect. *Newsweek* religion editor Kenneth Woodward, on assignment to write about Christianity in Africa, was on his way to worship services early one Sunday morning in Nigeria when his vehicle broke down. "We'd better get a mechanic in a hurry," he said to his fellow journalists, "because once he gets to church, he'll be there all day."[44] The African Christian, like the African-American Christians of my home community, know that the *fulness of joy* is found in the presence of the Lord even now, as we pray and praise God together and gather at his table.

But people like the afflicted family members who are so much in our prayers right now know that suffering in this life can be so great that a phrase like "the fulness of joy" can seem like nothing better than a mockery. That is why the Christian community is so indispensable. When we can't pray, the community prays for us. When we have no hope, the community holds the hope for us. When our suffering seems more than we can bear, the community comes alongside us in mute witness. From the standpoint of this vale of tears, we can experience this fulness of joy only in the form of promise. It is not yet; but it will come. We know it now only by faith. But it is not "only" by faith, because as Paul writes in Romans 5:1-5, the faith and grace "in which we stand" gives us the strength we need: "Suffering produces endurance, and endurance produces character, and character produces hope, and *hope does not disappoint us,* because God's love has been poured into our hearts through the Holy Spirit which has been given to us." That is why we have that Easter window in the back of the church, to remind us of what lies in the future for those who trust God. Christian hope cannot disappoint us because it is rooted and grounded in the Resurrection and guaranteed by the gift of the Spirit. The promise of abundant life, the hope of glory, the guarantee of the fulness of joy lie in our recollection of the mighty act of God who raised Jesus from the dead and has promised that we will be raised with him. We trust him for the future because in our own day we have heard afresh the ancient Easter message: "The Lord is risen! The Lord is risen indeed! Alleluia!" Let us therefore praise God together in the final words of today's Psalm, beginning with verse 8:

> I have set the Lord always before me;
>> because he is at my right hand, I shall not fall.
> My heart, therefore, is glad and my spirit rejoices;
>> my body also shall rest in hope.
> For you will not abandon me to the grave;
>> nor let your holy one see the Pit.
> You will show me the path of life;
>> in your presence there is fulness of joy,
>> and in your right hand are pleasures for evermore.

AMEN.

Endnotes

⎯⎯⎯∞∞∞⎯⎯⎯

Author's Foreword

1. Kenneth Leech, *We Preach Christ Crucified* (Cambridge, Mass.: Cowley, 1994), 88.

Part One: The First Day of Holy Week

1. All four Gospels contain three solemn predictions by Jesus of his suffering and death. The Messianic secret, so-called, in Mark is held until the moment of his death, when his identity is fully revealed to the Roman centurion (see below, "The New World Order"). The Gospel of John is specifically structured to move toward the Passion; the turning point is in chapter 12 when Jesus says for the first time, "My hour has come," instead of "my hour has not yet come."

2. The other, better-known mention is John 11:35, at the tomb of Lazarus ("Jesus wept"). See the title sermon, "The Undoing of Death."

3. Two young children horrified America in 1998 by shooting their school classmates in Jonesboro, Arkansas.

4. The Lamentations text actually says *"my* sorrow," but Christian tradition has always assigned these words to Jesus and they are sung with that meaning ("his sorrow") in the brilliant libretto for Handel's *Messiah* by Charles Jennens.

5. A several-times-repeated phrase from the letters to the seven churches in the book of Revelation.

6. Hymn 171 (Episcopal *Hymnal 1982*), "Go to Dark Gethsemane," by James Montgomery (1771-1854).

7. David Brooks, "The Organization Kid," *Atlantic Monthly,* April 2001, 40-54.

8. The B.C. (Before Christ) and A.D. (*Anno Domini,* year of Our Lord) dating sys-

tem reflects this Christian conviction. This system is being replaced in some quarters with B.C.E. (Before the Common Era) and C.E. (Common Era). Perhaps this will cause some Christians to reflect afresh on what we really believe.

9. As I was preparing this sermon for publication ten years later, I was struck by the continuing relevance of this observation. I felt no need to update the headlines for a new century. Harvard chaplain and professor Peter Gomes, when asked about the significance of the new millennium, said he thought it had no significance: "I suspect the same old people will be up to the same old things." Just so.

10. That is why the centurion utters the affirmation "Truly this man was the Son of God" at that moment in Mark. Mark's special emphasis is precious to the church for reasons that I indicate in this sermon; Matthew follows Mark to a great extent. Luke's and John's versions of the Passion are quite different. We need all these perspectives for a full picture. In the Good Friday sermon called "The Hour of Glory," below, the Johannine perspective is given.

11. There was a time when I thought, seeing Susan off for Liberia, that I would quite literally never see her alive again. However, the Lord has preserved her for new missions yet to be revealed; while in Liberia, Susan Leckrone met David Copley, a fellow missionary, and they are now married. As of this writing they are studying at Virginia Theological Seminary, preparing to be ordained. This is not the place for a full recounting of their travails during the past decade, but their faith and tenacity during severe trials continues to be a source of faith for many.

12. Howell Raines, ed., *My Soul Is Rested* (New York: Penguin, 1983), 56.

13. See "Ascension Day in Pretoria" in my book *The Bible and The New York Times* for a treatment of Bishop Tutu's witness at the time of the collapse of apartheid and the inauguration of Nelson Mandela.

14. Not their real names, but many readers will recognize them.

15. Craig Horowitz, "Divided We Stand," *New York,* 9 April 2001.

16. It *is* in the sense that an inalienable part of the story is its geographical and historical particularity, which distinguishes Christianity from religion in general. But it *is not,* because even if a hydrogen bomb, God forbid, were dropped on the Holy Land, the story would still be true and would still have the same living, saving significance for the present and for the future of the world.

17. "For it is written that Abraham had two sons, one by a slave and one by a free woman. . . . Now this is an allegory: these women are two covenants. One is from Mount Sinai, bearing children for slavery; she is Hagar. Now Hagar is Mount Sinai in Arabia; she corresponds to the present Jerusalem, for she is in slavery with her children. But the Jerusalem above is free, and she is our mother" (Galatians 4:22-26). We should remember that this same letter is the one in which Paul declares that "there is neither Jew nor Greek, there is neither slave nor free, there is neither male nor female; for you are all one in Christ Jesus" (3:28).

18. Jennie E. Hussey, *New Songs of Praise and Power,* 1921.

19. The location in Jerusalem where Jesus was crucified has two Biblical names, Calvary and Golgotha. Calvary is actually Latin, from the Vulgate translation

of Mark 15:22, the "place of a skull" (Latin *calvaria* for Mark's Greek *kranion*). Golgotha is a Greek transliteration of the Aramaic and Greek for "skull" (Matthew 27:33; Mark 15:22; John 19:17). It is not known why the place had that name, nor can it be shown where it was, except that it would have been outside the city wall. It is significant that the early Christians showed no interest in preserving relics of Jesus or memories of where his Crucifixion and Resurrection took place. This sort of preoccupation did not arise until the fourth century. For the early Christians, it was the living presence of Jesus through the Spirit that counted. Surely there is something for us to learn here.

20. C. S. Lewis, *Perelandra,* second volume in the "space trilogy" (New York: Macmillan, 1965), 111.

21. Patricia Lee Brown, "Preserving the Birthplaces of the Atomic Bomb," *The New York Times,* 7 April 2001.

22. Everybody would turn out, that is, except for the Jews of the towns. There is a lamentable history here, because Holy Week in Europe was a time for persecution of Jews. Holy Week preachers have a special responsibility to teach about this; many Christians remain woefully ignorant of these issues.

23. We don't really know very much about what happened when Jesus entered Jerusalem because the evangelists have interwoven the story with so much meaning from the Old Testament that we can't sort out the facts from the interpretation. However, it is precisely the interpretation, with the Old Testament prophecies woven in, that makes the facts live for us today.

24. That may be an exaggeration, but Matthew believes that the event was important enough to use the passive voice, as he does at other significant moments. "Was shaken" means that there was an outside agency at work, namely God.

25. Hymn 156 (Episcopal *Hymnal 1982*), words by Henry Hart Milman (1791-1868).

26. The full description from John Calvin's *Harmony of the Gospels* is worth quoting: "The ass was borrowed from some person, and the want of accoutrements compelled the disciples to throw their garments on it [Matthew 21:7], which was a mark of mean and disgraceful poverty. He is attended, I admit, by a large retinue, but of what sort of people? Of those who had hastily assembled from the neighboring villages. Sounds of loud and joyful welcome are heard, but from whom? From the very poorest, and from those who belonged to the despised multitude. One might think that he intentionally exposed himself to the ridicule of all . . ." *Calvin's Commentaries* 16 (Grand Rapids: Baker, 1984), 447.

27. Luke had another theological purpose in mind, which was well appropriated by Justin Martyr only a few decades later when he quotes the Lucan saying ("Father, into thy hands I commend my spirit") as an example for Christians who are facing death; see Raymond E. Brown, *The Death of the Messiah* (New York: Doubleday, 1994), 1068-69. The author of the Fourth Gospel seems to have had an altogether different tradition of Words from the Cross.

28. One familiar attempt to soften the Cry of Dereliction posits that Jesus was

simply speaking aloud the whole of Psalm 22. Without doubt, Jesus had the Psalm memorized, but the evangelists clearly intend to highlight the first verse only. Since this Word is the only one quoted in two Gospels, and since it is so scandalous, the saying is regarded as especially authentic.

29. Søren Kierkegaard, commenting on Galatians, gives voice to this scandal by contrasting it with Plato's descriptions of Socrates: "Socrates did not possess the true ideal, nor had he any notion of sin, nor that man's salvation required a crucified God: the watchword of his life could not therefore be: the world is crucified to me and I to the world [Galatians 6:14]. He therefore retained irony which simply expresses his superiority to the world's folly. But for a Christian, irony is not enough, it can never answer to the terrible truth that salvation means that God is crucified. . . ." *The Journals of Søren Kierkegaard* (New York: Oxford University Press, 1938), 403, entry 1122.

30. Someday, God willing, she will be better known; she is a Christian heroine right up there with Mother Teresa and Dorothy Day or anybody else you could care to name. She is almost always referred to with the honorific "Mrs." as a mark of respect.

31. Quoted in Charles Marsh, *God's Long Summer: Stories of Faith and Civil Rights* (Princeton: Princeton University Press, 1997), 22. Note the way that the speech of this almost illiterate woman, a despised sharecropper, takes on the cadence ("they know not what they do"), and therefore the rhetorical power, of the King James Version — the Bible she learned in her church from childhood.

32. The members of the TRC all paid a price for their service; years of listening to families describing how their loved ones suffered under torture and died took a terrible toll on them all. Barbara Brown Taylor has reported that all the members had become sick in one way or another (Bishop Tutu has cancer).

33. Desmond Tutu, *No Future Without Forgiveness* (New York: Doubleday, 1999), 270-72. In one case I have rearranged the order of the sentences, without changing the wording. This quotation is longer than the one used in the original sermon. My sense is that the reader can absorb more than the listener in the pew.

Part Two: Monday, Tuesday, and Wednesday of Holy Week

1. Statement by the National Association of Evangelicals.

2. Readers who suspect this of being anti-Roman Catholic are asked please to reserve judgment until they have read "My Taste Was Me" in the Eastertide section below.

3. It is impossible not to be deeply moved by Joan's life and specifically by her cries of "Jesus, Jesus" as she was burning. No derogation is intended; she is one of my heroines. I am making a different point, which can be illustrated by the example of Lady Jane Grey, whose head was cut off in 1554 when she was two years younger (seventeen) than Joan (nineteen) at her death a century earlier. Jane Grey was given a classical education and amazed everyone with her capacities; because she read Scripture

(in Greek and Hebrew!) under her Protestant tutor John Aylmer, she became a true theologian. See Paul F. M. Zahl, *Five Women of the English Reformation* (Grand Rapids: Wm. B. Eerdmans, 2001). A second point here is that the Christian faith itself has been the seedbed for liberation movements which have led to such things as education for the peasant Joans as well as the privileged Janes.

4. This was the movie that was pushing people's buttons in 1988-89. Every year it is something different. Madonnas with dung, crucifixes in urine, a female form on a cross in the Cathedral of St. John the Divine — the frequency of these controversies should have alerted us by now to let the fifteen-minute sensations die a natural death and concentrate our energies on the true meaning of Christ's mission.

5. Quoted in Marina Warner, *Joan of Arc: The Image of Female Heroism* (New York: Knopf, 1981), 268.

6. The earliest independent references to him are from historians like Josephus, who wrote four decades after Jesus' death and added nothing to our knowledge of him.

7. I am assuming a late date for the so-called Gnostic Gospels. Even if the Gospel of Thomas, so beloved of the revisionists, does contain some early Jesus traditions, it cannot be called a historical source. The fact is that we simply do not have access to the "historical Jesus," but only to the "living Christ." As Luke Johnson writes, the "faith perspective [of the evangelists] is not a problem but the point," and he continues with more than a little ironic understatement by adding, "For the historian, [the faith perspective of the Gospels] means that a high degree of authorial bias must be taken into account when assessing the historical character of the New Testament compositions." Indeed. (Luke Timothy Johnson, *The Real Jesus* [San Francisco: Harper-SanFrancisco, 1996], 88.)

8. The title has caused some difficulty for gender-sensitive translators. "The Human One" was proposed a few years ago, but was soon discarded after an outcry from Biblical scholars.

9. The German scholar Oscar Cullmann gave us an analogy years ago which continues to be helpful: the Cross and Resurrection are D-Day; the Second Coming of Christ is V-E (Victory in Europe) Day. A crucial point here is that there were many dangerous battles to be fought in between and many would die; but the victory was secure and the ensuing battles would be fought with confident certainty and even, if such a thing were possible, with gaiety. One thinks especially of Desmond Tutu of South Africa.

10. Origen, Gregory of Nyssa, and others. Some of their contemporaries repudiated the idea, however — among them, John of Damascus and Cyril of Alexandria. The notion of a ransom paid to the devil was swept aside in a definitive way by Anselm and Abelard at the turn of the second millennium.

11. Vincent Taylor, *The Gospel According to St. Mark* (London: Macmillan, 1952), 446. Taylor's commentary on the Greek text, at age fifty, shows every sign of being a classic.

12. Vincent Taylor's phrase, often repeated by others.

13. "We can never ransom ourselves, or deliver to God the price of our life; for the ransom of our life is so great that we should never have enough to pay for it" (Psalm 49:7-8).

14. We can readily see how predominant the ransom theme and the battle imagery were in the early centuries by looking at the Holy Week hymns of Venantius Honorius Fortunatus (540? 600?). For example:

> The royal banners forward go, the cross shines forth in mystic glow
> Where he through whom our flesh was made, in that same flesh
> our ransom paid.
>
> — Hymn 162, Episcopal *Hymnal 1982*,
> translated from the Latin.

15. C. S. Lewis, *The Lion, the Witch and the Wardrobe.*

16. Flannery O'Connor, *Mystery and Manners* (New York: Farrar, Straus & Giroux, 1969), 118.

17. A recent book by George Hunsinger is aptly titled *Disruptive Grace* (Grand Rapids: Wm. B. Eerdmans, 2000).

18. For the sake of brevity, this history has been somewhat oversimplified. The development of messianic expectation through the prophetic literature and on into the early apocalyptic period is a wonderful subject unto itself.

19. One could use larger issues to better effect, perhaps. For instance, it is easy enough to be "tolerant" of others if they are similar to us and cooperative with us, but if other groups want to emphasize their differences from us — whether it be ultra-observant Muslims, Hasidic Jews, intrusive Jehovah's Witnesses, whatever — we discover, if we are honest, that judgmental thoughts sneak unbidden into our psyches. I mentioned the relatively trivial issue of "praise music" in this sermon because I knew the congregation would recognize itself.

20. We don't know if there was actually a person with this name, since Malachi means "my messenger." The concerns and date (500-450 B.C.) of the author, however, are easily identified. Because Malachi so clearly points ahead to the coming of the appointed Day of the Lord and its fulfillment, it makes an extraordinarily fitting conclusion to the Old Testament. The Hebrew Bible *(Tanakh)* is arranged differently, with the Prophets in the middle and the Writings at the end.

21. The fashion in much of today's Biblical criticism would be to interpret the passage in terms of a power struggle between the Levitical priesthood and the prophet's disciples. Apparently the school of Malachi won this one. As to whether this exhausts the meaning of the passage, let the reader decide.

22. "[Jesus'] action is not merely that of a Jewish reformer: it is a sign of the advent of the Messiah." (Edwyn C. Hoskyns, *The Fourth Gospel,* 2nd ed. [London: Faber & Faber, 1947], 194.)

23. In capitalizing I AM in this sentence, I am taking a small liberty which seems right to me. In the Gospel of John, the *ego eimi* ("I am") sayings are strategically located in numerous places throughout the narrative to underscore Christ's messianic

authority and identity with God the Father. See especially John 18:5-8, where he says *ego eimi* three times in four verses, near the point of greatest crisis. The usage is dreived from the name of God, I AM WHO I AM (Exodus 3:14).

24. Alexander Maclaren, *Expositions of Holy Scripture* (Grand Rapids: Wm. B. Eerdmans, 1959), 7:41.

25. See, for example, Jeremiah 23:1-4; 50:6-19; Ezekiel 34; Zechariah 10–13.

26. The standing *Agnus Dei* with battle flag symbolizes not only victory but also continuing militancy against evil. The lying-down lamb with flag suggests well-earned rest after battle. The lamb standing or lying down on a book (often with seven seals) is reminiscent of Revelation 5:6, 12; 6:1: "Worthy is the Lamb who was slain. . . . I saw when the Lamb opened one of the seven seals. . . ."

27. All of this is described in the book of Leviticus.

28. It is now generally agreed that a "Sea of Reeds" is meant, but the telling of the story has developed so much rhetorical grandeur over the centuries as it has given meaning and hope to the lives of oppressed communities that it would be unthinkable to change it.

29. Most of the Cecil B. DeMille movie of *The Ten Commandments* is laughably dated now, but one scene that still has power is the depiction of the children of Israel as they prepare to leave Egypt.

30. For a fuller treatment of the Exodus narrative and its relation to the Cross and Resurrection, see "A Way Out of No Way" in my book *Help My Unbelief.*

31. Jewish Christians would have known all of this as their birthright, their meat and drink. Gentile Christians would have known it because they would have been taught it as catechumens (those being prepared for baptism).

32. This last phrase is from Eucharistic Prayer B in the Episcopal Book of Common Prayer.

33. It is often said, though it cannot be proved, that the Gospel of John depicts the Last Supper taking place on the night *before* Passover because he wants to show Jesus dying at the precise moment of the yearly ritual slaughter of the Passover lambs — thereby underscoring Jesus' identity as the Paschal (Passover) lamb. The other three Gospels identify the supper as a Passover seder. A significant number of scholars today think that John's dating is more likely to be historical, a development which has led many in recent years to question the appropriateness (though not the good intentions) of congregations holding seders on Maundy Thursday. A brief summary of the debate about the chronology of the Johannine account is given in Rudolf Schnackenburg, *The Gospel according to St. John* (New York: Crossroad, 1982), 3:34.

34. Note the remarkably apposite words of the Easter hymn called "At the Lamb's high feast we sing":

At the Lamb's high feast we sing praise to our victorious King. . . .
Where the Paschal blood is poured, death's dark angel sheathes his sword;
Israel's hosts triumphant go through the wave that drowns the foe.

Mighty victim from on high, hell's fierce powers beneath thee lie. . . .
Thou hast conquered in the fight, thou hast brought us life and light.

Hymn 174, Episcopal *Hymnal* 1982,
translated from a 1632 Latin hymn
by Robert Campbell (1814-1868).

35. In the interests of strict accuracy, *ephapax* is repeated three times in Hebrews (7:27; 9:12; 10:10) and the impression is of great emphasis. The words "once for all" appear in most English translations four times, because the idea is so clearly present in 9:26.

36. As this book goes to press, the latest examples come from Rwanda, where Catholic and Anglican clergy and religious are being brought to trial and some have already been convicted.

37. "Here is the Lamb of God" (NRSV) lacks resonance. It is flat, banal.

Part Three: Maundy Thursday

1. This is a reference to the widely criticized pardons given by President Clinton in his last days in office.

2. This last sentence is disputed. I have given the most widely-agreed-upon reading, the one that makes the most sense to me.

3. Edwyn C. Hoskyns, *The Fourth Gospel,* 2nd ed. (London: Faber & Faber, 1947), 446.

4. C. K. Barrett, *The Gospel According to St. John* (New York: Macmillan, 1955), 363.

5. Raymond E. Brown, *The Gospel According to John XIII-XXI,* Anchor Bible 29A (Garden City, N.Y.: Doubleday, 1970), 551.

6. This set of insights about Peter is partly drawn from William Temple's meditations on John's Gospel.

7. It is from this passage that we get the name *Maundy* Thursday.

8. St. Paul uses this "how much more" construction frequently when talking of God's love in Christ. See also Jesus' words: "What father among you, if his son asks for a fish, will instead of a fish give him a serpent; or if he asks for an egg, will give him a scorpion? If you then, who are evil, know how to give good gifts to your children, *how much more* will the heavenly Father give the Holy Spirit to those who ask him!" (Luke 11:11-13).

9. Much has been written about this "ransom saying." For a full treatment, see above, "The King's Ransom."

10. The last two sentences are not in the early manuscripts of Luke's Gospel, but they were known to the church as early as the second century and reflect first-century tradition about the suffering of Jesus. In the Great Litany we pray, "By thine agony and bloody sweat, good Lord, deliver us."

11. In a striking passage from one of her Good Friday sermons, Barbara Brown Taylor suggests that the seeming abandonment by God that reached its climax in the Cry of Dereliction actually began in the garden. (*Home by Another Way* [Cambridge, Mass.: Cowley, 1997], 81-85.)

12. In Nicholson Baker's novella, *The Everlasting Story of Nory* (New York: Random House, 1998), the main character, a little American girl, muses about the cathedral that dominates the English town where her family is living. "A cathedral is usually arranged in the shape of a crucifixion because Jesus died upon the cross. 'But why,' Nory wondered sometime, 'do they have to concentrate on the awful way he died?'"

13. OK, so maybe David didn't write Psalm 51 — but there is great wisdom and suitability in the traditional ascription to him.

14. I have made it sound as though verse 3 comes before verse 1, but I have not distorted Paul's argument in doing so because he repeats the same thoughts many times in different words.

15. It is very important to understand Trinitarian theology at this point. This is not a cruel Father punishing a victimized Son; God the Father and God the Son are doing this together. Another Holy Week hymn puts it well:

> Calvary's mournful mountain climb;
> There, adoring at his feet,
> Mark the miracle of time,
> God's own sacrifice complete. . . .

Hymn 171 (Episcopal *Hymnal 1982*),
"Go to Dark Gethsemane," by
James Montgomery (1771-1854).

The death of Jesus is *God's own* sacrifice. When we see Jesus, we see God (though, to be sure, we see him as God the Son). As Paul writes, "*God was in Christ* reconciling the world to himself" (2 Corinthians 5:19).

16. Hymn 313 (Episcopal *Hymnal 1982*), by John Brownlie (1859-1925).

Part Four: Good Friday

1. Tradition has it that Jesus' disciples Peter and Andrew were crucified, but if this is so (and it can't be proven one way or the other) these are the exceptions that prove the rule.

2. The King James Version is familiar to us from Handel's *Messiah:* "All we like sheep have gone astray; we have turned every one to his own way."

3. *In Retrospect: The Tragedy and Lessons of Vietnam* (New York: Times Books, 1995). Mr. McNamara confessed his complicity and deceit during the Vietnam War.

4. Impaling comes closest, perhaps, but that horrible method differs from cru-

cifixion in this respect: over the centuries it has been done to people of all classes and stations. Crucifixion was reserved for non-Roman citizens and, especially, for slaves.

5. There is a good book about all this by Martin Hengel, *Crucifixion in the Ancient World and the Folly of the Message of the Cross* (Philadelphia: Fortress, 1977).

6. To be accurate, we should note that the Gospel of John mutes the dreadfulness because the Fourth Evangelist has a somewhat different theological focus. The final words (called "discourses") of Jesus in John are addressed to future Christian communities. "Light is thrown in advance on the darkness of this event [the Crucifixion] and its frightfulness is diminished. The Johannine passion is therefore really a story of Jesus' victory and of the fulfilment of his work"; Rudolf Schnackenburg, *The Gospel according to St. John* 3:4. These themes are addressed elsewhere in this book; here I am concentrating on the Synoptic Gospels, Paul's Epistles, and Hebrews.

7. This may seem like a repetition of the "Lamb of God" sermon above, but it isn't. It is my hope that varying treatments of the same themes will serve not as repetition but, when read devotionally, as expansion and reinforcement.

8. Episcopal *Book of Common Prayer,* Holy Eucharist, Rite One.

9. "Now when John heard in prison about the deeds of Christ, he sent word by his disciples and said to him, 'Are you the one who is to come, or shall we look for another?'" (Matthew 11:2-3).

10. There are legitimate theological reasons for preferring the Christus Rex cross, or a plain cross. That was not the issue in this case. This woman did not want to have anything to do with anything distasteful at any level of her life.

11. This point will be repeated several times because of its importance and the deeply ingrained nature of the mistake.

12. Here we are quoting from Anselm of Canterbury who said that if we don't understand the Cross as some sort of compensation or satisfaction, then "you have not yet considered the gravity of sin" *(nondum considerasti quanti ponderis peccatum sit).*

13. Commenting on George Herbert's poem "The Agony," Diogenes Allen writes, "Herbert tells us that if you want to know what sin is, look at that man on the cross." ("Jesus and Human Experience," in *The Truth about Jesus,* ed. Donald Armstrong [Grand Rapids: Wm. B. Eerdmans, 1998], 154.)

14. John Lewis, James Bevel, James Farmer, Fannie Lou Hamer, Hosea Williams, Fred Shuttlesworth, Andrew Young, and numerous others. Kelly Brown Douglas, professor of theology at Howard University, has spoken of Dr. King's significant influence on the development of Christian theology. She notes that he drew a dangerously complacent American church into a cross-centered, Kingdom-oriented, active faith.

15. The Greek word *arrabon* (2 Corinthians 1:22; 5:5; Ephesians 1:14) means downpayment, guarantee, first installment, deposit.

16. The *Gloria Patri* that we say so frequently requires interpretation. "Glory be to the Father, and to the Son, and to the Holy Spirit, as it was in the beginning, is now and ever shall be, world without end. Amen" *cannot* mean that everything is going to remain the same forever and ever. The entire Biblical witness is that God will

do something completely new (especially Isaiah 40-55). See above, "The New World Order."

17. Hymn 551 (Episcopal *Hymnal 1982*), "Rise Up, Ye Saints of God," formerly "Rise Up, Ye Men of God," by William Pierson Merrill (1867-1954).

18. The Black Sash was an organization of white South African women opposed to apartheid. American nuns Maura Clark, Ita Ford, and Dorothy Kazel, and Jean Donovan, a lay worker, were all kidnapped, raped, and murdered in El Salvador in 1980 by members of the Salvadoran National Guard. It has been shown over and over that they were sisters of mercy and not supporters of violent rebellion as has so often been charged by the U.S. Department of State. Ita Ford's family, in particular, have been passionately committed to social justice and human rights for decades. The younger generation of Fords sees this as "the most precious gift" from their aunt; David Gonzalez, "Kin of Nun Slain in 1980 Keep Faith in a Cause," *The New York Times,* 6 November 2000.

19. Galatians 3:10-14 does not appear *at all* in the 1983 Common Lectionary or the 1992 Revised Common Lectionary.

20. Actually, the best translation for the word in English is *rectification,* but it's too confusing to get into that on Good Friday, so I'm staying with the more familiar word.

21. This idea is classically elaborated by J. Christiaan Beker in his various books about the Apostle Paul.

22. I am saying "religious people" here instead of "Jews" in order to make crystal clear the fact that we are not speaking about ethnic Jews in today's sense. Karl Barth, in his commentary on Romans and elsewhere, has shown us that the "Jews" of the New Testament can be understood as the good religious and/or moral people of today, that is, as ourselves when we trust in our own righteousness.

23. Hymn 685 (Episcopal *Hymnal 1982*), by Augustus Toplady, 1776.

24. Here I am capitalizing Death and Sin to emphasize their status as Powers — a point made repeatedly at various points in the New Testament.

25. J. Gordon Davies, *Holy Week: A Short History* (Richmond: John Knox, 1963), 47.

26. This famous remark was made at a dinner party at Mary McCarthy's. Miss McCarthy, writing about the incident later, essentially corroborates Miss O'Connor's version of the story but adds that she, as the hostess, was attempting to find common ground with her guest, who had been entirely silent up to that point. When Mary McCarthy, a lapsed Catholic, suggested that the Eucharist was a symbol, Flannery O'Connor reports that she replied "in a very shaky voice, 'Well, if it's a symbol, to hell with it.'" This is hilariously recounted at length in one of Miss O'Connor's letters; *The Habit of Being* (New York: Farrar, Straus & Giroux, 1979), 124-25.

27. Hymn 164 (Episcopal *Hymnal 1982*), words by Peter Abelard (1079-1142).

28. Paul uses these phrases in 1 Corinthians 4:13. He uses them to refer to the

difficulties of the apostolic mission, but there is no question whatever that he links this to the Cross.

29. This important verse is also addressed in the previous section of seven meditations, but not in precisely the same way.

30. The phrase, "the Man for Others," is associated with Dietrich Bonhoeffer, who died a martyr at the hands of the Nazis.

31. The references are to phrases written or collected by Thomas Cranmer during the English Reformation, preserved in the 1928 Prayer Book of the Episcopal Church. They are not much remembered by the younger generation, but are greatly beloved and much missed by those who used to say them.

32. Hymn 158 (Episcopal *Hymnal 1982*), fifth verse, words by Johann Heerman (1585-1647).

33. Three years later as this sermon is being edited, I am still buying Baobab cards for Easter. They definitely have more soul than "white" cards.

34. *The New York Times* reported the story of a woman who barely survived the September 11 World Trade Center attack. As she staggered northward on foot, choking, crying, and covered with dust and ashes, a stranger gave her a plastic cup of water. She said she planned to keep it the rest of her life; "it meant so much."

35. I don't mean to be entirely dismissive here. It is possible to argue, I suppose, that the lakeside path just isn't the right place for a reverent sculpture. From that perspective, I could be accused of a homiletical cheap shot in order to get the point across. At any rate, as this goes to press some years later, the carving is still there, protests or no protests.

36. More words from Cranmer's General Confession. This older form is not used much nowadays in the Episcopal church, but its resounding sentences are much more telling than the newer ones. *Two* books with the title *Devices and Desires* have been published in the last decade.

37. Once again, this phrase is from the 1929 Prayer Book, which in its turn was a revision of the 1549 and 1662 Prayer Books. The Collect for Purity, as it is called, dates from the eleventh century.

38. Hymn 168 (Episcopal *Hymnal 1982*), words by Paul Gerhardt (1607-1676).

39. This was written in 1999, the year of NATO's bombing for the purpose of halting Serbian dictator Slobodan Milosevic's program of "cleansing" Kosovo of ethnic Albanians.

40. Hymn 158 (Episcopal *Hymnal 1982*), first three verses, words by Johann Heermann (1585-1647).

41. "Solus ad victimam," by Kenneth Leighton (1968); *Anthems for Choirs* 1 (London: Oxford University Press, 1973).

42. This text is also expounded in the "Seven Meditations" above, but in a different way. Biblical passages, especially such rich ones, evoke multiple interpretations.

43. I have emphasized this point several times because in our day there has been bitter criticism of the theology of the Cross on this basis, especially from theologians

with feminist interests. It is widely recognized today that some of the nineteenth-century interpretations in evangelical circles did give the wrong impression. We must be careful to avoid this in the future. The doctrine of the Trinity will be our guide.

44. One such familiar illustration involves a man whose job it is to raise and lower a railroad bridge. One day he sees his small son playing in the bridge machinery as a train full of passengers approaches. The agonized father closes the bridge, crushing his son to death as the unheeding passengers smile and wave. In my opinion, this story should not be used to illustrate the Crucifixion because it perpetuates the idea that the Father is acting alone.

45. Hymn 160 (Episcopal *Hymnal 1982*), words by William J. Sparrow-Simpson (1860-1952).

46. The Easter cease-fire did not, of course, come to pass. Three years later as this book is being edited, the widespread popular perception in America is that "Madeleine's war" (Secretary of State Madeleine Albright) was a triumph. Thoughtful observers who know the situation thoroughly from inside (Misha Glenny, for example) are not so sure. Milosevic was toppled, certainly, but the aftermath has been one of profound misery for many, and the Albanians have revenged themselves upon the Serbs in a number of ways. More immediately relevant in 2001 was the bombing campaign in Afghanistan and the question of a Ramadan pause, much discussed but never seriously considered by the U.S. What everyone does seem to agree about is that these next decades must bring about great improvements in intelligence-gathering, "boots on the ground," language skills, deep understanding of cultures largely unfamiliar to us — in sum, an end to American isolationism and a new commitment to "closework" (article by Joe Klein, *The New Yorker,* 1 October 2001).

47. It is not possible or advisable in a liturgical setting to try to include too much information. When I say "the evangelists" I am aware that the Fourth Gospel differs from the others in presenting Jesus throughout as a conqueror. However, it is noteworthy that John is the only evangelist that depicts Jesus washing the disciples' feet, an unpleasant task allotted to slaves. Peter's response ("You will never wash my feet!") is exactly the sort of reaction one would expect from a disciple seeing his Master assuming the shameful posture of a slave. It is a hint of what is to come the next day. (See above, "Lord, Not My Feet Only.") John also emphasizes the mocking and the striking on the face "with the open hands" (John 19:3).

48. I don't mean to imply that Isaiah in the fifth century B.C. was consciously writing about the Crucifixion of God's Messiah. There are other ways of understanding the famous "Suffering Servant" passage of Isaiah 53. As noted already, it has always been understood by the church, however, as a prophecy in the Spirit and has long been a traditional Holy Week reading.

49. See "Nothing Virtual Tonight," in the author's *Help My Unbelief.*

50. An article in this week's *TV Guide* makes a distinction between "religion" and "spirituality." As far as I can see, it is a distinction without a difference. Neither is Christian because neither has the Cross at its heart.

51. The debate between the revisionist scholars (some of whom are members of

the Jesus Seminar) and those who stand squarely on the witness of Scripture and tradition has not yet exhausted itself, but many think it is growing increasingly tiresome. There is nothing wrong with publicity if it comes as a concomitant result of noteworthy achievement, but the very high publicity content of what is being called "the Jesus wars" does cast suspicion on the motives of many of these scholars. As a proud and grateful product of academia myself, I am most certainly not casting scorn upon it, but many have noted that few of the revisionist scholars have any ongoing connection to any local worshipping congregation. For a highly readable, even racy account of the "Jesus wars," see Luke Timothy Johnson's *The Real Jesus: The Misguided Quest for the Historical Jesus and the Truth of the Traditional Gospels* (HarperSanFrancisco, 1996).

52. Since 9/11, it is important always to emphasize that sin and evil are not located solely in terrorist dens. The war against sin and evil is waged among Christians as well, since God must root out the "old Adam" in each one of us.

53. *The Crucified God* is the name of an important book by Jürgen Moltmann (New York: Harper & Row, 1974).

54. Philemon is an exception, being a private letter from Paul to his friend.

55. Hymn 208 (Episcopal *Hymnal 1982*), "The Strife Is O'er," translated from the Latin by Francis Pott (1832-1909).

56. Note to possibly mystified Northeastern readers: in many American universities beyond New England, "Tri Delt" (Delta Delta Delta) is considered an elite sorority.

57. *New York*, 30th anniversary issue, 6 April 1998.

58. Paul Sevier Minear, *The Golgotha Earthquake: Three Witnesses* (Cleveland: Pilgrim, 1995).

59. It is advisable to avoid the term "New Age" in order to make clear that we are not talking about the sort of popular, eclectic spirituality that one runs into all over the place these days. Here I am calling it "the Age to Come"; earlier in this sermon collection I call it "The New World Order" (Palm Sunday section).

60. Again, when I say "St. John writes" I am following tradition; that doesn't mean that I believe there was a single person who wrote all of what we call the Johannine literature.

61. At the time of this preaching, Newt Gingrich was still Speaker and was indulging in a lot of futuristic talk. How ironic it seems now; his thoughts about the future did not include his own precipitous downfall.

62. "East Coker," in *Four Quartets*.

63. "Beloved, we are God's children now; it does not yet appear what we shall be, but we know that when he appears we shall be like him, for we shall see him as he is" (1 John 3:2).

64. Hymn 158 (Episcopal *Hymnal 1982*), words by Johann Heermann. I am aware that I have made this point many times in this collection of sermons. That is because it is so important to teach this at every opportunity. Very many Christian people are still unaware of the dangers in misunderstanding New Testament references to "the Jews."

65. Flannery O'Connor, *The Habit of Being* (New York: Farrar, Straus & Giroux, 1979), 360.

66. Kenneth Woodward, "Rethinking the Resurrection," *Newsweek,* 8 April 1996, 60-70.

67. *Newsweek,* 27 March 2000. The cover story itself includes Hindus, although the headline on the front omits them, probably because their numbers in America are much smaller than the increasing numbers of Buddhists and Muslims.

68. Jacques Ellul, *The Politics of God and the Politics of Man* (Grand Rapids: Wm. B. Eerdmans, 1972).

69. Nor did it appear as a twin of pre-Christian Celtic spirituality as some today would almost seem to suggest. Real Celtic Christianity is notable (and valuable) for its strong Trinitarian emphasis (see the hymn "St. Patrick's Breastplate").

70. The phrase "hints and suggestions" is taken from Stephen Sykes's splendid little book, *The Story of Atonement* (London: Darton, Longman and Todd, 1997). It is notable that his book is part of a "Trinity and Truth" series.

71. The worst instincts were certainly on display in June 2001 as Timothy McVeigh was executed in Terre Haute, Indiana, to the accompaniment of T-shirt sales. Even death penalty supporters seemed shocked, though they should not have been surprised.

72. I am indebted to the noted historian Peter Brown for this insight.

73. Peter Steinfels, "Beliefs" column, *The New York Times,* 3/19/99.

74. Hymn 158 (Episcopal *Hymnal 1982*), words by Johann Heermann.

75. W. H. Auden, "Christmas 1940," *The Collected Poetry of W. H. Auden* (New York: Random House, 1940), 118-20.

76. Jürgen Moltmann, *The Crucified God* (New York: Harper & Row, 1974), 7.

77. See "The Three Signs on Calvary."

78. Roger Cohen, "In a Town 'Cleansed' of Muslims, Serb Church Will Crown the Deed," *The New York Times,* 7 March 1994.

79. "The Judge Judged in Our Place" is the name of a chapter in Karl Barth's *Church Dogmatics,* IV/2.

80. Hymn 662 (Episcopal *Hymnal 1982*), words by Henry Francis Lyte (1793-1847).

81. *The Wall Street Journal* (15 October 2001) ran a story about what the morning of 9/11 was like for the executives and air controllers at American and United Airlines. Three days after the attack, Andy Studdert, COO at United, received a sympathetic phone call from an old friend. "How you doing, kid?" he asked. Mr. Studdert replied, "There is no kid left in me any more."

82. *The New York Times* Op Ed column, 29 September 2001.

83. *The Wall Street Journal,* 21 September 2001.

84. Jennifer Steinhauer, "A Symbol of Faith Marks a City's Hallowed Ground," *The New York Times,* 5 October 2001.

85. John Calvin, *Harmony of the Gospels.*

86. "See amid the winter's snow," by John Goss (arr. David Willcocks), *On Christmas Night,* The Choir of King's College, Cambridge.

87. Our revels now are ended . . .
> The cloud-capp'd towers, the gorgeous palaces,
> The solemn temples, the great globe itself,
> Yea, all which it inherit, shall dissolve. . . .
>   (Shakespeare, *The Tempest,* Act IV, Scene 1)

88. *The New York Times,* 3 October 2001.

89. In 1998, Westminster Abbey unveiled twelve statues in the previously empty niches over the main façade. They are twentieth-century Christian martyrs, male and female from countries all over the world.

90. On October 17, 2001, just a little more than a month after her husband's death, Lisa Beamer flew from Newark to San Francisco to embody once again that dauntless courage in the eyes of the whole world. In a striking symbolic action, she took the same flight that Todd had taken on the fateful morning of September 11. While in San Francisco she met with the business people that Todd had been scheduled to see that day.

91. Shaila K. Dewan, "Beyond Calamity, Death Goes On," *The New York Times* 17 October 2001.

92. Episcopal *Hymnal 1979,* Hymn 665, words by Robert Seymour Bridges (1844-1930) after Joachim Neander (1650-1680).

Part Five: The Day of Resurrection

1. Orpheus is the exception that proves the rule.

2. In a striking conception, Thomas Keneally, the author of *Schindler's List* (the book, not the movie), uses various phrases to describe the Nazi death camp which indicate its status as an actual *realm:* "Planet Auschwitz," "the dreadful kingdom," "the Auschwitz duchy," "the grand necropolis" (New York: Simon & Schuster, 1982).

3. Many Bibles used to include an illustration of Peter and the beloved disciple running. You could tell from the picture that the artist means us to think that the two men are already imagining the unimaginable. There is nothing in the text to suggest this.

4. There are other explanations for the folded cloths. On radio station WJMJ (Hartford), a Catholic priest said that Jesus had folded them up himself, leaving them behind. In any case, it was the sight of the cloths that convinced the beloved disciple of the inconceivable.

5. When Jesus says "he" here, he is speaking to a woman. It is an address to the individual human being in this case, not generic humankind. It is very awkward to change the Greek for "he," obviously intended to mean a person of either gender who believes in him, to a generic pronoun like "one."

6. See the sermon called "Strange Ending, Unthinkable Beginning" in my book *The Bible and The New York Times*.

7. Raymond E. Brown writes: "There can be no question that the evangelists themselves thought that Jesus' body did not remain in the grave but was raised to glory. . . . Underlying all [the] variations [in the Gospel narratives] is a solidly attested tradition by all four Gospels that the tomb was empty on Easter morning. . . . I maintain that the Biblical evidence points to the fact that Peter and Paul preached a risen Jesus whose body had not corrupted in the grave. There is not an iota of New Testament evidence that any Christian thought the body of Jesus was still in the grave corrupting. Was the body that was placed in the tomb raised into glory so that it no longer remained in the tomb or rotting in the earth? And that question I answer affirmatively according to the Biblical evidence" (*The Gospel According to John XIII-XXI*, 967, 978).

8. Notice that nothing is said about anyone saving the grave clothes. These transforming Easter events occur in an atmosphere very unlike that of subsequent centuries, with its True Cross relics and Shroud of Turin. Among the New Testament Christians, these things were of no importance. It was the living presence of the Lord that was important.

9. That's why the life of the Christian community is so central. The love of Christ is now mediated through our own embodied care and love for one another. There isn't any other kind of care and love.

10. Those with theological curiosity will want to know more. The issue at stake with immortality vs. resurrection is that immortality assumes there is some constituent aspect of the human being (usually called the "spirit" or "soul" of the person) which already possesses this divine attribute. This is erroneous on two counts: first, it posits a body-soul split which is Greek, not Hebraic (Biblical anthropology depicts the human being as a psychosomatic unity); and second, it teaches that there is a part of us that does not have to yield to death or hand itself over in radical trust to the God who alone has the power to raise that which is dead.

11. This was a remarkable tribute from Rabin's seventeen-year-old granddaughter. Her remarks were translated and published in full in *The New York Times*, 17 November 1995. Here is the relevant portion: "Grandfather, you were the pillar of fire in front of the camp and now we are left in the camp alone, in the dark, and we are so cold and so sad. . . . Others greater than I have already eulogized you, but none of them ever had the pleasure I had to feel the caresses of your warm, soft hands, to merit your warm embrace that was reserved for us, to see your half-smile that always told us so much, that same smile which is no longer, frozen in the grave with you." This is a near-perfect evocation of the irreplaceability of bodily presence.

12. In 2001, *The Dying Animal* by Philip Roth was published (Boston: Houghton Mifflin). If there is a more powerful depiction anywhere in literature of the unity of body and soul, I don't know what it is. The epigraph is from Edna O'Brien, who wrote, "The body contains the life story just as much as the brain." Another striking example would be "Parker's Back," one of Flannery O'Connor's short stories.

In an essay she commented, "When [Ralph Waldo] Emerson decided, in 1832, that he could no longer celebrate the Lord's Supper unless the bread and wine were removed, an important step in the vaporization of religion in America was taken. . . . When the physical fact is separated from the spiritual reality, the dissolution of belief is eventually inevitable" (*Mystery and Manners*, 161-62).

Part Six: Easter Week

1. This was the month in which the members of the "Heaven's Gate" cult, imagining that a spaceship concealed behind the Hale-Bopp comet was about to arrive, committed mass suicide.

2. "Now when they saw the boldness of Peter and John, and perceived that they were uneducated, ordinary men, they wondered; and they recognized that they had been with Jesus" (Acts 4:13).

3. With regard to "and women," it is now believed that the person formerly designated Junias (Romans 16:7) in English translations is actually Junia, a woman. The Greek suggests a woman, but earlier translators did not think that there could be a woman apostle. Lydia appears to have been the leader of the church in her house in Philippi (Acts 16:40), and we know that Euodia and Syntyche were important leaders in Philippi, for Paul writes "they have labored side by side with me in the gospel" (Philippians 4:3).

4. Jacqueline Kennedy, at the time of the President's assassination. For a much more positive assessment of Mrs. Kennedy see reference below in "The Undoing of Death."

5. The book of Revelation is appointed to be read in Easter season in Cycle C of the Revised Common Lectionary.

6. The *Newsweek* story, 27 March 2000, is, as usual, the exception. It was written by Kenneth L. Woodward, longtime religion editor of the magazine. I have expressed my great appreciation for him in the author's foreword.

7. Jeffrey L. Sheler, "Why Did He Die?" *U.S. News and World Report*, 24 April 2000, 50-55.

8. From a review of Thomas Cahill's book about Jesus, *Desire of the Everlasting Hills: The World Before and After Jesus* (New York: Nan A. Talese, 1999).

9. It is conceivable that one of them could have been a woman, since women were clearly part of Jesus' circle though not identified in the Gospels as part of the Twelve. (It is noteworthy that Paul, in his letters, names many more women in leadership than the Gospels do.)

10. "Who is the third who walks always beside you?" T. S. Eliot, "The Waste Land."

11. Emily Dickinson, poem #187: *The Complete Poems of Emily Dickinson* (Boston: Little, Brown, 1951), 88.

12. This is especially true in the Psalms. It is noteworthy that the Psalmists

overcome their horror of death simply by praising God and resting in his larger purposes, rather than in hoping for life beyond death. See below, n. 13.

13. Susan Sontag, *Illness as Metaphor* (New York: Farrar, Straus & Giroux, 1977), 55.

14. Such hints, along with the teaching of the resurrection of the dead, began to appear in the late postexilic period (see Isaiah 26:19 and Daniel 12:2 for the only two canonical examples) and became common in the decades before the time of Jesus, but not before. Job 19:25-27 ("I know that my redeemer liveth") has always been understood by Christians as an affirmation of hope in the Resurrection, but its meaning in its original context is ambiguous.

15. A phrase of Søren Kierkegaard's.

16. William Stringfellow, *Count It All Joy* (Grand Rapids: Wm. B. Eerdmans, 1967), 52, 89.

17. *The Habit of Being,* 552.

18. *The American Way of Death,* by Jessica Mitford (New York: Simon and Schuster, 1963), was a scathing treatment of the funeral industry. For some years after it was published it strengthened resistance to the industry's blandishments and marketing practices, but in an interview before she died, Ms. Mitford lamented that matters had become worse than ever.

19. I have capitalized Death when I especially want to draw attention to its status as a Power.

20. Hymn 208, "The Strife Is O'er" (Episcopal *Hymnal 1982*).

21. For a great many Anglicans, the most disappointing liturgical misfire of recent years was the funeral of Diana, Princess of Wales, at Westminster Abbey. Virtually nothing remained of the classical Order for the Burial of the Dead. Two and a half billion viewers worldwide were given almost nothing that they would not have seen at a secular memorial service. One of the few vestiges remaining of the traditional liturgy was the opening choir anthem, Purcell's funeral music, beautifully sung in the best English choirboy style but mostly inaudible to those who did not already know the words by heart ("Thou knowest, Lord, the secrets of our hearts; suffer us not for any pain of death to fall from thee").

A few weeks after the funeral I wrote an article lamenting the lost opportunity and received more than seventy-five letters in support, more than I have ever received for anything else I have ever written. Surely that says something about the longing of many for the traditional Anglican burial rite.

22. "[Jesus] did not, with Stoic resignation, view death as a very natural transition, but as something horrible, not willed by God — in Paul's words the 'last enemy'"; Oscar Cullmann, *The Christology of the New Testament* (Philadelphia: Westminster, 1959), 96.

23. Shakespeare, *Hamlet,* act 5, scene 2, line 345.

24. Traditional words for the imposition of ashes on Ash Wednesday.

25. Shakespeare, *Macbeth,* act 5, scene 5, lines 22-26.

26. Revelation 1:8; 22:16; Malachi 4:2; Isaiah 9:6; and the final question is Jesus to Martha in John 11:26.

27. It will be obvious that this sermon was preached in rural New England. Not long after this sermon, just as one might have expected, a feature story in a local paper heralded the arrival of a cosmetic surgeon in the area.

28. From a post–September 11, 2001, perspective, I would obviously have written this paragraph somewhat differently. However, an article in *The New York Times* noted that there had been an uptick in cosmetic surgery since 9/11 ("When Times Get Tought, Some Go for Plastic Surgery," SundayStyles section, 21 October 2001). One doctor said that patients were in search of instant gratification; "people want to live a bit more in the moment." There have been many other signs that we still look for life in all the wrong places.

29. It astonished everyone when this hitherto respected Westchester County (NY) judge was convicted of obsessive stalking and dangerous harassment of a former lover. Sol Wachtler, *After the Madness: A Judge's Own Prison Memoir* (New York: Random House, 1997).

30. After September 11, 2001, when the bombardment of Afghanistan had begun, Peter Steinfels wrote in the "Beliefs" column in *The New York Times* that violence sometimes actually does put an end to violence. He is thinking in the "just war" tradition, and especially of World War II. In the aftermath of 9/11 it is not a point that one wants to argue. Nevertheless, the brutalizing effects of war affect the "good" guys as much as the "bad." Many a gentle person has been hardened into a callous, even cruel one in wartime. See, for example, the horrific descriptions of Americans at war in the Pacific in "The Hardest War," by John Gregory Dunne, *The New York Review of Books,* 20 December 2001.

31. Cartoon by Robert Mankoff, *The New Yorker,* 4 May 1987, 107.

32. It should be noted that a considerable amount of criticism has been published about her work, especially in its later stages. For example, "Is Acceptance a Denial of Death? Another Look at Kübler-Ross," by Ray Branson in *The Christian Century,* 7 May 1975, 464-68. In a review of Kübler-Ross's book *To Live Until We Say Goodbye,* Rachel Mark writes that her message is "cruelly misleading" and that she uses "the language of evasion. Dr. Kübler-Ross does battle with fearsome death by denying its existence"; *Wall Street Journal,* 3 January 1979.

33. Further remarks quoted in this (undated) article include Kübler-Ross's dictum that the child should not be taken by a person who "finds death traumatic."

34. *The Habit of Being,* 552.

35. Deirdre Carmody, "Two Lives, One Fact: Terminal Cancer," *The New York Times,* 12 April 1976.

36. I quote more or less verbatim because I took notes.

37. Hymn 203 (Episcopal *Hymnal 1982*), "O sons and daughters, let us sing," words attributed to Jean Tisserand (15th cent.), translated by John Mason Neale (1816-1866).

38. Hymn 196 (Episcopal *Hymnal 1982*), "Look there! the Christ, our Brother, comes," words by John Bennett (b. 1920).

39. Phrase from the Nicene Creed.

40. The traditional designation of fifty days was taken from the books of Luke and Acts. The Gospel of John, idiosyncratic as usual, depicts Jesus bestowing the Spirit on the evening of Easter Day.

41. In his unique book, *Early Christian Rhetoric* (Cambridge, Mass.: Harvard University Press, 1971), Amos Wilder shows how a new form of speech — a "language event" — entered the world with the apostolic Christian preaching. Here are some of the phrases Wilder uses to denote the new thing: "the great cosmic turning-point," "the world-drama of salvation," "the hinge of history," "a world-changing transaction of conflict, death and glory," "a reversal of the story of the race as hitherto understood." Wilder's book is an extraordinary encouragement to preachers. Another sample: "When we hear [the Biblical passages preached] . . . we hear pledges of that last Word which will finally overrule all fates and tyrannies."

42. There is much dispute about the sermons in Acts because they differ in certain significant ways from Paul's preaching, which we know firsthand from his own much earlier letters. These differences are important and fruitful for further in-depth study — ultimately one must prefer the Paul of the letters to the Paul of Acts — but it is not necessary to go into that from the pulpit. Acts has its own marvellous contributions to make.

43. Eduard Schweizer, "ἀναψύχω," in *Theological Dictionary of the New Testament,* ed. Gerhard Kittel and Gerhard Friedrich (Grand Rapids: Wm. B. Eerdmans, 1974), 9:663-64.

44. Opening line of "The Waste Land," parodying the opening line of Chaucer's *Canterbury Tales.*

45. *The New York Times,* 1-7 April 1991.

46. Robert Frost, *New Hampshire* (New York: Henry Holt, 1923), 84.

47. "You are those who have continued with me in my trials; and I assign to you, as my Father assigned to me, a kingdom, that you may eat and drink at my table in my kingdom, and sit on thrones judging the twelve tribes of Israel" (Luke 22:28-30).

Part Seven: Eastertide

1. As we have already observed earlier in this volume, there is one exception to this and that is, of course, St. Paul, who never knew Jesus in his earthly life and was in the process of persecuting the new Christian movement when he was intercepted by the risen Christ on the road to Damascus. ("Have I not seen Jesus our Lord?" Paul wrote with some heat to those who would question his apostleship; 1 Corinthians 9:1.) This illustrious exception speaks to us of the freedom of God, who is able to reveal himself to whomever he pleases.

2. "He appeared to more than five hundred at one time" (1 Corinthians 15:6).

3. The older form of the words used at Communion are suggestive: "Take and eat this in remembrance that Christ died for thee; and feed on him in thy heart, by faith, with thanksgiving." These words were written with the greatest care, to show that receiving Jesus is never ours by right; it calls forth an act of trust on the part of the recipient — and indeed, not just a single act of trust or faith, but the repeated giving over of our entire existence. The words just quoted are the "Zwinglian" second half of Thomas Cranmer's words of administration in the Book of Common Prayer, which stress the idea of remembrance; the first half is more "catholic" ("the body of our Lord Jesus Christ which was given for thee"). The two forms were joined in the 1559 Book, giving a nice balance (very Anglican, one might say!).

4. Alternatively he could be thinking of the Roman triumph, a grand procession led by the victorious generals and ending with the prisoners of war. Either way, the point is the same. See for example Gordon D. Fee, *The First Epistle to the Corinthians,* New International Commentary on the New Testament (Grand Rapids: Wm. B. Eerdmans, 1987), 174-75.

5. A disciple is one who is taught, one who sits at the feet of a master. An apostle (Greek *apostolos,* "one who is sent") is one who is commissioned to go out as an agent plenipotentiary (with full powers) of the One who commissions.

6. For an appreciation of a heroine in Acts, see "Lydia: The First Christian in Europe" in my book *Help My Unbelief.*

7. One of the most rewarding sights in London for lovers of Bible stories is the hall of Raphael cartoons at the Victoria and Albert Museum, showing scenes from Acts.

8. I never have. This is its only appearance outside its original setting. These sorts of stories should be told with great reticence lest we tempt the Holy Spirit.

9. "We are his workmanship, created in Christ Jesus for good works, which God prepared beforehand, that we should walk in them" (Ephesians 2:10). Paraphrased in the Episcopal Book of Common Prayer, the Thanksgiving after Communion: "We humbly beseech thee, O heavenly Father, so to assist us with thy grace, that we may continue in that holy fellowship, and do all such good works as thou hast prepared for us to walk in. . . ."

10. Many Episcopalians today have rejected the Protestant roots of Anglicanism, but I believe this is a great mistake. Ironically, since the 9/11 attacks on America, numerous voices have been heard calling for a Reformation of Islam — at the moment when the Episcopal Church is turning its back on the Reformation.

11. Julia Preston, "Helmet Instead of a Miter for the Bishop of Chiapas," *The New York Times,* 16 June 1998.

12. Eric Konigsberg, "Marcus Canby Was Nobody to Play With," *The New York Times Magazine,* 22 April 2001, 70-75.

13. "Holocaust" means "burnt offering." The suggestion that it was in any way a sacrifice is offensive to many. "Shoah" means, simply, "catastrophe."

14. Gerard Manley Hopkins, "I wake and feel the fell of dark, not day," *Poems,* ed. Robert Bridges (London: Humphrey Milford, 1918), no. 45.

15. There has been much scholarly discussion about why Jesus calls him "Simon,

son of John." It seems to distance Peter a little, as though Jesus were testing him. It is also logical to assume that Jesus is recalling his very first address to "Simon son of John" when he called him to be a disciple. In Matthew the name of Peter's father is Jonah.

16. To be sure, Peter says these words in Matthew, not in John, so strictly speaking we cannot insist on this point. But it is an inspired linkage nevertheless.

17. It is generally agreed that the three questions asked by Jesus correspond to the three denials of Peter.

18. This doesn't imply papacy in the subsequent Roman Catholic sense. Clearly, however, Peter achieved primacy in the church very early, as the entire New Testament attests. The hero of the Fourth Gospel is the Beloved Disciple, but Peter's importance even to the Johannine Church made it essential that he be equal to the Beloved Disciple. See the very helpful book produced by a committee of scholars from various traditions, *Peter in the New Testament,* ed. Raymond E. Brown, Karl P. Donfried, and John Reumann (Minneapolis: Augsburg; New York: Paulist, 1973).

19. Bruce Feiler, *Walking the Bible: A Journey by Land through the Five Books of Moses* (New York: Morrow, 2001).

20. Daniel Mendelsohn, "Holy Schtick," *New York* Magazine, 16 April 2001.

21. Claudia Smith Brinson, "Death Penalty Foe Says Death Can't Heal," *The State* (Columbia, SC), 9 October 2000.

22. Sara Rimer is covering death penalty issues for *The New York Times.* This is from her article of 19 April 2001.

23. As this goes to press, it has become ever more apparent that world peace will never be possible until there is a resolution of the Israeli-Palestinian conflict. The September 11 attack and its aftermath made this very clear to the Bush administration, which almost overnight began to show signs of modifying its former isolationist position. Praying for the peace of Jerusalem, in its literal geopolitical form, will remain a priority for Christians.

24. *The State* (Columbia, SC), 26 April 2000.

25. Actually, the vote was taken in a committee of the County Council, but for simplicity's sake I have omitted that detail from my pulpit copy. Final approval of the plan was scheduled for July 2000.

26. Seth Mydans, "Cambodia's Latest Plague: Lynch Law," *The New York Times,* 13 April 2000.

27. I realize that many readers might think this disingenuous. However, there are several reasons that I refer often to Tibetan Buddhism: (1) I have been seriously interested in Tibet all my life; (2) I know more about Tibetan Buddhism than any other non-Christian religion; (3) Tibetan Buddhism has been highly visible in America recently, and the continuing romanticization of it is a genuine news story.

28. Steven Kinzer, "As the World Heals, Tibet's Exiles Feel Forsaken," *The New York Times,* 24 June 1999. For a thorough discussion of the West's sentimentalizing of Tibet, see Orville Schell, *Virtual Tibet: Searching for Shangri-La from the Himalayas to Hollywood* (New York: Metropolitan, 2000); and Donald S. Lopez, *Prisoners of Shangri-La: Tibetan Buddhism and the West* (Chicago: University of Chicago Press, 1998).

29. *Mystery and Manners,* 147-48.

30. The anthropologist Lionel Tiger is only one of many who has written about this.

31. Douglas Southall Freeman, *R. E. Lee: A Biography* (New York: Scribner's, 1934), 2:462.

32. Firefighters gave extensive interviews after 9/11; they frequently spoke about their love of the action.

33. Israel Finkelstein and Neil A. Silberman, *The Bible Unearthed: Archaeology's New Vision of Ancient Israel and the Origin of Its Sacred Texts* (New York: Free Press, 2001). Review by Phyllis Trible, *The New York Times Book Review,* 4 February 2001.

34. It is important to be aware, however, that there are strong countervailing voices to this "minimalist" trend. For example, see William G. Dever, *What Did the Biblical Writers Know and When Did They Know It? What Archaeology Can Tell Us about the Reality of Ancient Israel* (Grand Rapids: Wm. B. Eerdmans, 2001).

35. For the sake of simplification in this particular sermon, I have omitted the phrase "died *for our sin,*" but we should not forget that this is at the very center of Paul's preaching and the proper subject of an infinity of sermons — as we have seen in the Holy Week sections.

36. An Old Testament expression denoting God's powerful activity.

37. In saying this we recognize that there is a huge complex of problems related to the relationship of Christianity and Judaism, and a ghastly fallout from those problems. That, however, is the subject for more extended treatment elsewhere. Interested readers might try *Jews and Christians: Getting Our Stories Straight,* by Rabbi Michael Goldberg (Philadelphia: Trinity Press International, 1991).

38. J. Christiaan Beker, *Paul the Apostle: The Triumph of God in Life and Thought* (Philadelphia: Fortress, 1980).

39. Words from Job combined with 1 Corinthians — as in the libretto of G. F. Handel's *Messiah.*

40. The Burial of the Dead, Rite One. This is Thomas Cranmer's version of an older Latin hymn. Martin Luther and Miles Coverdale also translated this hymn for use in burial rites. See Marion J. Hatchett, *Commentary on the American Prayer Book* (New York: Seabury, 1981), 485.

41. I have reversed the order of the two clauses for the purposes of this sermon.

42. Maybe Paul didn't write Ephesians, but as theologian Paul L. Lehmann used to say, "If he didn't, he should have."

43. Phrase from the Episcopal Book of Common Prayer.

44. Kenneth L. Woodward, "The Changing Face of the Church," *Newsweek,* 16 April 2001, 46-52.